Problem Solving in Recreation and Parks

5th Edition

Joseph J. Bannon

SAGAMORE
PUBLISHING

Publishers: Joseph J. Bannon and Peter L. Bannon
Sales and Marketing Manager: Misti Gilles
Director of Development and Production: Susan M. Davis
Production Coordinator: Amy S. Dagit
Graphic Designer: Marissa Willison

ISBN print edition: 978-1-57167-795-2
ISBN e-book: 978-1-57167-796-9
Library of Congress Control Number: 2016962239

Printed in the United States

1807 N. Federal Dr.
Urbana, IL 61801
www.sagamorepublishing.com

This book is dedicated to:

Charles Brightbill
Who taught me the meaning and importance of leisure.

"THE" George D. Butler
The Chairman of the Board at my first job
in Leonia, New Jersey.

Allen Sapora
Who guided me through my master's thesis and PhD at the
University of Illinois, and a great personal friend.

CONTENTS

CASE STUDIES

FOREWORD

The following was written by George Butler, a true pioneer in the field of parks and recreation and the mentor to me. He served as the chairman of my first job in Leonia, New Jersey. His comments are as relevant now as they are for our future. His wisdom still holds true.

Everyone who has had responsibility for the conduct of recreation programs or the administration of recreation or park service has been faced with a variety of complex problems. There are few departments that have not experienced abuse of their facilities and buildings, failure of supposedly popular programs, lack of cooperation between volunteers and paid workers, and misinterpretation of their policies and proposals by news media. Cooperation promised by other departments is not always forthcoming; in fact, it may turn into open opposition. And interagency jealousy sometimes prevents the fulfillment of well-conceived plans. In some localities, political considerations influence appointments and appropriations, and board members have been known to advance their special interests at the expense of the total program.

Problem Solving in Recreation and Parks has been written by Joseph Bannon, who has wide experience in dealing wisely with such problems. He correctly states: "Success in the recreation and park field depends on one's ability to solve problems." The need for this ability applies not only to the administrator but also to the supervisor and the recreation leader. To achieve success, they must think creatively and face their problems directly. There have been situations when mounting difficulties have caused administrators or boards to close their eyes in the hope that these problems would disappear. Such inaction can only result in failure.

The purpose of this volume is to provide guidelines to park and recreation professionals to develop a systematic and creative approach to the problems and vital issues they face.

The book should be equally useful to recreation educators in carrying out their responsibility for preparing men and women for effective service in recreation and parks. The need for such a book is apparent, because few recreation or park curricula include courses in problem solving. Furthermore, little published material deals with this subject. It is true that many texts dealing with recreation administration describe policies and procedures that have proved effective and successful, but they do not deal with obstacles that have been met or the manner in which they have been overcome. Clarification and discussion of these matters seem the appropriate responsibility of instructors in college courses and in in-service training programs.

Problem Solving in Recreation and Parks therefore fills a gap in the literature currently available. In it, Dr. Bannon not only clearly sets forth the importance of solving problems in a creative manner, but also describes a tested method that can be applied in a range of diverse situations. Every recreation and park worker and board member can benefit from a study of this method and from its application, when called upon to make a decision designed to eliminate a problem.

The last part of this book, composed of 100 case studies, illustrates the scope, nature, and diversity of problems encountered by personnel at various levels of responsibility. In a sense, it provides a picture of the activities, functions, and relationships involved in the operation of a recreation or park department, as reflected in the problems faced by its workers. Another value, perhaps not anticipated, is that it gives prospective workers a fuller, more comprehensive description than is available elsewhere of the complications that they are likely to encounter in their profession. It will help dispel any danger that they may be misled as to the role of the recreation worker, a role that other texts have been accused of portraying as "foreordained in an antiseptically pure environment."

All of the problems confronting recreation and park departments will not be solved by using this book, for the rapid expansion of services provided by these agencies will surely give rise to increasing difficulties. However, for his contribution toward tackling problems and solving them creatively, Dr. Bannon deserves the gratitude of all who are concerned with increasing the effectiveness of recreation and park services.

George D. Butler
Sarasota, Florida

PROLOGUE

I am honored four times in writing the Prologue to this fifth edition of *Problem Solving in Recreation and Parks.* First, I am honored to follow the Foreword written by George Butler, Director of Research for the National Recreation Association for 43 years. Second, I am honored to be a student of the work of Charles Brightbill, a giant in the field of parks and recreation, who articulated the importance of and challenges associated with leisure in our lives. Third, I am honored to be in the company of Allen Sapora, founder of the University of Illinois's distinguished curriculum in parks and recreation. And fourth, I am honored to endorse the thinking and writing of Joseph J. Bannon, Sr., for whom this fifth edition has been a labor of love in this, the 85th year of his young life.

My enthusiasm for this book has spanned my own career of 40 years, and this fifth edition retains, just like Dr. Bannon, a youthful exuberance in its innovative approach to preparing college students and park and recreation professionals alike for meeting the day-to-day trials of public service in recreation and park management, administration, and programming. Dr. Bannon does a masterful job of readying his readers for their immersion into 100 new case studies presented in the latter part of the book by first acquainting them with the theoretical foundations and nuts and bolts of problem-solving techniques. The book works because it ties together the abstract world of ideas with the relevance of those ideas to the world of professional practice. There is a pragmatic quality about the book that is sorely missing in many academic texts. The case studies provide a "hands-on" learning experience for students and practitioners alike and in so doing constitute a rich learning environment from which students, practitioners, and interested others can draw important lessons about the vicissitudes of working with and for people in a variety of problem-solving contexts. As I have recently written with my colleagues in "Pasteur's Quadrant: A Conceptual Framework for Bridging the 'Great Divide' Between Higher Education and Professional Practice in Parks, Recreation, and Tourism "(*Schole: A Journal of Leisure Studies and Recreation Education,* Vol. 31, No. 2, 2016, pp. 3–10), Dr. Bannon's *Problem Solving in Recreation and Parks* illustrates how the "great divide" between book learning and experiential learning can be bridged, as well as demonstrating how the "great divide" between theoretical propositions emanating from the "ivory tower" can be relevant to the "real world."

Books that make it to a fifth edition do so for a reason. I believe the reason for the staying power of *Problem Solving in Recreation and Parks* can be attributed to the fact that while times, contexts, and problems change, successful problem-solving techniques and strategies are enduring. The challenge for students, educators, and practitioners alike is learning how to apply those problem-solving principles and practices that have stood the test of time to constantly changing contemporary conditions. Dr. Bannon's book is a great resource for any management, administration, or programming course in parks and recreation, or, for that matter, any introductory course that aspires to give learners a sense of what the field is about and what working in it entails. It should also be useful in staff training. *Problem Solving in Recreation and Parks* has a "let's roll up our sleeves and get down to work" quality about it that shows the strength of role-playing exercises that immerse learners into the day-to-day fray of professional practice. Amidst the give and take of back and forth debates, readers can suspend their disbelief and begin to feel what it must be like to be a park and recreation professional. What more could be asked of a book?

Daniel L. Dustin
Professor
Department of Health, Kinesiology, and Recreation
University of Utah

PREFACE

To find solutions to the critical problems facing the recreation and park profession, its leaders must become effective problem solvers. This book offers a problem-solving model that should aid such leaders in developing a systematic approach to the vital issues they confront. It also includes a series of case studies depicting typical day-to-day problems faced by administrators, supervisors, leaders, and recreation and park boards and commissions.

Certainly, a book of this type should not be limited to classroom use. It is hoped that its concepts and ideas can also be effectively used in staff development programs and in-service training, as well as by park and recreation boards, military installations, hospitals, conservation agencies, penal institutions, commercial recreation enterprises, colleges and university administrations, state departments, and other agencies concerned with recreation and park problems. What is important is that the problems a person is likely to encounter, and these are for the most part predictable, are those for which students and practitioners have been prepared.

I attempt to combine practical with academic approaches to problem solving, offering both the theoretical and pragmatic viewpoints, combining these wherever possible. For these reasons, this book should be useful not only for teaching park and recreation students how to handle hypothetical problems systematically, but as an update and refresher for those involved with actual problems in agencies and organizations. Regardless of whether a person is a student preparing for a career in parks and recreation or a related area or a professional already working in the field (not to mention those who serve on advisory boards and commissions), the concepts and ideas presented in this book should (1) increase the reader's problem-solving ability, (2) offer a systematic multi-idea approach to problem solving, and (3) improve the reader's performance as a student or a worker as the result of the reader's more effective problem-solving and decision-making skills.

In addition to all the chapters being substantially revised, 100 new case studies have been added. These case studies represent a wide array of current problems, but the issues facing park and recreation professionals change as rapidly as the times. What was relevant 6 or 7 years ago is far less pressing today. On the other hand, other issues and confrontations not touched upon in the previous edition are given voice in these case studies. More prevalent than before, in addition to the usual case studies on vandalism and personnel matters, are issues related to equal rights, women's rights, liberation movements pressed by a variety of groups, as well as ecological and environmental problems. These are all presented in case studies relating to park and recreation organizations, though they can be modified for other human-services organizations as well.

There is no need for this book to be confined to classroom use only. It can be readily used in staff development programs and in-service training, by park boards, or in a variety of social and educational situations. This text is a proven one. The mere fact that this is the fifth edition attests to its credibility and vitality. Those of us who have used it understand its usefulness. Those discovering it for the first time will quickly realize its value and application. There are scores of new case studies included, updated critical references, and resources devoted to small-group concepts. Students, administrators, educators, and volunteers will find it an excellent resource, one that will hone their skills as decision makers and problem solvers. It also affords greater insight into the nature of park and recreation operations and the myriad of situations that park and recreation professionals encounter in their provision of opportunities for meaningful leisure expressions.

Joseph J. Bannon
Sagamore Publishing

ACKNOWLEDGMENTS

A number of individuals provided input for this book on problem solving. Some provided advice, some provided reviews of case studies, and some provided source materials. I wish to extend thanks and appreciation for their contributions. Below is a listing of contributors:

- Ron McCarwille, Professor and Associate Dean, University of Waterloo
- Glens Falls, NY, *Post Star*
- David Austin, Indiana University
- Don Decker, Director Parks and Recreation, Weston, Florida
- Joe DeLuce, Executive Director, Champaign Park District, Illinois, and Megan Kuhlenschmidt
- Prince George CT Riversdale, Maryland
- David Halberstam, Halby Group
- Marcia Carter, Re.D.
- Heather Andersen, Ed.D.
- Stephanie Esters, *The Southern Illinoisan*
- Emily Attwood, Managing Editor, *Athletic Business Magazine*
- Donna Weiner, Maryland, University of Miami Miller School of Medicine
- Claudia Hoffacker, Minnesota Publication Manager
- Dan Waldinger, Director of Park and Recreation, Mahomet, Illinois
- Sam Banks, Director, Boys and Girls Club, Champaign, Illinois
- Emma Ockerman, Editor-in-Chief of *The Post,* Ohio University, authors Janet Nester and Jen Strawn, staff writers.

AUTHOR

Dr. Joseph J. Bannon, Sr., has over 40 years of experience in the parks, recreation, and leisure field and in publishing. A recognized leader in both fields, Dr. Bannon has received numerous awards for outstanding service. He began his career in 1957 as the director of Parks and Recreation in Leonia, New Jersey, and moved on to Topeka, Kansas, as the director in 1962. In 1966, he joined the staff at the University of Illinois, and in 1972, Bannon was appointed the head of the Department of Leisure Studies.

Dr. Bannon developed *Management Strategy* in 1977. The publication was dedicated to disseminating management information to park and recreation professionals throughout the world. Dr. Bannon has also written many articles and authored and coauthored more than 10 books. Dr. Bannon retired from the University of Illinois in 1991 and now works full time acquiring and developing titles for Sagamore.

CHAPTER 1
PROBLEM SOLVING: A PROFESSIONAL NEED

Students of recreation and park administration face the challenge of absorbing information, understanding theoretical concerns within the field, and at the same time gaining practical experience with problem solving in their chosen profession. This situation is prevalent among young scholars entering this field of study. With an education usually obtained away from the rest of society, graduates are expected to take on the demands and responsibilities of professional life. They are able to secure professional positions primarily because of their advanced education. Few educators or curricula train students in problem solving or practical skills, trusting them to have been acquired elsewhere or to be known instinctively.

As recreation and park educators, we are interested in teaching and researching the more arcane aspects of leisure studies. We also must be concerned with training students in the more pragmatic skills necessary for recreation and park administration. If the student's problem is balancing intellectual matter with more practical experience, the educator must incorporate such skills into the curriculum while training students in the administration of recreation and parks. For instance, a student with a degree in recreation and park administration should be able to design an 8-week summer camp program, develop and implement an adult recreation program, plan basic marketing strategies, and understand tax levies and the financial management of a park and recreation agency. However, few students are trained to systematically handle the common challenges associated with vandalism, labor negotiations, low program attendance, poor community relations, or the broader effects of complex social problems that affect the profession.

The opportunity to obtain a college education does not solely address these challenges. Rather, students must learn to think clearly and logically, to judge, to select, and to predict outcomes. Most important, this field requires individuals to have the ability to make decisions and create sustainable solutions to problems. These skills are the key components of a person's ability to problem solve. These challenges were identified in earlier editions of this book, and they continue to exist throughout the field of parks and recreation in the new millennium. Where are the new and creative ideas that will turn such aims into reality?

Such aims are good, but it is difficult to carry out programs without considering the broader context in which they are situated. Over the past 20 years, the climate of Congress and state legislatures overwhelmingly supporting the efforts to clean water, protect open spaces, and develop urban areas has changed and often leads to highly contentious debates. The challenges deriving from economic recessions, ideological differences, and lack of trust in governmental oversight are chief concerns that park and recreation professionals must balance with the daily challenges of public acceptance of and/or engagement with the agency, as well as program and fiscal management. These challenges suggest that students must gain important problem-solving skills through their university education to prepare them for entering this field.

Many challenges that park and recreation professionals will face do not have clear-cut answers. Today, problems often involve multiple factors that require the professional to consider various perspectives (Walsh & Wicks, 2014). As a result, park and recreation professionals must become creative thinkers and gatherers of information to solve problems thoughtfully. Colleges and universities must evaluate their curricula to address this skill acquisition among students so they become accustomed to addressing challenges in the field (Gregory, Hardiman, Yarmolinskaya, & Rinne, 2013). When recreation and park staff are hired, preference should be given to those who consider creativity an important aspect of their work.

In the late 1960s, the Stanford Research Institute (SRI International) suggested that students in creative-problem-solving courses believed the classes reduced their imaginative inhibitions and broadened their perspectives when seeking solutions to complex problems (Edwards, 1968). The best problem solvers are creative and pragmatic, which are qualities equally necessary for today's information and innovation-driven society (Gregory et al., 2013). To solve most complex problems, practitioners must forge relationships with individuals of differing experiences to achieve a creative solution. For instance, a transdisciplinary course was piloted to develop a creative and sustainable solution to Louisiana's coastal wetland degradation, with students from three science disciplines: environmental management, geology, and landscape architecture (Walsh & Wicks, 2014). Student teams were arranged to ensure all three disciplines were represented in the groups throughout the projects. Each student brought a unique perspective and intellect from his or her discipline that, when combined with the other knowledge areas, created a more comprehensive solution for addressing the state's wetland challenges.

Many people think more creatively if they are shown how to draw more effectively on their own imagination and to trust it. Especially when they are children, most people are naturally imaginative, but because of various cultural pressures, including compulsory and formal education, they are too often taught to distrust the products from their own minds. Einstein once said, "I am enough of an artist to draw freely upon my imagination. Imagination is more important than knowledge. Knowledge is limited. Imagination encircles the world."

There is much teachers can do, especially on the college level, where education may be more relaxed, to wean students from the habit of thinking as others do, to encourage their creativity, and to support the outcome of such efforts. It is through departure from traditional methods of teaching and learning that people's imaginations are freed. It is only when students truly feel that their ideas will not be squelched that they become more creative thinkers, and new ideas are limited only by boundaries of individual skill and imagination. Gregory et al. (2013) identified eight guiding principles teachers can use in their classrooms to foster creative thinking among students:

1. Supply students with a wealth of information in specific context areas, and take steps to ensure that students retain that information, which allows them to use the information flexibly.
2. Ask students to offer multiple ideas to any open-ended prompt and remind students to make each solution as varied as possible.
3. Encourage idea generation by posing questions or problems that have more than one correct response.
4. For each potential solution that a student suggests, ask the student to also think about implications and implementation.
5. Include group work opportunities when presenting multipart problems.
6. Give students a novel relationship and have them generate items that, when related, exemplify that relationship.
7. Provide students with two or more unrelated ideas and ask them to find a novel relationship.
8. Include outside resources in certain group work situations. (pp. 47–48)

The park and recreation administrator who must answer the question of whether it is now time to submit a bond issue referendum to the voters should do so only after knowing (a) if people understand the need for the additional revenue, (b) the extent voters are willing to pay, and (c) if enough community support can be raised to pass the bond. Some problems are so complex and the amount of information about the problems is so limited that it is often impossible to make the decision alone. Such problems depend more on the administrator's network of colleagues, expertise, and ability to gather multiple perspectives. Only through this personal insight can an effective solution be realized. The solution to problems of parks and recreation must be found within the profession. There is no substitute for effective leadership. The responsibility is ours—shall we accept it or let it drop by default?

The concepts and ideas in this text are designed to (a) increase problem-solving ability, (b) offer a systematic, multi-idea approach to problem solving, and (c) improve performance through more effective problem-solving and decision-making skills.

References

Edwards, M. (1968). A survey of problem solving courses. *Journal of Creative Behavior, 2*(1), 33–51.

Gregory, E., Hardiman, M., Yarmolinskaya, J., & Rinne, L. (2013). Building creative thinking in the classroom: From research to practice. *International Journal of Educational Research, 62,* 43–50.

Walsh, M. M., & Wicks, C. (2014). Introducing transdisciplinary problem solving to environmental management systems and geology students through a case study of disturbed coastal systems. *Journal of College Science Teaching, 43*(3), 48–53.

CHAPTER 2
THE PROBLEM-SOLVING MODEL

People often compliment intuitive and perceptive problem solvers, or those who respond creatively to problems, by telling them, "It's easy for you." Such a compliment completely overlooks *why* it appears easier for them to solve problems. Are they instinctive problem solvers, or do their experience, patience, background, personality traits, and the like affect their talent? What appears to be an intuitive problem solution is often revealed to be a systematic approach to problems. Although a line is often drawn between intuitive and systematic thinking, it should be a thin one. Chaos is not creativity, nor is plodding systematic. A problem solver, especially one who encounters problems in the park and recreation profession, is simultaneously systematic, creative, and sometimes willing to step back and look at the big picture, because researchers cannot always isolate and measure such approaches. It is important not to classify people as one type or the other, because most people draw on (to the best of their ability) a systematic intuition.

The graphic model in this section includes a step-by-step approach to problem solving. As the illustrated model shows, generally, nine steps are included in problem solving of this nature:

1. Defining the problem situation.
2. Defining objectives for a solution.
3. Identifying obstacles to a problem solution.
4. Observing change and conflict.
5. Identifying factors that influence change and conflict.
6. Brainstorming for solutions.
7. Selection of alternatives.
8. Decision making.
9. Strategies for implementing decisions.

Problem solving, though it can be analyzed to some extent, is complex and often uncertain. As students and practitioners read the following chapters, they will readily see why the problem-solving model depicted requires much skill, insight, and ingenuity if it is to be successful. Because there are many frustrating and unexpected obstacles in problem analysis, it is important that problem solvers, novice or otherwise, accept that some problems are *not* soluble. If there are constraints on a problem solution over which they have no control, either the problem is not soluble to their satisfaction or they must compromise with a less than ideal solution. In fact, ideal solutions are seldom effective. Take, as an example, land use for recreation purposes. Recreation and park specialists constantly face a common dilemma in land-use planning for recreation purposes. They wish to develop or maintain a natural, complex, semi-wilderness area for campers and other vacationers. But the more attractive the area is, the more campers it entices, leading eventually to the destruction of the very qualities for which the site was selected or designed. Such a dilemma has no ideal solution; someone will suffer. Sometimes, the problem is not truly soluble, and the area is entirely closed to campers to forestall irreparable damage to the ecosystem caused by the destructive intrusion of "nature lovers."

But if students and practitioners study and follow the problem-solving model presented here, they will certainly improve their mode of analyzing problems, improve their patterns of thinking about problems, and strengthen their personal and professional decision-making and problem-solving abilities. In the simplest terms, a problem exists when a person encounters difficulties in obtaining a desired objective; that is, a problem is an "unwanted effect—something to be corrected or removed brought about by some specific event or a combination of events" (Kepner & Tregoe, 2013). The case studies presented in Part III corroborate these definitions of a problem situation.

References

Amer, A. (2005). *Analytical thinking*. Cairo, Egypt: Cairo University.

Kepner, C., & Tregoe, B. (2013). *The new rational manager*. Princeton, NJ: Princeton Research Press.

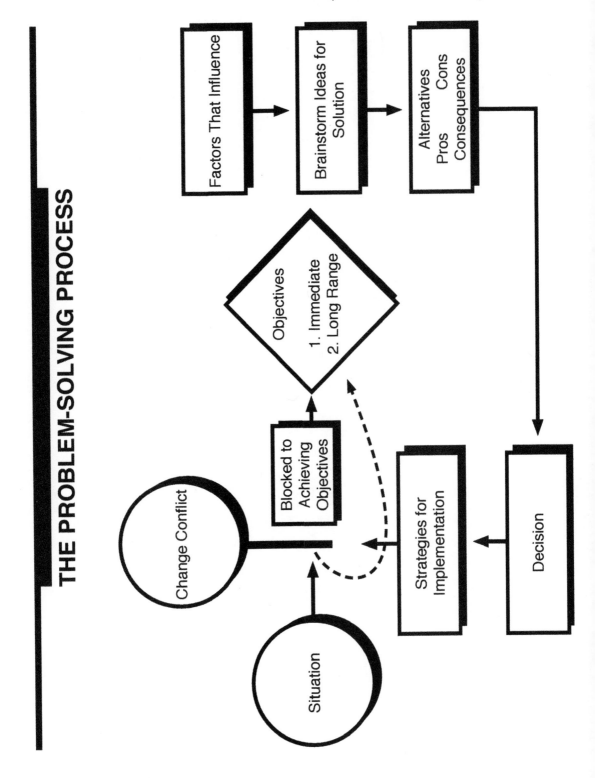

THE PROBLEM-SOLVING PROCESS

Factors That Influence

Brainstorm Ideas for Solution

Alternatives
Pros   Cons
Consequences

Objectives

1. Immediate
2. Long Range

Blocked to Achieving Objectives

Change Conflict

Situation

Strategies for Implementation

Decision

CHAPTER 3
USE OF THE CASE STUDY METHOD IN PROBLEM SOLVING

The Case Study

The analysis of case studies is among the most challenging assignments for a student. Case studies are far from "busy work." If approached in a proper fashion, case studies can be extremely formative in career preparation for the field of parks and recreation management. When students are presented with the challenge to develop their decision-making skills under proper tutelage in the classroom, it helps them meet the expectations of their postgraduate career.

The case study as an aid for management training was first developed in the early 1950s at Harvard University's School of Business Administration. Based on the longtime practice of using court cases in legal training, the case study approach was one of the first teaching methods in the social sciences to depart from more traditional lectures, in which information was transmitted to rather than elicited from students. Students today tend to be inductive learners and may retain more knowledge and develop stronger skills through application to real-world situations (BU Center for Teaching and Learning, 2015).

Case studies are generally divided into three types or combinations of these three:

1. The *individual problem* involves a specific person in an organization and a difficulty that may be affecting the person's job as well as the organization.
2. The *isolated incident* involves an unusual occurrence in an organization not covered by regulations and procedures, but disruptive to the organization.
3. The *organizational problem* may be a labor-relations conflict or a sales or recruiting difficulty affecting the entire organization.

A case study should also contain three fundamental details (Dunne & Brooks, 2004):

1. A question (problem) or series of questions (problems) that necessitate imperative solutions.
2. Problem context (although a case study may be presented with limited information to imitate real-world decision making, in which quick decisions are necessary despite the lack of data).
3. Supporting data to engage students (e.g., URLs, newspaper articles, social media, video clips, images, or audio files).

One limitation of case studies, or one reason for their failure in training, is that too much is expected from them. As an *aid* to teaching, they are not meant to replace other methods of learning and obtaining information. Cases attempt to represent real situations faced by agency leaders, but they may underrepresent the difficulty or severity of decisions. In the technology era, they can also overwhelm students with information because of the mountain of data they will need to sift through. In the end, a good case study should help students make important, quasi-permanent decisions under severe time constraints.

Case study training is intended to help students learn how to make decisions with greater ease, reduce the time required to make decisions, and increase the frequency and quality of decision making (National Center for Case Study Teaching in Science, 2015). One purpose of the case study approach is to teach students *indirectly* how to solve problems and how to make specific decisions. The case study should not be used, therefore, in more sophisticated management training programs in which qualified, successful managers are seeking more erudite techniques.

Instructors use different case studies for different audiences. Undergraduates, new to the use of case studies, new even to the practice of problem solving, require simpler cases than do graduate students, and certainly, experienced managers are given cases that are more complex. Regardless of the audience, case studies should not merely be a "filler" in a course of instruction or a form of entertainment. Such abuses only negate their possible advantages, time is wasted, and everyone will feel cheated. There must be a reason for using case studies, and it should not be trivial.

- What do I want to achieve in this session?
- What case, if any, will best aid me in this?
- How can I best present the case?

The criticisms of case studies in teaching often stem from their inappropriate use: They are used when not needed, are not of apparent value, or are not treated seriously by the instructor or the students.

Case studies are generally valuable for four types of management training:

1. Awareness training: Defining precisely the pressures and environments managers are likely to encounter, and making students more aware of them.
2. Technique training: Teaching specific skills, such as interviewing or being interviewed, and giving students practical experience in them.
3. Illustration of a specific point: Isolating a particular solution and indicating its pros and cons, such as reorganization, and revealing to students the implications of them.

Perhaps the greatest advantage of case studies is that they force a student to think, first alone, then with a group. They also require concentration and introspection. Participating in evolving solutions, especially if a case is handled seriously, may be a more successful experience for students than hours of note taking. For many students, especially if the instructor is well prepared with in-depth case studies, experiences in solving case studies are a highlight of their education.

Teaching With Case Studies

Students and instructors must be prepared to use case studies in the classroom because they change the relationship among student, instructor, and material to be learned. Although no longer lecturing to a passive audience, the instructor is still in control.

To the experienced instructor, the case method is not adequately described as a completely nondirective approach to teaching. Rather, it involves direction in the most exquisitely subtle sense of the word. The instructor must listen carefully to what students say—not only to words, but also to meanings as expressed in feelings and attitudes.

This indirect mode of teaching requires some restraint by the instructor to not force a solution on and not put pressure on students who are baffled by the obvious. The instructor can give clues to a suitable solution, but the purpose of a case study is to encourage insight and self-direction.

For the case method to be effective, the instructor must know the students fairly well, be a skilled and enthusiastic discussion leader (not a lecturer!), and be well versed in the subjects of the case studies. The instructor must be able to anticipate the responses of students, ask the proper questions at strategic times, and maintain a relaxed atmosphere during discussions. Obviously, these qualities are not acquired quickly. Instructors who use this teaching aid must be prepared for a great deal of study and practice; above all, they must have patience. Teaching with case studies is difficult, but it can be extremely rewarding for students and instructors.

It is important for the instructor to select carefully the students who will participate in the problem-solving sessions. It would not be advisable, for example, to include students who have much experience in recreation and parks with those who have relatively little. Those with experience may view problems from a much different viewpoint than that of those with little practical experience. This is not to say that inexperienced students should never be mixed in with experienced students; it is only to alert the instructor to potential difficulties in mixing groups unintentionally.

Students are important to the success or failure of using case studies. Those who come to the session unprepared, not having done their background homework, will not be good discussants. Students also must be prepared to discuss the case study intelligently. If a case deals with, say, the development of a therapeutic recreation program, students must at least be aware of the planning principles, budgetary requirements, and administrative practices of operating such programs.

Role-playing is an innovative way to involve students in the case study. This is an active way to engage students, and it allows them to take a fresh look at the perspectives of each stakeholder in the case study.

When used properly, role-playing can move individuals away from seeing the problem only in black and white or as right and wrong. Creativity and imagination are playful ways to explore real-life situations, tempered with factual consequences that keep the simulation from random meanders. Role-playing generally pertains to problems of individuals and problems of groups. The values of role-playing for training in these two areas include the following (Matwiejczuk, 1997):

1. It requires participants to act out a thought or decision, emphasizing the distinction between *thinking* and *doing.*

2. It allows group members to practice various actions so they realize that good human relations requires as much skill as any other acquired talent.

3. It enhances *attitude* training by placing practitioners in the positions (roles) of others, teaching them that attitudes are not merely the result of personality, but also of situation.

4. It helps participants to become more aware of and sensitive to others, especially when relating to subordinates and groups. In role-playing, listening skills are enhanced because more focus and attention are being placed on the situation.

5. It reveals practitioners to themselves, notably behavior faults or control of emotions and feelings when these disrupt decision making.

6. It allows practitioners to practice various approaches to difficult or unfamiliar situations. Situational experience and increased confidence are important outcomes for participants (Torrance & Murdock, 1996).

Anything to help students visualize the situation is helpful. Videos or field trips to the study site are helpful if time allows. Reading assignments are especially effective as well to help students understand a concept or method of analysis (Dunne & Brooks, 2004).

With case studies, students must develop their own rationale for decisions, accept responsibility for the decision, and be prepared to defend it. This will make them more rigorous in problem analysis; knowing that they may be judged by classmates, they will be more thoughtful of their final decisions.

Case studies encourage students not only to think independently, but also to work cooperatively in teams. Many decisions are the result of group discussions. For example, it is essential that a recreation and park board cooperate in formulating sound policies. A sound policy can be reached only by independent thinkers who recognize the importance of listening to other viewpoints. A recreation professional must work closely with boards, commissions, executive committees, advisory units, and other community groups. The recreation manager's success depends on the ability to think rationally, first as an individual, then with a group.

The following are procedures to assist instructors and students in making case studies a productive teaching aid:

1. In presenting a case, the instructor should ask students if anything about a particular case is not clear. In each case, certain assumptions are made; it is important that every discussant's analysis of a case be based on comparable assumptions. For example, for a case on planning a comprehensive community recreation program, the problem solver makes certain assumptions about the amount of funds available for the program. If one discussant approaches the problem with the perspective that limited funds are available and another with the perspective that funds are no problem, the group discussion will be confusing, if not a waste of time.

2. The instructor must create an informal atmosphere for discussions; all ideas should be heard. No student should worry about "inappropriate."

3. The instructor should not monopolize the discussion, otherwise the students will quickly lose interest in the discussion. The main responsibility of instructors is to help students build problem-solving abilities and effective thought processes, not to demonstrate that they have all the answers.

4. The instructor should keep the discussion focused on case details, their relationships, and their implications.

5. The instructor should not anticipate the direction of the discussion or lead participants to specified lines of thought. Violating this rule denies students the responsibility they will need if they are to be independent problem solvers.

6. The instructor should be alert to students who alter case facts. If overlooked, the discussion will drift from the principal aspects of the case study.

7. The instructor who knows the outcome of a case study should not reveal it until students have had an opportunity to explore the case thoroughly. Doing otherwise would bias the discussion.

An instructor's course objectives should guide the case study process, but a systematic approach to analyzing case studies should provide a good starting point (BU Center for Teaching and Learning, 2015):

- Thoroughly read the case and supplemental readings.
- What is the central issue?
- Define the goal of this case.
- What is the context for this case?
- What are the constraints of the central issue?

- Identify key facts.
- Identify relevant alternatives.
- Select the best alternative, with reasons behind the choice.
- Develop an implementation plan.

Obviously, this is demanding. Students are required to think not as their instructor wishes, but as employees faced with a problem would. Creating such independence in students is a constructive outcomes of case studies. It brings reality into the classroom by insisting that students reach a decision and are responsible for its consequences. It also requires that they become deeply involved in problem solving and through this become more successful decision makers.

References

BU Center for Teaching and Learning. (n.d.). Using case studies to teach. Retrieved May 2, 2015, from http://www.bu.edu/ceit/teaching-resources/using-case-studies-to-teach/

Dunne, D., & Brooks, K. (2004). *Teaching with cases.* Halifax, Canada: Society for Teaching and Learning in Higher Education.

Matwiejczuk, K. (1997). *Role play: Theory and practice.* London, England: Sage.

National Center for Case Study Teaching in Science. (2015). Retrieved May 1, 2015, from http://sciencecases.lib.buffalo.edu/cs/

Torrance, E., & Murdock, M. (1996). *Creative problem solving through role playing.* Pretoria, South Africa: Benedic Books.

CHAPTER 4
THE PROBLEM SITUATION

"Something is wrong" is the simplest definition of a problem. A problem is a departure from some preferred or desired state and exists when someone is concerned enough with the deviation to recognize the need for change. If no one articulates a deviation from some preferred state, it can be argued that a problem does not exist. Recognition and articulation are required to determine if there is a problem. As soon as someone notes the deviation, the problem can begin to be defined, no matter how intangible it seems at first.

What seems an obvious deviation to some people may not be a problem at all, but rather *symptoms* of a more critical problem. For example, consider the problem to be a levee that is not built high enough, which leads to periodic flooding, when siltation from runoff or environmental abuses that have affected the global climate may be the real problems. Concentrating on building a taller and wider levee to the exclusion of the "larger variables" that have brought about this symptomatic difficulty is to eradicate the symptoms of a problem without touching the problem itself.

The separation of symptoms of a problem from the problem itself is the main skill of a talented problem solver. We, as problem solvers, also use self-restraint, for eventually all problems can be seen to be related to larger and larger issues, until we are exhausted by the enormity of the situation, and nothing is accomplished. A director must decide at what level of awareness to begin defining and solving a problem, at what cutoff point to cease defining soluble problems as symptoms. Because analysis of the *problem situation* is the first step in the problem-solving process or model, it is also the most critical in determining how effectively a problem will be handled. Problem definition is problem analysis. We have to analyze the problem situation before being able to state accurately what is wrong. The problem solver has to understand the crux of the situation before moving unprepared to the next step. The "doer" has to be kept under control, and the "thinker" contemplates the entire situation.

How to Analyze a Problem

Often, agencies have what appear to be multiple problems at a recreation center or park. But one of these problems, as yet undefined, is the key problem. The other problems either are related to the KEY problem or are symptoms that should diminish once the main problem is isolated and solved. Many people are tempted to solve simple problems or remove symptoms first, hoping that the larger issue will disappear in the interim. These interim solutions, except when done intentionally, are shortsighted and often confound the larger problem. We have to know how to isolate the *correct problem.* Interim solutions should be clearly identified as such and not treated as the problem solution.

Objectives

If the problem is defined as a deviation or departure from some preferred state, this departure is from an explicit or implicit standard established by, in this case, the recreation center. Most problems are deviations from a mixture of explicit, implicit, and normative standards. That is, standards are clearly stated, are understood but not stated, or are what *should be* the desired state. The latter are normative standards or objectives (e.g., "We should have more attendance").

If the recreation center has deviated from some measurable standard and this causes a problem, the objectives that the center wishes to reach have to be stipulated during problem analysis. Objectives are closely related to problem analysis, for they are the measure against which alternative solutions will be gauged. Objectives not only entail correcting a deviation, but also often include future objectives. Such objectives are not merely an attempt to catch up with the past, but also a means to forecasting and planning. For instance, if participation at a special event was greater than it is now, this does not mean the center should be satisfied with a return to previous levels of participation as a future objective. The center may want to increase the amount of out-of-town visitors that come to the special event, or it may want to target a minority group that does not typically attend. On the other hand, the center should not set unrealistic objectives, frustrating all attempts at solving the problem more modestly.

Delegation of Authority

Although the topic is not explored in depth in this text, delegation of authority is worthy of attention for those studying problem solving. The growth and complexity of today's organizations (nonprofit, governmental, or commercial) require leaders to consider new roles for their employees beyond completing a task list. Numerous management theories and practices are focused on broadening employees' decision-making capabilities so leaders can tackle larger and more significant decisions regarding the direction of the organization (Marx, 2015). Because problem solving is a principal component of a manager's responsibilities, the associated tasks and responsibilities may also be shared between the ranks of employees. Although many managers will admit to the value of and need for shared authority, few are able or willing to delegate such decision-making responsibilities. Several definitions of delegation can be found within management or medical-related literature. For instance, delegation occurs when authority is granted to an individual other than the primary decision maker in the organization (Rees & Porter, 2015; Pettinger, 2012) or, put more simply, when other individuals are allowed to complete work or make decisions for an authority figure (Mullins, 2013).

Viewpoint

The personal and professional viewpoints of those in problem solving or those likely to be affected by its outcome must be anticipated and examined during the problem-analysis stage. The viewpoints of everyone involved or implicated are part of the problem.

No one concerned about a problem or likely to be affected by its solution should be excluded from problem analysis. All viewpoints must be considered. For example, after the phenomenal amount of campus unrest during the 1960s and early 1970s, it is now more common for academic problem solving to include the viewpoints of the parties affected by problem solutions. The perspectives on problem solving in an academic setting would include the viewpoints of students, faculty, administrators, and local and state involvement of these diverse groups in problem analysis and throughout the entire problem-solving process is either dictatorial or doomed to failure in a democratic setting.

All viewpoints must be reflected in analyzing a problem situation and considered judiciously. For instance, when a recreation and park board attempts to provide a recreation program for young people, if the program is planned from the viewpoint of the board and recreation staff alone, a meaningless program is most likely. The program will be unsuccessful because those for whom it was "designed" had nothing to say about what went into its creation. No matter how well we believe we can represent others' viewpoints, the people involved have to represent themselves.

A director or administrative staff will often enter a problem situation that has been reviewed by staff several times. An appropriate question for us is, *have the people in the neighborhood(s) surrounding the problem area (park, recreation center, special event, etc.) been asked for their opinions?* If staff members continue to analyze the problem without the serious involvement of those for whom the amenity was intended, no worthwhile solution is likely to emerge. For example, answers must be found for several questions, such as do citizens in the neighborhood feel reluctant to volunteer or use their recreation center, do neighborhood residents feel that adequate funds are spent on recreation programs, and are these funds considered adequate by other stakeholders? Another equally important viewpoint is that of municipal authorities, the mayor, or a city council, who appropriate funds for special events, centers, parks, and programs. As they form an opinion on the issue, it cannot be assumed that their opinion will be compatible with the problem solver's opinion or that of the staff. What is the viewpoint of the citizens outside of the district or municipality?

For those who receive county tax support, do these other residents consider the work worthwhile, do they have suggestions for defining the problem, and will they support a tax increase if it is needed to improve the problem? We must obtain their views in addition to the views of those more directly involved.

Symptoms

We begin now to look more closely at the actual problem, to separate it from the multiple symptoms that may exist in a case study. As we begin trying to solve a particular problem, it may seem that much of the talk and suggestions deal with related incidents and peripheral concerns. We talk around a problem, not because of reluctance or hesitation to state the problem, but because we simply do not know the real problem. Although we spend most of our time describing, isolating, and classifying symptoms, we still believe we are accomplishing something! As a result, potential solutions are missed or overlooked. For example, the mayor and council members of an East Coast city complained because they had not received a pay increase in nearly 10 years. To receive such an increase, they needed a yes vote from the voters. Their so-called "problem" was stated frequently: How can the budget be increased to cover a new salary schedule? What is a legitimate salary increase? How should the issue be presented to the electorate? When should the salary increase become effective?

Certainly, many of these issues are relevant to the problem, but they are *not* the problem. Until the viewpoint of the citizens is considered, the mayor and the council cannot possibly isolate the real problem and propose a solution for salary increases. One council member finally asked why the voters had been reluctant to approve a salary increase. In an attempt to answer this question, it was discovered that the public image of the officials left much to be desired. Citizens were critical of matters such as poor street maintenance and lighting, excessive spending, insufficient planning and zoning, and inadequate recreation and park services.

Therefore, solutions to their "problem" ignored the larger problem. As these officials further explored the problem situation, they found that salary increases could not be obtained until they confronted the real problem: *What can be done to improve the image of public officials?* If the mayor and council had not defined the problem properly—the need to improve their public image—they would have continued to discuss only symptoms. As it was, once a more accurate problem statement was formulated, which reflected the true problem, their problem could be solved more directly.

Unfortunately, problem symptoms are often more demanding, more visible, and seemingly more soluble than a problem. It is understandable why they gain so much attention and scrutiny. However, what is still ignored is the statement of the problem and solutions to the problem. We must always differentiate symptoms and problems.

In citing deviations from the norm or from some desired standard, we must be careful not to lump them under one general problem: "The morale of the recreation center's staff is low" or, more broadly, "We all are burnt out and unhappy." Such general problem statements, although perhaps philosophically refreshing, often hamper attempts to form a more precise problem statement.

Even if true, such generalizations are more likely to be overt symptoms than to be the problem itself.

Priorities

After listing the problem symptoms, we must rank them. One is more important than the others, though which one is not known at this point. To help determine which is most important, we need to pose these three questions:

1. How urgent is the symptom?
2. How serious is it?
3. What is its potential for improvement?

That is, which of these symptoms, if alleviated, would improve the center as a social institution, and which of these symptoms, if alleviated, would also have a positive effect on the other symptoms? Ideally, problem specification must be free of problem speculation, biases, and assumptions. We need to draw on as many relevant and accurate facts as possible. This is a somewhat systematic, mechanical action that requires discrimination as we decide what to consider and what to discard. To do so, we must ask more specific questions:

1. What is the action, behavior, or condition that is different than normal?
2. Where is it occurring?
3. When does it appear?
4. How large is the deviation from normal standards and expectations?
5. Whom does the deviation involve or affect?

The question, *why?* is not asked at this stage, because we are seeking the cause of a problem as much as its definition. *Why* will come once the problem has been isolated and stated clearly. To seek the cause of a problem before it is properly stated is a dead end, no matter how good our hunches. A legitimate problem statement reflects the viewpoints of those who should be represented in solutions considered. It is legitimate not only because it is equitable, but also because it is realistic, with as many points of view as possible. Furthermore, a problem statement is legitimate if it reduces biases or assumptions that result from one viewpoint dominating all others.

A biased approach to problem definition limits the possibility of obtaining an accurate problem statement. After considering the various facets of problem definition—objectives, priorities, symptoms, and viewpoints—we are ready to state a tentative problem statement and to begin gathering facts and information that appear relevant to that problem. The problem statement should be as concise as possible. Because this statement will be conveyed to others, it is best to compose as precise a statement as possible before showing it to others.

It is important to write out the problem statement: Unless you put a problem into words, you do not give it form. If it is formless, it does not exist in a manner that permits solution. Putting the problem statement into writing gives others a better opportunity to assist in finding a solution. It keeps us focused on the problem and not on peripheral issues that continually arise.

A tentative problem statement for the East Coast city practitioners seeking a raise could be as follows:

Park and recreation practitioners have not received a raise in our city in 10 years, but they failed to consider their residents' satisfaction with their work.

Such a statement remains tentative because it does not answer all questions, such as what the city council wants to accomplish and what the real problem is. This statement is more of a symptom statement than a problem statement. It must be reformulated to focus on the ultimate objective in solving the problem. A reformulated statement of the problem could be as follows:

What is the best way to change the public image of the East Coast city practitioners?

Related to this statement of the problem, the following questions arise:
1. What are the best methods for using social media and news outlets?
2. How can the practitioners be more accessible?
3. What are the residents' needs and desires?
4. Are residents happy with the physical appearance and cleanliness of their park and recreation facilities?
5. How can community residents be involved in future planning activities?

This is a problem because at this point the main problem seems to be poor image. This East Coast city council has a poor image with its residents and hence many other problems, including low staff wage. After this is established as the problem definition, the city council then realizes that the city's image cannot be improved without making substantive changes. In other words, the council must now ask how this can be achieved and what ideas would help achieve the objective of an improved image? After the council reconsiders the problem statement, a statement closer to reality and more capable of solution emerges.

It seems that the *crux* or *real* problem is the involvement of residents in city activities. Such involvement could improve the city's image. The following problem statement is then suggested:

How can the people in the city become involved in the strategic planning process?

This concept is illustrated more clearly in Figure 4.1.

The assumption is that if residents are involved in planning, the symptoms will diminish or vanish. That is, if parents or guardians assist in planning programs, they will also be more likely to concern themselves with reducing undesirable activity. This, in turn, will greatly improve the city's image. As involvement increases, the desirability of creating and/or serving on an advisory board will also increase. As a result, the advisory board will become a more influential force in city activities. Once the problem is defined, the symptoms can be seen more clearly as subordinate to it.

Fact Finding

When we begin to collect information related to the problem, one of our most important roles is to attempt to weed through the opinions, speculation, and inferences to find *facts* (Fawcett et al., 2013).

As we continue to analyze the problem statement and situation, we immediately recognize that fact gathering is essential. Most problem-solving specialists agree, however, that gathering all the facts is almost impossible. The most difficult skill is to ensure that the facts gathered are relevant to the problem. The more valid the facts, the better the chance to make a logical problem statement.

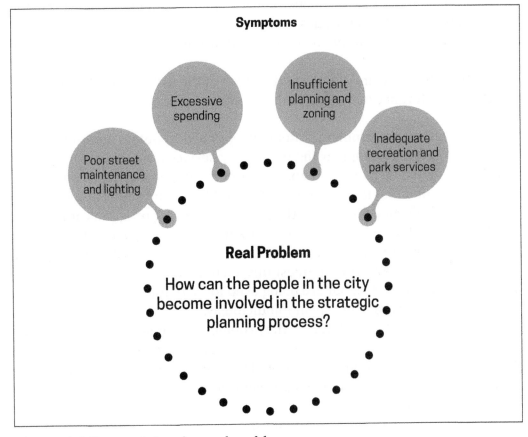

Figure 4.1. Determining the *real* problem.

We should not simply look for quantity, but also for the facts gathered to be relevant to the situation. We can determine the relevancy of facts using these methods (Beecroft, Duffy, & Moran, 2003):

a. Scientific investigation: This can occur through interviews, focus groups, surveys, and personal observations.

b. Opinions of experts: This step can be as simple as gathering information from employees and management at an agency. Or this step can include seeking the counsel of mentors in the same field and other professional opinions (lawyer, consultant, etc.) via phone or virtual conversation.

c. Personal judgment.

d. Demands of the problem analysis.

e. Online databases: The Internet contains a wealth of comparative information from various research groups, such as PEW or Standard and Poor, that may contain relevant and useful information related to the problem.

It was also noted that the facts to be considered should be measured and classified by three characteristics:

1. "The degree of confidence one has that the so-called facts are indeed facts,

2. "The direction and degree of the effect of the fact on the situation,

3. "The relevance of the fact to the problem situation."

To strengthen the problem statement, we need to obtain additional facts. The exact number of people using the agency services should be determined. This figure should be compared with the number of people in the community. We may then find that use is not low. We should also determine at what times usage is low. This may reveal that the agency is offering programs at inconvenient times. Another point is that adequate funds are being spent to carry out an effective program. We must determine the exact amount being spent and for what purposes. Answers to questions such as these may reveal that adequate funds are provided, but are being used for activities that do not interest the participants or are being spent injudiciously.

As additional facts are obtained, the problem statement will be revised and perfected. Many potentially useful facts are not given in case studies. Ignorance of such facts will not produce a solution. The following is a classification of additional facts needed for a more comprehensive solution:

Vandalism and Crime:

- What is the nature of the vandalism?
- Where does it occur?
- Does it occur at any particular time?
- Have arrests been made as a result of the vandalism?
- What is the extent of police protection in the area?
- Do police patrols make regular tours through the area? If so, how often?

- During these patrols, do the officers get out of their cars?
- What kind of checks do they make at the recreation center?
- Is the police department aware of problems at the center?
- What is the relationship between the police department and the recreation and park department? What is the crime rate in the area in contrast to the rest of the city?

Attitudes:
- Is accurate information available about the general attitude of the people toward the recreation center program (i.e., has an attitude, interest, and opinion survey ever been done)? This information can be secured from the city planning commission, from welfare planning council records, or at local universities.

Comparability:
- Are agencies such as the YMCA, YWCA, Boy Scouts, Girl Scouts, after-school activities, and church groups experiencing problems similar to those of the recreation and park department? This information can be elicited from agency personnel.

Facilities:
- What is the physical condition of the parks and facilities and the surrounding area? How does it compare with other amenities in the city? Are buildings old or new? Are they well maintained? Is the lighting outside buildings sufficient for night activity? Is the equipment used in the programs up to date? Is equipment replaced when necessary? How much equipment is available for program activities? Is there a variety of equipment?

Staff:
- Do personnel have the proper skills to conduct the programs? What is the relationship of the staff with participants, advisory board members, and neighborhood residents? Are the staff respected? Do the staff live in the community?

Race:
- Is there evidence of racial tension in the community? What evidence? Are programs inclusive? To what extent? Is the advisory board inclusive? Are schools and other agencies experiencing racial tension?

Programming:
- What efforts have been made to involve residents in planning? Do the residents believe the recreation and park department wants them? Has the advisory board made suggestions for improving the program? If

they have, what action was taken? Was the action communicated to the advisory board? How was it communicated?

Publicity:
- How have the news media been used to inform the public about the programs? What is the department's relationship with newspapers, radio stations, and TV stations? Have the programs been communicated to schools or churches? Do other agencies, such as the welfare department, know about the recreation programs?

The quality and quantity of facts gathered will depend on the money and time available as well as the assumptions for their evaluation. To review the affordability of facts, each grouping must be evaluated as follows:
1. Make a preliminary analysis of the situation on the basis of facts that are immediately available at the time you first become aware of a problem.
2. On the basis of your personal judgment, from clues furnished by the preliminary analysis, list the specific additional facts you would like to have before undertaking a final analysis.
3. By the application of appropriate research techniques, discover as many of the desired facts as time and money will allow.

Collecting facts can be tedious and time consuming. Therefore, do not spend time collecting irrelevant facts. Gathering facts can also be frustrating because many are simply not available. For example, if a park and recreation department has kept poor records, it will be impossible to determine accurate figures. Additionally, if the agency maintains poor financial records, it would be impossible to determine how much and for what purpose funds were being spent. Make every effort to secure all possible facts, but do not become discouraged if these are not as precise as desired.

Implications of Problem Analysis

After the facts are gathered, they must be evaluated to ensure that false assumptions or biases have not been permitted to persist. Bias is a problem throughout the problem-solving process, but it is critical to gathering and evaluating data. Many facts are based on an assumption that the situation will not change and will remain fairly static into the foreseeable future. Such an assumption is risky. We must anticipate, as much as possible, the probable changes that may occur in the facts that affect the problem. For instance, if we select objectives against which to measure the solution, will these merely be short-range objectives, or will there be long-range and interim objectives as well?

Finally, when we seek to involve others in decision making, we have to involve them seriously and not just keep them informed on what happens. If we want to have the viewpoint of the participants, we will have to give them responsibility and power. Without a relinquishment of power and responsibility to the residents, their desire for participation is shallow. Such power, frankly, entails the appropriation of money and other decision-making authority to others outside of the department.

References

Beecroft, G., Duffy, G., & Moran, J. W. (Eds.). (2003). *The executive guide to improvement and change.* Milwaukee, WI: ASQ Quality Press.

Fawcett, S. B., Francisco, V. T., Shultz, J. A., Nagy, G., Berkowtiz, B., & Wolff, T. J. (Contributors). (2015). Our model for community change and improvement. In *Work Group for Community Health and Development, Learn a skill.* Retrieved January 5, 2016, from http://ctb.ku.edu/en/table-of-contents/overview/model-for-community-change-and-improvement

Marx, T. G. (2015). The impact of business strategy on leadership. *Journal of Strategy and Management, 8,* 110–126.

Mullins, L. (2013). *Management and organisational behaviour* (10th ed.). London, England: Pearson.

Pettinger, R. (2012). *Management: A concise introduction.* Hampshire, United Kingdom: Palgrave Macmillan.

Rees, W., & Porter, C. (2015). Delegation - A crucial but sadly neglected management skill. *Industrial and Commercial Training, 47,* 320–325.

CHAPTER 5
DEFINING OBJECTIVES

The second step in the problem-solving model is setting objectives. These include shortand long-range objectives for evaluating the solutions selected. Objectives are used as specific goals or measurements to evaluate other solutions developed in the problem-solving model.

We should keep in mind, however, that when the problem-solving model is followed, these steps should not be taken in a rigidly prescribed order, nor is one step necessarily separated from the others. These steps are separated for discussion purposes here, but usually are part of an interrelated flow from start to finish.

To solve a problem and to know if the solution was effective, we must be able to measure or evaluate it. These measures are known as goals and objectives. They are either short range (interim) or long range, and their intended duration and impact must be stated in advance. We must clearly state the goals and the process we intend to follow to reach them. This is one step in the model that requires precision.

How do we know if we have poor objectives? What guidelines or criteria can be used? We must be as disciplined in our formulation of objectives as in the scrutiny of assumptions and biases during the fact-finding stage. A problem may be stated as follows: *How can people in the recreation center's neighborhood become involved in planning programs?* One of the objectives is included in the problem statement. This is not unusual, because a well-formulated problem statement should specify at least one objective, though this is often done in general terms.

To be able to state, clarify, and rank objectives in terms that can be understood, we must first analyze the objectives of the organization as stated in bylaws or policies. That is, we should determine what the objectives of the recreation center are and how these policies are related to the problem statement. If the attendance figure is low, we need to define a low measurement. Is there a policy, formal or otherwise, stating a percentage or degree of involvement from which the center has deviated? Did the recreation board establish a policy stating the desirable objective to achieve for neighborhood involvement with identified penalties when not reached? Comparisons with actual measures in mind can yield specific, measurable objectives.

Is the problem a deviation from a formal policy, an implied or informal organizational policy, or neither? Does policy influence the problem? Unfortunately, comparing formal policies with the problem statement does not always produce objectives. Many intangible factors, seemingly unrelated to the organization's formal policy, are important. Even though recommended attendance figures in policy statements are not being met, they may not be far from the recreation director's expectations. The director may have ignored formal policy and decided alone what is feasible and practical, based on previous attendance markers.

If such intangible policies exist, and often they do, they must be reflected in any problem analysis of formal organizational policies. If they are not examined, their implications will be hidden and their impact unrealistically diminished. These are real concerns—political, personal, or whatever—and are important, no matter how intangible or embarrassing. This is especially true if the problem solver is an outside consultant, who may waste many hours before discovering these unwritten policies.

Not all implied policies are contrary to stated objectives. Burying such policies causes the difficulty, forcing us to deal with incomplete information. For example, if we set an objective to increase attendance by 10%, we should not do so when our real intention is to reach only 5%.

Any organization's objectives have to change to keep pace with the needs of the people being served. For these objectives, we have to consider any factions seeking reform within the organization as well as the grievances of those closest to the problem. However, if we feel our traditional objectives remain worthwhile, a goal can be set that reaffirms the related objectives for those involved as a way to reeducate them. Radically altering policies is not necessary when the organization's objectives are still valuable. This is seldom the case, but is mentioned because change in itself is rarely the best solution when the original plan has not been carefully analyzed.

We must carefully define the specific objectives leading to the best solution. Objectives are not meant to be final at this stage (though they may be), but we modify or change them as we approach the solution to the problem.

Other objectives are intentionally selected as steps leading to other goals and are called *interim goals*. These are a way of eventually obtaining a longer range goal. For example, if the reduction of vandalism is an interim goal, a 24-hour guard or security cameras could be placed at the center. This goal is intended as a stopgap, until we can begin to deal with the problem that causes such vandalism. However, if we feel that eliminating vandalism alone will resolve the attendance problem in the long run, we are misusing interim goals. Vandalism is one symptom of the problem, not the problem itself.

Although the value judgments, opinions, and expertise of those concerned are important to setting objectives and cannot be ignored during problem solving, the strongest determinants are economic and analytic. What resources are available? What resources can be expected to achieve various objectives? For instance, how many staff members would certain objectives require? Is there enough financial support? Is a special appropriation necessary? What time limits govern the objectives? What facts are required for the statement of objectives? For instance, a recreation director who is determining how a bond issue is to be passed must also be concerned with the development of community long-range plans encompassing or affecting the role of the organization in the community. The employment of a drama specialist, as another example, may eventually give impetus to the development of a cultural arts program. This outcome should be anticipated when an interim goal to hire a drama specialist is set. The unexpected outcome is not always a desirable objective. A clear set of objectives will largely determine how successful we are in solving a problem and the direction resulting from the solutions.

We must decide whether the solution is merely a stopgap or a lasting solution to a problem. When we label objectives according to intention, duration, or flexibility, we know their aims before attempting to identify a solution. (See Figure 5.1.)

As the recreation center staff discuss the problem, they must determine what they are seeking to accomplish. If the objective is stated simply as increasing attendance at the center, and if no thought is given to involving the neighborhood residents surrounding the center, little progress can be expected in the larger problem. Of course, the recreation staff should be concerned with the immediate attendance problem, but any objective must be evaluated for its effect on the greater impact of the center's programs and activities. For example, a citywide event attracting patrons from the entire city on a particular day would not solve the problem. This program would involve many people for a short time in the center, but it would do little to increase continuing neighborhood attendance or alleviate the purely local symptoms of the problem. This idea could be a supplementary or complementary objective for the center, but not be a main one.

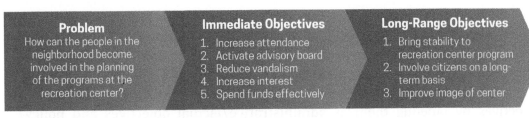

Figure 5.1. Objectives: Immediate–Long-Range

Defining objectives is not simple. We must know what we are attempting to achieve and how to do it. These conceptions are best stated in quantitative and qualitative terms, as specifically as possible. Only with such a plan in mind can we begin to formulate *sound* objectives. Objectives can be visualized as a skeleton of the problem-solving model with the outer substance determined by the major steps of the model. As a skeletal dimension, objectives help remind us whence we have come, and where we are going, and what we hope to achieve. They are checkmarks along a route that must be rigorously stated at the start. We must state our attendance objectives in number and kind.

Many objectives used in public administration, such as park and recreation agencies, are *value objectives* (Molina, 2009), based on value elements rather than on only facts based on the data gathered. Factual statements are observable and empirically measurable. Value statements must have a set of criteria or assumptions commonly agreed on by those solving the problem. If at all possible, some tangible weights should be quantitatively assigned to these values.

These quantitative weights must be worked out *before* incorporating any value objectives into problem solving. There is no way of rationally testing these values for validity later. To recognize that problems have a value or an ethical component does not diminish the factual elements of problem solving. Both are interrelated in any statement of objectives. Values are intertwined in public administration, whereas no one person's personal values should outweigh another individual's or organization's. In public administration, Goodsell (1989) identified five value perspectives:

1. Means: Administrator concerned with values such as efficiency, effectiveness, and expertise.
2. Morality: Administrator concerned with values of equality, honesty, justice, and fairness.
3. Multitude: Administrator concerned with values such as pluralism, inclusiveness, and responsiveness to citizens.
4. Market: Administrator concerned with values of entrepreneurialism, limited government, and free-market solutions to public problems.
5. Mission: Administrator concerned with values such as institutional integrity, advancing organizational programs for the common good, and exercising discretionary authority in the public interest (Molina, 2009).

This perspective suggests that park and recreation administrators may have different value perspectives. However, their values or the individual values of their employees can be greater than the organizational values that they are working toward for the betterment of the community.

Usually, a fairly clear line can be drawn between *factual* and *value* objectives by labeling them as administrative/factual objectives and policy/value objectives, because this is how they usually are developed in practice. Administrative concerns are more often factual information and objectives, whereas policy concerns stress values, broad social achievements, and goals.

In recreation, when a superintendent recommends policy decisions for board approval, these policies incorporate the superintendent's value objectives. When the board approves these recommendations, it is assumed that the board members are aware of values underlying the policy. Their concern is achieving values, not facts. The decision and implementation strategies are the primary concerns of the administrators. They must formulate measurable objectives for the process toward meeting the value goals initiated by the superintendent and board. Both types of objectives combine and make up the means by which the solutions are evaluated, as illustrated in Figure 5.2.

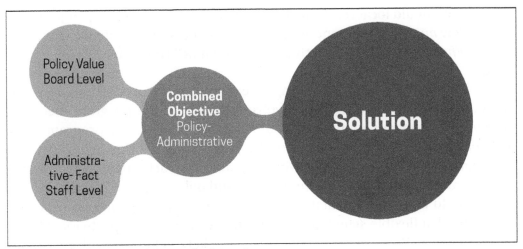

Figure 5.2. Value and factual objectives.

No matter how broad-ranging and inspiring the stipulated objectives, if we fail to meet them because of ambiguity or generality, we also fail to solve the problem. Failure due to trying to achieve too much may be consoling to some, but when it involves the setting of vague objectives for an organization, it is simply poor planning. As with personal aspirations, we do not often get a second chance to solve a problem, because of such unrealistic or ambitious goals. Thus, objectives add an element of specificity to a problem statement, without necessarily limiting the scope of that statement.

If we desire to increase the advisory board's involvement, for example, our objective may be to increase board size from five to 15 community members. This objective reflects that there is more work for the board to address as well as the value for increasing community involvement in the center. If we want to publicize the activities of the center or the final decision it makes for the problem, we may set as an objective the release of several (three or more) publicity news releases per week, especially when beginning to implement a solution. We could also set as practical, measurable objectives a reduction of vandalism by 10% and an increase in monthly attendance from the present average of 400 to 750. Such factual objectives consider the values we seek to represent.

Any modification in objectives should be a compromise among those concerned about previously stated and agreed objectives of the organization. For instance, the recreation director and staff, the neighborhood youth and their parents, and the city government officials should collectively formulate the objectives. It is unlikely that all parties will agree to similar objectives. Compromises must be made as those concerned seek to set *equitable* and *constructive* objectives for the problem.

When we begin to formulate factual objectives for involving residents more with the local park and recreation agency, we should ask questions such as the following:

- *How* should local residents be involved with the agency's programs?
- *How much* involvement in the programs and activities do we want?
- *When* and *where* should this involvement be? How often?

Such questions aid in formulating objectives that are precise in time, place, and quantity. Thus, "We wish to involve residents in the program" becomes "We wish to involve *x* number of youth and residents in our programs on a daily basis for *x* number of weeks of the year." "We wish this involvement to be in planning activities as well as in participating in activities." "This involvement is intended to include administrative and policy matters." "Such involvement should allow the residents to hire a community organizer or a leader able to work a flexible schedule to meet the needs of youth participants on a personal basis." Because some objectives are likely to be met with resistance from officials, we should anticipate and prepare "sales" pitches to use when speaking with policy makers.

With objectives stated, we may then begin to evaluate proposed solutions. At this point, we can discard tentative solutions simply because they do not meet our objectives. For example, an attempt to alleviate the attendance problem by having special announcements for citizen groups regarding the next season's programs does not meet the objectives of serious neighborhood involvement. This action simply announces already concluded program plans and does not invite resident involvement in the program design and implementation.

On the other hand, in an economically constrained situation, this solution may lead us to reconsider our objectives. Objectives come from two viewpoints: results that are expected and resources that are needed to achieve results. If there is no possibility of obtaining additional money from the city to involve the residents in the center—by delegating power and money to neighborhood groups—it may be that a large neighborhood meeting announcing predetermined programs is the best solution we can offer in the financial circumstances. It is not intended as an interim objective, because the next step of greater involvement may not be taken for some time.

Even with economic constraints, we should consider the value of involving a few key neighborhood representatives—if financially feasible—in the center's programming activities in lieu of designing programs without such involvement. A small but qualified involvement by the neighborhood may offer a *better* solution within the limited resource limitations. This is what is intended when we weigh and judge objectives and solutions against one another.

After we have formulated, stated in measurable terms, and weighed objectives that we feel are important to the problem, we must classify and rank them by importance. This is a critical distinction that helps us to list our objectives in relation to different levels of resources. Objectives are often categorized into one of two processes: fundamental or means-end oriented (Shields, Solar, & Martin, 2002). The fundamental process organizes the objectives, which are typically situation based, according to the impact level, with the most significant objectives placed at the top. The fundamental hierarchy arrangement often resembles a tree, with lines drawn from each objective that identify the implementation or evaluation attribute for that objective (Shields et al., 2002). A second process called the means-end network provides a structured order that is directly connected to an organization's value structure. In short, the objectives are ordered according to the value identified by the organization. The objectives directly connected to organizational values are placed at the top, with the fundamental, situation-based objectives following (Shields et al., 2002). The distinction between these objective types overlaps at times, which makes organizing objectives challenging (Bond, Carlson, & Keeney, 2008). The most important element is to fully consider how the objective will lead to the outcome and the individuals who will be involved in the process.

To formulate goals more effectively, we have to invite and welcome the individuals concerned with the problem. If they state that they wish to expand the concept and role of recreation in the community, this objective is not likely to stir the imagination of anyone but the director and staff. The concern is too broad and not immediate enough to the neighborhood residents. This is a fundamental objective because it is desirable but not necessary to solve the immediate problem.

We often achieve this goal indirectly by not even including it in our short list. Rather, we connect this process to a means-end objective. If we improve the image of the center through residential involvement in programming, we indirectly expand the concept of recreation beyond that of offering predetermined programs to citizens. Community involvement in recreation planning and programming indirectly increases the scope of recreation without stating it as an absolute objective. We, therefore, solve the problem effectively without altering the conception of recreation at all. As mentioned, ambitious objectives do not necessarily lead to ambitious results; often quite the contrary, they draw attention away from the real problem.

We should also be sure that our objectives are not personal or vindictive. For instance, if we wish to expand the role of recreation in the center simply because it will improve our chance for promotion or transfer, without regard for its effect on others, this is shortsighted. Similarly, citizen involvement in the process of developing goals and objectives presents an equally challenging situation because some individuals arrive to the process with a predetermined agenda. Smith and McDonough (2001) described one citizen's reason for dismay with the public engagement initiative: ". . . Some of the meetings I quit going to because they were loaded and they were orchestrated, so why attend when you knew the outcome was gonna be what they wanted . . ." (p. 245).

Personal and organizational goals can coexist, but we should be able to differentiate them. Mixed goals are not necessarily incompatible, but should be distinguished. If we can honestly excite the group about a personal career goal that would promise organizational benefits to all involved, this is fine. Assuming that a "good" ambition will lead to good objectives is specious reasoning. All organizations exist to meet their own goals as well as the employees' individual goals. Personal goals are an important stimulus for solving organizational problems, but their motives must be understood and distinguished.

Although we are perhaps able to understand and recognize personal motives, we also have to be on the lookout for the personal goals of other participants: staff, residents, and city officials. If one resident has ambitions to become an advisory board member, the resident may favor flamboyant objectives (however shortsighted) to make a good (and flashy) impression on the voters. This resident may seek to ignore or downplay organizational objectives as of little concern. In such a case, we must defend the organizational objectives that were agreed on. These objectives must be compatible with personal and professional concerns, yet they presumably have an equal or greater importance than purely personal objectives.

The closer an objective is to a person's concerns, the more interested the person becomes in the solution. By delegating the initial formulation of objectives to those who are closest to the problem, we often receive well-formulated and specific objectives to integrate within the broader objectives.

As we gather the various measurable objectives, we must project, as much as possible, the effects of the objectives on the environment in which we operate. We will encounter many difficulties because of environmental fluctuations that we did not anticipate when the objectives were designed or from our own conceptual limitations.

References

Bond, S. D., Carlson, K. A., & Keeney, R. L. (2008). Generating objectives: Can decision makers articulate what they want? *Management Science, 54,* 56–70.

Goodsell, C. (1989). Balancing competing values. In J. Perry (Ed.), *Handbook of public administration* (pp. 575–584). San Francisco, CA: Jossey-Bass.

Molina, A. D. (2009). Values in public administration: The role of organizational culture. *International Journal of Organization Theory and Behavior, 12,* 266–279.

Shields, D., Solar, S., & Martin, W. (2002). The role of values and objectives in communicating indicators of sustainability. *Ecological Indicators, 2,* 149–160.

Smith, P. D., & McDonough, M. H. (2001). Beyond public participation: Fairness in natural resource decision making. *Society and Natural Resources, 14,* 239–249.

_____ CHAPTER 6 _____
FACTORS THAT INFLUENCE PROBLEM SOLVING

This chapter focuses on the factors leading to the initial problem situation as well as on the factors affecting the attainment of objectives. In considering these factors in an analysis, we need to understand the effect on the overall solution. Although we must recognize as many factors as possible, we also need to distinguish the most important factors for examination. Good judgment is particularly important when making this distinction.

Change as a Factor

The most important factor in the problem environment is change. Changes that affect the problem, either positively or negatively, can be complex or simple, radical, or routine. A change, in its simplest form, is something different in an environment from what had originally been perceived. Change is either natural or intentional. Before a problem was discovered, some factors had not yet emerged to affect the environment. In problem analysis, we are more interested in negative changes because they more drastically limit a situation, causing a problem to be discerned.

When setting objectives, we should distinguish between what a situation actually is and what we feel it should be. Any shift from actual to normative is change, either spontaneous or intentional. In problem analysis, we try to identify the actual change and reason for occurrence. Additionally, the analysis determines the direction and duration of the change. The prime change will be the cause of the problem. Once the cause is known, we may then begin to devise solutions.

To discover the cause of a problem, we need to distinguish it (Hicks, 2013). For instance, what if we received the following feedback: "Residents and youth do not attend our programs as often as we feel desirable." The desirable number should be stated as a quantitative objective. Such a distinction could provide the reason for _limited_ participation. Such factors—a blighted, poor neighborhood; an old center building; and a negative image—are important to recall in seeking the reason for poor attendance. By isolating changes in the environment, we begin to recognize the symptoms of the main cause of the problem. As we once had to distinguish the real problem, we now need to seek the real cause.

As with logical analyses, one distinction is often built upon or precedes another. These distinctions are a closer view of the symptoms. What do they say about what caused the problem? Earlier, we delayed determining the cause of the problem. It was premature to focus on the cause of a problem rather than on its definition. It is now time for such focus when approaching the formulation of solutions. These solutions must be related to the cause of a problem, or what is believed to be the cause.

It is possible to solve a problem without knowing its cause. If we randomly suggest a variety of solutions to the problem, *without* investigation, it may be possible—by chance alone—to discover an effective solution.

Such conjectural solutions may be justified only when we feel the solution is the best we can come up with after thorough analysis or in a situation in which we have nothing to lose. For instance, we could now try some "experimental" solutions, such as increasing the budget or personnel for the agency, better lighting in parks and facilities, wellness posters in the lobby, or social media blasts related to improving the image of the agency. But we must realize that if these solutions do not solve the problem, they may be costly. We have to take chances in problem solving, but these should be realistic, not merely intellectual or experimental exercises. This is not to say that speculation has no role in making distinctions in a problem situation. If we speculate about what changes would affect attendance, we often find a much deeper cause than anticipated. However, speculation should still only be seriously used after we have exhausted more straightforward searches for causes; that is, speculation should never replace rigorous analysis. If through speculation we are led into larger areas of concern, we should pursue them only if they seem worthy of further analysis. If we discover, for example, that recreation interests and needs have changed within the community population, we should pursue these changes, which most assuredly does affect the situation.

We should never assume that a larger or more complex change is the cause of the problem. For example, if we speculate that racial difficulties have affected the park and recreation department's image and attendance, we may feel justified in pursuing improved community police relations, alternative programming, or community–center relations. However, the prime cause of the attendance drop may be as simple as a lack of locker space! We must not be overly ambitious in attempts to pinpoint causes.

As we begin to distinguish distinctions and changes in the situation, the specific cause is the one nearest and most pertinent to the problem. Is the cause of the problems social malaise, lack of resources, poor security for participants, or perhaps the suspicious attitude of staff toward youth? We must determine which if any of these causes is the key cause. As we discover and analyze the causes, we should rank them as to which is likely to be the cause.

It is now clear why we defined the problem situation before seeking its cause. By having a clearly defined problem statement, we can compare various causes with the problem statement, discarding those with no causal relationship. We should begin to consider the most obvious causes first, those that we already have in mind from dealing with the problem. We should deal only with relevant or possible causes at the start, for these are more likely to reveal the cause and thus end the search. Hicks (2013) suggested the process of synectics is useful when identifying diverse problems and ideas toward solutions, "when our need is to 'open up' the problem situation, view it from many angles and give ourselves a reasonable chance of checking that we are attempting to solve the right problem" (Hicks, 2013, p. 21). To accomplish this process, a diverse group of stakeholders engages to identify the true nature of the problem, and through facilitation multiple solutions are identified to address the issue.

Whatever causes and changes we begin to examine, these are testable in relation to the problem. As with the problem statement, the more specific and rigorous the change statement, the easier it will be to select a solution to the problem. Again, if more information is required to prepare a specific change statement, we would gather additional facts. Fact gathering is not a cutoff point in the model, but continues throughout problem solving as needed.

When examining some of the more obvious causes and preparing hypothetical statements on them, we may begin to uncover other subtle or less evident causes. These may be aspects of change that no one wants to know, such as a serious drop in the quality of programs offered at various facilities and the effect of this on attendance or racism by the staff. Nonetheless, we must pursue such analysis if we feel that these changes are part of the problem.

Change as a Block

Awareness of one change leads to another. After revealing what we believe are the changes that caused the problem, we then consider solutions to the problem. Such solutions invariably will entail another change. If we are going to increase participation of residents in park and recreation programs, this change may cause difficulty. Such blocks to setting and achieving objectives are cultural, perceptual, emotional, or even physical (Hicks, 2013).

Attitudes Toward Change

Early theorists (Lewin, 1952) conceptualized resistance to change as a significant negative outcome. Over time, this perspective has waned, and in the late 1990s, a shift in this perspective occurred to view resistance as a normal component of individual or organizational attitude toward change (Ford, Ford, & D'Amelio, 2008). Most individuals are not resisting the change itself, but rather they are anxious over the looming effect it will have on them (Dent & Goldberg, 1999; Oreg, 2006).

We must recognize that most people are more comfortable with a familiar situation and resist the unknown, no matter how trivial. Extensive research has been conducted for several decades regarding the process of change for individuals as well as for organizations (e.g., Bareil, 2013; Ford et al., 2008; Lewin, 1952). Such research has been concentrated on changes (or innovations) as desirable and planned. Random or chance changes were rarely considered in the beginning, but now we must plan for the unexpected to create change in their organization (Bareil, 2013). One of the difficulties of such research is how to introduce change effectively. No matter how much a change may benefit those involved in the problem, we should never assume that people will accept the risk of change. Nothing should be assumed about the positive aspects of any change.

The process of change can no doubt elicit fear and anxiety. Ford et al. (2008) suggested three primary elements to consider when undertaking and addressing change with the individuals who will be most affected:

1. Recognize and address the change to recipients' public behavior rather than contemplating the possible internal feelings.
2. Understand that bringing preconceived notions of stakeholder resistance can also induce resistance.
3. Keep the relationship between the change agent and recipient in perspective.

The ideal atmosphere for solving problems is one in which management has an open attitude and flexibility toward change and has substantiated it. No matter how appealing or nostalgic traditions are, we must reconcile them during the problem-solving process. To hear, for the hundredth time, "We have never done it that way before" is tiresome and depletes our energies. Nonetheless, this perspective should not be viewed negatively. When seeking changes, we should consider an employees' hesitancy to change as a counteroffer (Ford et al., 2008). In truth, this employee is nervous or anxious about the effect of proposed changes on his or her personal position in the organization (Dent & Goldberg, 1999)

Residents and possibly elected officials may be simultaneously resistant to and open to change because of a desire for change coupled with mental blocks against that change—for example, the thought that the current situation does not appear beneficial and seems to lead nowhere. Change within any organization can elicit anxiety or hesitation from the individuals involved, and higher education is no exception. Lane (2007) listed suggested approaches to intro duce change at an academic institution:

1. Manage the process.
2. Convey the importance or urgency of the need for change.
3. Acknowledge and protect the strengths of the current system.
4. Educate the organization on the nature of complex change.
5. Seek to understand fears and concerns.
6. Assess levels of resistance over time and plan accordingly.
7. Acknowledge and manage conflict appropriately.
8. Maintain knowledgeable, consistent leadership.
9. Provide sufficient time for complex change to be planned and implemented.
10. Create a strong proposal.
11. Provide evidence to support proposals when available.
12. Use demonstrations and pilot studies when appropriate to convey value of proposal.

13. Communicate frequently.
14. Encourage wide participation, including that of external stakeholders.
15. Communicate effectively, using multiple methods to collect and convey information.
16. Appeal to intellectual and emotional concerns.
17. Use various individuals (student, junior faculty, senior faculty, leaders) as opinion leaders to help build consensus.
18. Maximize face-to-face communication as much as possible.

These suggestions demonstrate the need for us to plan the change process, recognize and value the individuals who will be most affected, and maintain consistent communication to ensure information is consistently and correctly disseminated.

Various assumptions about problem analysis can cause serious blocks for reaching any solution. If we want to involve residents in the planning process, this objective has multiple assumptions. The principal assumption of any proposed solution is that all those involved in the problem will appreciate the need for a solution. Because a group has been working earnestly on a problem does not guarantee that they will see the value of any one solution. Lack of rapport or agreement about a solution can seriously block its implementation.

There must be continual staff and administrative support for resident participation in problem solving and planning. Lack of support from those who direct the center will create a major block to any lasting solution. If we are not serious about involving residents in programs, we face a potentially serious block to any solution. Involvement by residents also requires additional resources, which we have to consider. In such instances, lack of knowledge of various blocks is a deterrent to problem solving.

It is assumed that staff and residents are aware of how much time and energy such involvement will require. The amount expected from everyone should be calculated in advance. Nothing should be left unstated, because it appears obvious to us. It may be obvious only to us once a solution is proposed.

We must examine the structure of an organization before making any changes in the relationship between those within the organization and those who will be involved in the problem solving. For instance, if we are going to recruit residents for decision making—giving them the power to spend funds and hire special staff—a structural review of the organization is mandatory. We cannot adjust to new personnel—volunteer or paid—without knowing their function in the organization. New personnel need to know their relations with existing personnel. A weak structural analysis can preclude a solution.

Mental Blocks

Other blocks to meeting objectives, closely related to attitudinal blocks, are those in the ability to solve problems. These blocks range from a mental set for or against a particular solution, to rigidity when confronted with changes. People set their minds for or against something, which then hampers them in solving problems. Everyone has a mental block about one thing or another, so look for these in problem solving.

The three mental blocks inhibiting a person's creative ability to solve problems are perceptual, cultural, and emotional (Hicks, 2013). To a great extent, these blocks are extensions of the person's value system.

Many people exhibit perceptual blocks when they are unable to transfer expertise from one area to another. For instance, if a problem solver is keen on solving personal problems, but is incompetent in business for which comparable skills are needed, that person has a mental block. If an administrator sees the need for keeping detailed records of home finances, but does not keep good business records, that person is unable to perceive the need for good records in both places. The administrator has the skill, but is unable to make the link between the two "worlds."

A chief cause of poor perception is the influence of culture on problem-solving techniques. These values are standards for behavior to which people conform to survive or succeed in a group. For instance, if racism is one of the cultural norms with which a person has grown up, it may persist as an unspoken or assumed standard in the person's organization. Thus, if the problem solver at a park and recreation agency wishes to involve members of a particular racial community, there may be unexpected resistance from the staff. The same sort of implicit values may exist for personal ambitions within an organization. If a new staff member has new ideas for solving a problem, that person may encounter resistance from other staff members. The staff members do not wish to exert themselves too much, because cultural blocks cause them to frown on anyone exceeding implicit norms of ambition in the group. The group is content; the new staff member should be also if that person wishes to get along with the group. On the other hand, a cultural block by others also may cause a person to be overly ambitious. Unless the individual is strong or willing to leave an organization, that person usually succumbs to group cultural pressures, adopting group conceptions of what is acceptable.

Take an example of affection in our case study. If we have affection for either a staff member or a community resident, this can be personally satisfying. However, if we let a decision be overly affected by this emotion when this person is a factor in the decision, this can be a block. For instance, the community person for whom we have affection may not be the best representative of the community. Thus, if we insist on involving this person in the center, we may be satisfying our own needs at the expense of the community.

The same applies to giving not-so-talented staff members positions they are not qualified for simply because of an affection for them. The person must be qualified for the task. We must be able to be critical of shortcomings to avoid letting this emotion become a block: "I am really fond of John, but he has no 'feel' for the community problem."

Fear is probably the greatest emotional block in problem solving. If we are fearful of setting innovative objectives or of dealing with a problem because of expected repercussions, our problem solving will be severely hampered. Another fear is not knowing enough about a problem to make a decision. This is a common fault for many, based on fear of or anxiety about having to make a decision. There is nothing wrong with emotions—they are usually healthy or necessary—but we must be aware of them as potential blocks.

Summary

In today's society, people talk a lot about the "little man," but rely almost exclusively on professionals for work that volunteers or paraprofessionals could handle. For example, a suggestion is made that a park and recreation department use an outreach worker in the community. Those imbued with the myth that professionals are the only ones who can handle services to the community will resist this suggestion.

On the other hand, we can achieve community involvement while still harboring latent resentments toward the community. If we change our minds and values and wish to convert this into action, we may still be led astray. If we feel strongly that community involvement is crucial, we can overstress this viewpoint to the exclusion of other components.

If we see solving problems in a social vacuum, we would need only to consider our blocks to a problem. However, we are dealing with others and have to anticipate blocks that are likely to occur. As we anticipate such blocks, we have to be realistic about which we have control over and which we do not. Not all blocks can be removed or circumvented.

In regard to ignorance and resistance to change, we can begin to attack by attempting to educate those resistant to new ideas and viewpoints. If city officials and board members feel vandalism at the center is the prime problem, they may insist on immediate law enforcement. As discussed in other examples, however, such shortsighted solutions do not get at the real problem. We have to educate the board and officials about what we feel are the long-range aspects of the problem. We must be alert throughout the entire problem-solving model to the blocks that constrain or enhance our attempt to solve the problem.

References

Bareil, C. (2013). Two paradigms about resistance to change. *Organizational Development Journal, 31*(3), 59–71.

Dent, E. B., & Goldberg, S. G. (1999). Challenging "resistance to change." *The Journal of Applied Behavioral Science, 35*(1), 25-41.

Ford, J. D., Ford, L. W., & D'Amelio, A. (2008). Resistance to change: The rest of the story. *Academy of Management Review, 33,* 362–377.

Hicks, M. J. (2013). *Problem solving in business and management: Hard, soft, and creative approaches.* New York, NY: Springer-Science+Business Media.

Lane, I. F. (2007). Change in higher education: Understanding and responding to individual and organizational resistance. *Research and Education Reports, 34*(2), 85–92.

Lewin, K. (1952). *Field theory in social sciences: Selected theoretical papers.* London, England: Tavistock.

Oreg, S. (2006). Personality, context, and resistance to organizational change. *European Journal of Work and Organizational Psychology, 15,* 73–101.

CHAPTER 7
BRAINSTORMING

Creative Thinking

As noted earlier, the study and dissection of creativity and creative people have been of great interest to many researchers. In fact, more ideas and notions can be offered on what constitutes creativity than are given to an existing problem! With so many definitions of creativity, it seems the most creative thing to do is to let the subject rest. It is *never* the creative person who examines or researches creativity, but the onlookers, those who wonder if they are missing something. Creative people are too close to the quality, too involved to concern themselves with examining it. If asked to do so, they are often evasive, baffled, annoyed, or sarcastic.

Most creativity researchers conclude that a creative person is a maverick: restless, independent, a loner, rarely working in organizations (perhaps with the exception of academia, where impoverished creative people often corner a fellowship). The creative mind is invariably a solitary mind, even when forced to operate in organizations. Thus, researchers concentrate instead on how less creative people can be made more creative or how organizations can restructure themselves to become more attractive to these solitary, creative individuals.

Creative writers, perhaps of all artists, are best able to express themselves on creative inspiration. Whenever reading their descriptions, people realize quickly that this is far from the realm in which groups and organizations operate. Emily Brontë in the closing lines of her poem "To Imagination" calls her imagination and creativity, which she considers a gift, the God of visions: "Speak, God of visions, plead for me, / And tell why I have chosen thee!" It is a cheap shot to say creativity is not magic. If there is anything left under the sun that reason and logic have not destroyed, it is the hidden magic of creative imagination. That it cannot be measured or subjected to the researcher's gaze does not mean it is nonexistent. That is the worst research fallacy possible.

The creativity concern here is that which can be taught or learned, examined, and evaluated. As shown in Figure 7.1, this kind of creative thinking comes closest to artistic inspiration, but is still the "organized mind wandering." It does not favor one mode of thinking over another, but distinguishes different ways of thinking.

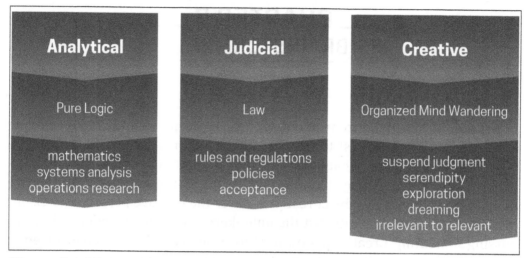

Figure 7.1. Ways in which we think.

Many administrators have difficulty shifting from more analytical and judicial modes of thought to creative ones, just as creative persons have difficulty with analytical and judicial modes of thought. Too often, analytical thinkers equate a wandering mind with a troubled mind. Many people are afraid of being creative or are hostile toward those they feel are more creative. This chapter focuses on one method—brainstorming for ideas—that enables those used to more rigid methods of thinking to move into the realm of group creativity. The concern here is not so much with how to attract creative persons to work in group settings and organizations.

J. P. Guilford, when president of the American Psychological Association, devoted his inaugural address to "education's appalling neglect of creativity." In response to this indictment, Osborn, an advertising executive, published *Applied Imagination* in 1953. The premise of his book is that anyone can be trained to use his or her imagination more effectively and that many can increase their productivity. Much of the material in this chapter pertains to these ideas because most current research is centered on Osborn's foundational work.

Creativity can be increased or at least enhanced by training. In a meta-analysis of creativity training programs, Scott, Leritz, and Mumford (2004) concluded that creativity training works and is effective for a variety of people. Furthermore, "techniques where people are shown how to work with information in a systematic fashion, were positively related to the success of training" (Scott et al., 2004, p. 382). In other words, even those who do not think of themselves as creative can be more creative if they have the right tools.

Many problems for recreation and park administrators can be easily solved by stimulating creative thinking, such as brainstorming sessions. Brainstorming is a method for generating ideas, in this case, suggesting solutions to the problems. One person can use the method, but it is usually more successful with groups. In brainstorming, ideas are encouraged from more subconscious levels of the brain, setting off a chain reaction of free association.

Osborn developed the brainstorming conference technique, which his advertising firm, Batten, Barton, Durstine, and Osborn (BBDO), then used with great success. Many organizations and institutions throughout the United States have tried this technique. In these sessions, six or more people, informally seated, are presented with a problem statement. The more specific it is, the better. Everyone is encouraged to offer as many ideas as quickly as possible for solving the problem. At this stage, no overt judgment of ideas is permitted.

Unusual approaches, creative solutions, and chance notions are the raw material of a brainstorming session. Everyone participating is encouraged to build on other people's ideas. The successful problem solver sees that the seemingly irrelevant idea may be relevant to the problem.

For those not familiar with its premises and use, brainstorming may seem to require little training or discipline, to be a bull session for quickly producing solutions to problems. Nothing could be further from the truth. Brainstorming *potential* solutions to problems. Brainstorming is an important aspect of problem solving, not its replacement. It is the creative ingredient of conventional styles of problem solving.

Osborn (1979) viewed brainstorming simply as "a workable way of jointly producing more and better ideas than is possible through the usual type of conference in which judicial judgment jams creative imagination" (p. 168) Brainstorming has a seductive quality and may first appear as a substitute for more logical approaches to problem solving. This seductive quality, probably more than any single factor, has led to its misconception and misuse.

Brainstorming is a technique for problem solving that encourages a person to generate radically new ideas, a technique that does not initially combine *good* judgment with *good* ideas. Rather, problem solvers are encouraged to ransack their brains for ideas. As Osborn (1979) stated, it is an attack on negative thinking, or on "positive" thinking that prizes critical judgment and immediate solubility of a problem as measures of worth.

Brainstorming encourages the suspension of judgment to encourage ideas without the constraints of critical evaluation. Speculation flourishes and is encouraged by brainstorming. Judgment is *deferred* to when it is more valuable, rather than during generation. Critical evaluation of ideas follows the brainstorming session, usually the next day.

It is hypothesized that people are more creative in a group if they are sure that their ideas will not be attacked or criticized. This fear has been termed *evaluation apprehension,* and studies have shown that it can affect the productivity of group brainstorming sessions (e.g., see Camacho & Paulus, 1995).

If judgment is temporarily suspended, the generation of ideas is usually improved, both qualitatively and quantitatively. Deferred judgment is important, although formal education stresses that logic and creativity should occur simultaneously. As a result, problem solvers tend to suppress potentially useful and innovative ideas because their own or others' "cold" judgment is used too soon. When judgment is deferred, many more alternative ideas are created from which to choose.

The concept of suspended judgment has been reflected in many books on how to think more creatively, notably de Bono's (1992) *Serious Creativity* in which he discusses his method of lateral thinking. He contrasted lateral with vertical thinking. In vertical thinking, logic controls a person's thoughts; in lateral, logic is at the service of a person's thoughts when it is needed. Vertical thinking goes deeper and deeper into a thought, regardless of how successful it is. Lateral thinking, on the other hand, moves on to consider other ideas and possibilities.

Group brainstorming can increase a person's ideas. Group interaction is another key principle of brainstorming. Group brainstorming procedures require individual idea generation before and after each session, as well as alternating group and individual idea generation. The combination usually produces the best results. Brainstorming can be done by an individual or in a group because it is not exclusively a group process. In either case, *individual creativity* is the key to effective problem solving.

Group brainstorming has been under attack in recent years. Some claim it is less effective than other idea generation techniques (most notably the nominal group technique whereby participants generate ideas individually). However, Isaksen (1998) reviewed 90 studies on group brainstorming and noted that brainstorming has rarely been tested under real-world circumstances:

> The overall "reality level" of most previous brainstorming research is fairly low. Most studies used untrained students working in artificial groups on relatively meaningless tasks with little or no concern for measuring anything but sheer quantity of ideas produced. (p. 21)

In a similar vein, Sutton and Hargadon (1996) argued that the measure of effectiveness used in most studies of group brainstorming—the number of ideas generated—is inadequate to reflect the true value of this process. They conducted a qualitative study on IDEO, a product design firm renowned for innovation, and noted that brainstorming contributed to many important outcomes in the company. The authors concluded that the effect of brainstorming should not be judged solely on the quantity of ideas it generates.

Participation in traditional group conferences can also be substantially improved by training in brainstorming. *Quantity breeds quality* in brainstorming. Brainstorming generates so many ideas that some are likely to be useful. The generation of ideas is relatively easy and not time consuming if the rules of brainstorming are carefully heeded. Osborn's firm (BBDO) held 401 brainstorming sessions and produced 34,000 ideas, of which 2,000 (6%) were good.

Even if many of them had proved unsuccessful, brainstorming is still a useful way for getting a group to come up quickly with solutions to problems.

In setting up a session, brainstormers need to remember the type of problem that they are "storming." The four rules originally formulated by Osborn (1979) are guidelines for any session. These rules are stated at the beginning and reiterated throughout each session:

1. *Critical judgment is ruled out.* It is believed that education and experience have trained most adults to think critically rather than creatively. As a result, they tend to impede their fluency of ideas by applying their critical power too soon. When judgment is deferred, it is possible to think up substantially more and better ideas. Although critical evaluation is forbidden, it is only open criticism and evaluation that is not allowed. It should not be forgotten that there is no way to control subjects' internal control and evaluation that may be operating before the suggestion of an idea. Therefore, it seems better to assume that judgment is not completely ruled out but minimized.

2. *Freewheeling is welcomed.* The wilder the ideas are, the better for creative thinking; it is easier to tone down than to think up.

3. *Quantity is wanted.* The greater the number of ideas, the greater the likelihood of achieving new and effective solutions to the problem.

4. *Combination and improvement are sought.* In addition to contributing ideas, participants are urged to suggest how the ideas of others and their own can be turned into better ideas or how two or more previous ideas can be joined onto still another idea (hitchhiking).

Who is asked to participate in a session is determined by the problem. Generally, the factors to consider before setting up a brainstorming session include (1) the mix of various employment levels, (2) the best number of people in any group, (3) the gender mix of the group, and (4) the time and location of the session. Much of the literature on brainstorming suggests that an optimal brainstorming session has from five to 15 persons. (Personal experience has shown the ideal size to be seven: six participants and a leader or coordinator.) The use of successful group brainstorming sessions has been reported with much larger groups (50 to 100) and smaller groups (two or three). Our preference is still seven.

Furthermore, people of antithetical behavior should not be mixed if possible, such as extroverts with shy people or active people with more contemplative ones. Such extremes in behavior and personality are not likely to stimulate the session; opposites do not necessarily aid in brainstorming. There is a likelihood the session might focus on differences among participants rather than on the problem. The intention is not to bring together participants of identical temperaments, as much as to avoid mixing *radically* different types.

Osborn (1979) found that having men and women in brainstorming sessions stimulates the flow of ideas. However, if not enough men or women are directly involved in a problem, there is no need to have equal numbers of both.

The composition of a group also reflects the type of problem, the type of organization, and the people concerned with solving the problem. The same group should never be used to solve different problems or work at one problem too long. Groups have a tendency to become rigid in their approach quickly. To maintain its effectiveness, brainstorming is best when used not too often or for too long with the same group. If not, it begins to resemble the rigidities of more traditional conferences.

A trained facilitator should lead the brainstorming session. A major theme Isaksen (1998) identified in his review of brainstorming research was the effect of the facilitator:

> One of the most effective ways to overcome social loafing, free riding, evaluation apprehension, uniformity pressure and production blocking is to utilize a facilitator during brainstorming sessions. It is the role of the trained facilitator to observe the interaction patterns, energy, and evenness of participation during the brainstorming session and provide an appropriate array of idea-stimulating techniques to support the general guidelines. (p. 21)

A facilitator should not overstate the value of brainstorming to the group. The technique is *supplemental* to other techniques for creating solutions to problems, not a replacement. If it is not presented this way, disappointments are inevitable. The facilitator's role is crucial. To ensure that the tone and mood of sessions are serious, without dampening the freewheeling aspect, the facilitator must be serious about brainstorming and not treat it as an experiment.

Research and experience have shown that when a superior or supervisor attends sessions with staff members, the sessions are usually less successful. Some success has been reported if higher level personnel observe the session but do not directly participate. Criticism and risk in a group cannot be artificially suspended if employees are arbitrarily mixed with employers. The session must be as relaxed as possible for full cooperation from participants. Ideally, the group should include people of the same employment level, in various areas of a specialty.

The location of the session should be *unlike* the usual place of work: perhaps at a nearby motel, a private home, a resort area, or even a special facility within the organization. A place away from the usual work environment and away from the usual locations for conferences is conducive to creativity and the freewheeling exchange of ideas. However, participants need a real connection to the problem so they can work on it before and after sessions. Brainstorming requires total removal. The participants are likely to take the sessions more seriously if the materials for working on a problem are brought to the special location.

Brainstorming should *not* be a marathon to drain people of ideas. A normal 8-hour workday, with no more than 2 hours devoted to brainstorming is more than suitable. A first session for participants should not run more than 20 minutes: People are less creative when they are tired. Brainstorming can be intensive but should not be exhaustive.

The seating arrangement, room layout, and decor should add to the "serious informality" of the occasion. Name tags or cards should be provided to participants if they do not know each other; the coordinator should be visible and generally accessible. There is no need to maintain formality in seating. Allowing participants to rearrange their seating literally offers them a new viewpoint, especially after a break.

Brainstorming in Recreation and Park Administration

In planning for a brainstorming session, the facilitator must first review the problem statement. The intention at this point is to be sure the problem is simply yet specifically stated. Because the aim of brainstorming is to generate many possible solutions, yet not be too vague.

After a specific problem statement has been formulated, the facilitator sends a one-page summary to those selected to participate in the sessions. The memo should summarize the problem, giving at least two examples of the kinds of ideas the coordinator feels could be solutions. The coordinator should have a longer list of possible ideas to use as stimulators if the group bogs down, but these should not be included in the initial memo. This memo should be sent at least two days before the session so participants will be prepared for the session. This advance notice should serve to stimulate ideas. Brainstorming is not to be sprung on an unsuspecting group, but is to be expected and planned. Spontaneity comes from suspension of judgment, not from surprise.

The facilitator should be ready with some idea-inspiring questions in case there is a lull in the brainstorming session. Most of the following questions were originally proposed by Osborn (1979).

The acronym SCAMPER is a good way of remembering them.

Idea-Spurring Questions: SCAMPER
- *Substitute?* Who else instead? What else instead? Other place? Other time? *Combine?* How about a blend, an assortment? Combine purposes? Combine ideas?
- *Adapt?* What else is like this? What other ideas does this suggest?
- *Modify?* Change meaning, color, motion, sound, odor, taste, form, shape? Other changes?
- *Put to Other Uses?* New ways to use as is? Other uses if modified?
- *Eliminate?* What could you take out? How could you simplify?
- *Reverse?* Opposites? Turn it backward? Turn it upside down? Turn it inside out?

If the group is unfamiliar with brainstorming, a thorough orientation to the concept and a warm-up is needed. A warm-up session should be used each time until the group is familiar with the procedure. The orientation should cover the background of brainstorming as a concept, as discussed by Osborn (1979), and then move on to hypothetical test problems. For instance, some of the more successful problems we have used in 2-minute warm-up sessions are, "How many other uses could you brainstorm for a paperclip?" and "If you woke up tomorrow and were twice the size you were, what would you do?" In three sessions in which this was used for the second problem, we received 47, 34, and 36 ideas, respectively. Another is, "What other uses could you brainstorm for a toothbrush?" Again in three sessions, we generated 61, 65, and 60 ideas, respectively, all within 2 minutes!

Another successful warm-up is to use pictorial jokes and to ask the group to brainstorm other captions for them within the 2 minutes allowed.

After orientation and a brief warm-up, the coordinator asks for solutions to the problem. The coordinator quickly recognizes those who raise their hands. If several hands are raised at once, the coordinator goes around the room and lets each present one idea in turn. Participants are never allowed to read off lists of ideas that they may have prepared before the meeting. Only one idea should be offered at a time by anyone, otherwise the pace is likely to be slowed. The facilitator especially encourages ideas that are directly sparked by a previous idea (hitchhiking). This chain reaction is enhanced by asking participants to snap their fingers, as well as raise their hands, whenever they have hitchhikes to offer. If several hands are up, the coordinator gives priority to finger snapping, making the most of the power of association.

An assistant to the facilitator, someone other than a participant, should be designated as a secretary to record all suggestions offered. This person should be seated next to the facilitator, in a direct line of communication. The secretary should write down the ideas. Some groups have found it helpful to have two secretaries taking notes, for greater accuracy and clarity. In this case, one secretary takes the even numbered ideas and the other records the odd numbered ones. Or one secretary records the ideas from the participants on one side of the room, the other from those on the other side. Some organizations tape brainstorming sessions. This enables the secretary to recheck the list of ideas recorded during the meeting.

Regardless of how the ideas are recorded, it is helpful to write a few on a blackboard or chart as the session proceeds. This offers visual stimulation to participants. The coordinator can refer the group to these ideas in case of lulls, encouraging combination and hitchhiking.

Each idea should be numbered, enabling the coordinator to know how many suggestions have accrued at any point in the session. The coordinator can then encourage the participants as follows: "Let's each of us come up with one more idea before we close." This encouragement sometimes uncovers a new idea that sets off a chain of others. It is recommended that no idea be identified by the person who suggested it. The same idea also may have occurred to another participant, or it may have resulted directly from a suggestion made by someone else earlier.

Failures in Brainstorming

Although this overview of a typical brainstorming session seems smooth, there are many pitfalls to its success, as noted by Osborn (1979):

1. Failure to properly indoctrinate the participants about brainstorming.
2. Failure to gain the support of the director and other key personnel to hold such a session.
3. Failure to describe the problem correctly or to orient the participants to the *real* problem.
4. Failure to evaluate and process the ideas effectively.
5. Failure to implement the ideas.
6. Failure to ask provocative, idea-spurring questions when session slows down.
7. Failure to keep focused on *real* problem.
8. Failure to seek specificity of ideas that were too general.
9. Failure to warn participants that many ideas at the beginning of a session are not too creative, and not to be discouraged.
10. Overselling the technique before there are any results to show.
11. Stating the technique as a replacement for individual, judicious thinking.
12. Failure to distinguish between freewheeling atmosphere and one that has moved away from the problem or become out of control.

Unless these obstacles are anticipated or avoided in brainstorming, its value will be greatly decreased. That is why it is crucial the leader of a session understand the method and be alert to modifications or innovations that might improve a session.

The session coordinator sees or phones all participants the following workday for further ideas. If any idea is complex, the participant may be asked to put it into a memo. Because the participants will have "slept" on the problem, some of the most valuable ideas are likely to come after the session.

The session secretary should prepare a list of all ideas suggested during the session and afterward. The coordinator then edits the list, making sure each idea is succinctly yet clearly described. At the same time, the coordinator puts the ideas into logical categories, usually five or 10. Under each classification are placed the numbers of the individual ideas (from the original list) that should be included in that section.

References

Camacho, L. M., & Paulus, P. B. (1995). The role of social anxiousness in group brainstorming. *Journal of Personality and Social Psychology, 68,* 1071–1080.

de Bono, E. (1992). *Serious creativity: Using the power of lateral thinking to create new ideas.* New York, NY: HarperCollins.

Isaksen, S. G. (1998). *A review of brainstorming research: Six critical issues for inquiry.* Buffalo, NY: Creative Research Unit, Creative Problem Solving Group-Buffalo.

Osborn, A. F. (1953). *Applied imagination: Principles and procedures of creative problem-solving.* New York, NY: Scribner.

Osborn, A. F. (1979). *Applied imagination: Principles and procedures of creative problem-solving* (3rd rev. ed.). New York, NY: Scribner. (Original work published 1953)

Scott, G., Leritz, L. E., & Mumford, M. D. (2004). The effectiveness of creativity training: A quantitative review. *Creativity Research Journal, 16,* 361–388.

Sutton, R. I., & Hargadon, A. (1996). Brainstorming groups in context: Effectiveness in a product design firm. *Administrative Science Quarterly, 40,* 685–718.

CHAPTER 8
SELECTING ALTERNATIVE SOLUTIONS

This chapter focuses on the various solutions obtained from brainstorming. The ideas suggested are evaluated *creatively* and *judiciously*. We must imagine and judge the consequences of each solution. The criticism suppressed during brainstorming is now allowed to surface. If a problem is simple and we already have a solution in mind, analysis of alternative solutions is not needed. Some problems have an obvious solution, and if we already have a suitable answer, little can be gained from an elaborate evaluation.

For instance, if participants say they do not use the Arcola Recreation Center because there is insufficient locker space, it would be foolish to assume that there is a greater problem. The solution is simple: Install lockers! But if we have determined at this stage in the model that such a complaint is merely a symptom, we should continue to seek a better solution.

Now we turn to a judicious *evaluation* of the various solutions suggested from the brainstorming session. Throughout problem solving, we have been evaluating the various solutions that arose before the brainstorming session. Now we will concentrate on evaluating the ideas developed in the brainstorming session, as well as those from other sources. As already mentioned, brainstorming is only one method for generating ideas.

Other solutions come from many sources. There is no best or proven source. Ideas can be offered by staff at the Arcola Recreation Center; these can be staff notions about what solution might best work or the ideas of a consultant or recreation specialist. Whatever the source of ideas, we have to reduce the number so we can analyze a few key solutions in depth. Before evaluating ideas obtained from the brainstorming session, we must first list and classify the ideas by *type* of solution. This editing task combines like ideas, eliminates those that do not meet the attendance objective at first glance, and adds last-minute ideas suggested by participants after the session. We usually begin screening and classifying these ideas the next workday after the brainstorming session. Before doing so, however, we ask the participants for additional thoughts on ideas suggested at the session or for their ideas. The participants have had an opportunity to sleep on the problem, and many times offer excellent ideas the following day or so. Thus, it is not necessary to cut off a session at its formal ending. A simple method of collecting these follow-up ideas is to call each participant the next day to obtain their additional thoughts. This procedure should be as informal as possible and not in any way pressure the participants for last-minute ideas. Only ideas that have occurred after the session, and which the participant feels have worth, should be recorded. After brainstormers have slept on a problem, they sometimes generate the most valuable ideas. In one brainstorming session, ideas were developed in 33 minutes. Then the harvesting of the afterthoughts added 23 more. Four of the latter turned out to be better than any of the first suggestions.

We then incorporate the ideas into one list and then classify and edit them according to similarity, relatedness, and applicability. This editing can be by any classification desired: by similarity of ideas, by the *resource* most needed to attain it, by time to carry out the solution, and so forth. For example, a list of solutions could be classified by those involving people and those involving *methods.*

Using a worksheet method of classification and evaluation developed by Parnes (1969), listing ideas by *People* or by *Method,* we can begin to perceive the different solutions.

> The worksheet . . . is where you now begin to assemble the various factors that can help you toward your problem solution. Copy in the statement of the problem you have been working with . . . copy in the most important criteria for measuring your ideas . . . select the best possible ideas and group them by categories. . . . (Categories will usually be related groups of ideas; different approaches to the problem; cost, time, or manpower groupings, etc.). (Parnes, 1969, Worksheet 13)

If an idea is not clearly stated, during editing we can reword it more clearly. We and any associates concerned with problem solving review the list, selecting the most promising ideas for a solution. Usually these associates are not the same people who participated in the brainstorming session, though they may be. Those responsible for solving the problem usually evaluate the ideas. Thus, if the director of the Arcola Research Center is the problem solver and is responsible for finding a solution, the director may have the staff or others brainstorm for ideas. Then the director and the associate or assistant (who had also not participated) would evaluate them. For most participants, their function ends with the session, except to follow progress on the problem and the final solution.

For the initial review of ideas,

> C. Frank Hix of General Electric has warned against screening out the far-fetched ideas too quickly. He believes that from a list of brainstorm suggestions, it is sometimes possible to pick the seemingly silliest and, by probing in and around it, to develop it into the best idea of all. (Osborn, 1965, p. 202)

While evaluating and selecting promising ideas, we can also restate and combine ideas for better formulations of related ideas. The solutions we evaluate are closely related to the objectives set earlier for the problem. If we stated the chief objectives as an increase in attendance at the Arcola Recreation Center and an improvement in the center's image and security measures, we must compare the various solutions with these objectives.

Objectives are, therefore, the first and constant measurement for screening and evaluating problem solutions. We should not change objectives because a solution, which does not meet the objectives, appeals to us. Our objectives should remain fairly constant.

We are looking for one solution or a mix of solutions. We want the solution that relates to the main cause of the problem. We must select carefully among different solutions, evaluate their known and conjectured consequences (both pro and con), state the risks of implementing or not implementing each, and then be prepared to make a final selection.

It is also possible to use brainstorming again to elicit possible pros and cons for each solution and the risks in not implementing each solution. That is, we could conduct a "negative" brainstorming session on what could be wrong (or right) about each solution, what might happen if each was implemented, and what might happen if each was not implemented.

We should write down the *known and suspected advantages and disadvantages.*

> Do it as rapidly as possible. Especially, don't try to judge whether the advantage or disadvantage being listed is important or even cogent. Don't even worry about whether the item being listed is really an advantage or whether it might turn out to be a disadvantage. Just list the ideas as they pop into mind. (Schnelle, 1967, p. 71)

We would then evaluate these pros and cons as we did with the solutions. The session on pros and cons would be conducted as would any other brainstorming session, with suspended judgment, even though the group is closer to solving the problem and presumably has better hunches about the ultimate solution. Whether or not brainstorming is used at this stage, the evaluation and elimination of various solutions ranges from an intuitive rejection of some ideas to in-depth research on and analysis of others.

Selecting a final solution requires a candid evaluation of the possible consequences and risks of doing or not doing something about the problem. Evaluation of most ideas is a simple screening process. For instance, we can evaluate the idea of holding more citywide sporting events at the Arcola Recreation Center. If this solution is compared with the objective, we see that its *consequence* is not likely to meet the main objective: It will increase attendance for the period of the event or tournament, but will not increase daily community attendance. This solution is also not likely to have a lasting positive effect on the center's image. Therefore, we discard it. Suppose, for example, that a consequence of holding the citywide event is a lasting positive effect on the attendance and image of the center. We must still consider and evaluate its other consequences because no solution would have only one consequence.

The event could cost more money than the organization could hope to obtain from the city, or it could overstrain the staff who are not familiar with citywide events, and so forth. Even a solution that at first appears to solve the problem has to be examined further to ensure its tractability for the situation. *All* the known consequences must be anticipated or controllable to some extent.

After exhausting the possibilities of known consequences and listing these with each solution, we search for unknown or probable consequences. These are as important as the anticipated consequences. Figure 8.1 illustrates the consequences of adult education programs.

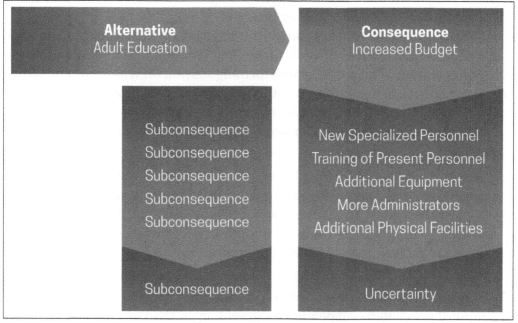

Figure 8.1. Consequences of offering adult education classes.

To evaluate ideas judiciously, we must establish criteria for the environment in which we attempt to solve the problem. This can be done by brainstorming. The possible criteria for evaluating the solutions to the Arcola Recreation Center problem could be as follows:

1. Will the staff be able to handle it?
2. Can the budget of the Arcola Recreation Center sustain it?
3. Will it be what the people want?
4. Will it include both adults and youth?
5. Will it require changes in existing programs?
6. Will it fit into patterns of future programs?
7. Will it improve accessibility to the center?
8. Will the people support it?
9. Will the people understand it?
10. Will it increase attendance?
11. Will it racially integrate the center and neighborhood?
12. Will people be able to get to it?

In addition:
   "Is the idea simple enough?
   "Is it compatible with human nature?
   "Is it timely?
   "Is it possible?" (Osborn, 1965, p. 201)

These criteria are not used to prevent an idea from being considered, but to indicate how a potential solution must be evaluated. Criteria are different from objectives: The former are a desired framework within which to judge ideas, and the latter are a constraint against which to measure solutions. In evaluating each idea, we use our desires (objectives) and our means (criteria) as determinants of its worth.

We can classify and reclassify ideas in many ways as evaluation continues: those that would cost *money*, those that would require additional *staff*, those that can be applied in the *short run*, or those that are more *long range.* For instance, are we seeking an immediate solution with long-range effects, or are we willing to wait for a longer range solution with few interim benefits?

This is something we must decide for each problem solution. If the main concern is money, we should evaluate and classify *by cost* those ideas that meet the objectives and criteria. If the constraint is staff, we should evaluate and classify *by personnel.*

Whatever the focus is, it must be the determinant of the classification: Is an inexpensive solution or a quick one needed? Can we obtain the money? Will we have difficulty procuring qualified staff?

If we feel an idea is good and re willing to strive for additional resources to implement it, the classification will remain the same, and we begin to think of ways of "selling" the idea to others.

Another way of evaluating ideas is to test them. This method, of course, cannot apply to all ideas. However, if we feel, for example, that newspaper publicity might be an answer to poor image and low attendance at the center, we can test this idea. If it fails, we cannot use this as our *best* solution. Nonetheless, we can hold this idea for possible use after we have chosen another solution, because it may be a good way of implementing the other solution.

In evaluating ideas, in addition to the criteria, objectives, and consequences, we have to be aware of what solutions may have been tried in the past or elsewhere to alleviate comparable problems. If the center had extensive press coverage and publicity in the past with no discernible increase in attendance or image improvement, this idea should be eliminated. We must choose a few practicable alternatives that clearly have a good chance of solving the problem. It is important, therefore, for either us or an assistant to know the history of the center, the community, and the research and/or experiences of other centers in comparable situations. Outside consultants are valuable, too, because they are not overly enmeshed in the inner workings of the center, personal politics, or seemingly insoluble constraints. They can bring a much needed objective viewpoint. They are also aware of the research and experiences of other agencies with related problems. Outside consultants are not essential, however, especially if we are familiar with the research and experiences of other centers.

During the fact-gathering stage, if information was not solicited from other organizations with similar problems, we do so now. In addition, we consider field observations or a community survey if this was not done during fact gathering. We should not frown on research at this stage in problem solving as being too taxing or too late. On the contrary, we are now better equipped to analyze facts and better able to design a comprehensive and well-formulated research approach. Resources would be better spent on quality research at this point because we have greatly reduced the solutions. We should research for new or old solutions to the problem. We should not think a previously unsuccessful solution elsewhere might work for us. If a case history is comparable, its precepts should be reflected in the evaluation. If our solution, if successful, would help others in comparable situations, the reverse is true. We should draw on available research and experience other than our own to avoid treating our situation as novel or atypical. We do not blindly accept the judgment of another's experiences, but we carefully consider the conditions in which a problem was handled and its outcome. An old solution may be useful for our problem, but we should be careful about simplifying similarities between problem environments.

It is important to reduce the number of ideas to consider because usually there are not enough resources to evaluate many. We suggest selecting from no more than four or five ideas. Considering the practical and theoretical considerations, but also relying, in large measure, on the reported experience of many analysts, we recommend selection of neither fewer than three nor more than seven alternative courses of action. Five frequently seems to be the best number of alternatives to investigate (Schnelle, 1967).

In the Arcola Recreation Center case, suppose we have narrowed the possible solutions to four. This screening may have used any or all of the aforementioned evaluation steps or simply common sense. There are now four ideas or combinations of these:

1. Convert the center to include adult education programs.
2. Provide free transportation to the center.
3. Employ a roving recreation leader.
4. Balance cultural and athletic programs.

Adult education is good in that it would increase attendance at the center by expanding the current programs (now athletic activities for youth). Such programs would actively involve adult residents in the center. We kept the suggestion of providing free transportation because it may have an immediate practical value for the problem. By offering free buses each afternoon at local schools to bring youth to the center, we hope to increase attendance. A roving leader in the community has appeal because it might offer a way of increasing attendance and improving the image of the center. Finally, the combined cultural and athletic program has potentially the same value as an adult education program, offering arts, crafts, and other cultural activities for residents.

Now we begin to focus on selecting the most likely solutions to the problem.We must remain critical of those that do *not* match the criteria and objectives. Even if all four solutions appear to meet the objectives, we must analyze the consequences of implementing them. For instance, we selected adult education programs because this appeared to be a good way to increase attendance by increasing the appeal of the center. As shown in Figure 8.1, we must still anticipate *all* the consequences of each solution.

The idea of modifying center programs to include adult education activities met the MUST objective on first analysis. Its appeal is broader than merely recreation programs because it offers adults an opportunity to learn useful vocational skills. But there are consequences to this decision. Such a revision would require, at the least, a change in center programs and facilities as well as in center staff and budget needs. Within these consequences are subconsequences: the need to modify the present facility and purchase equipment for new uses, to hire educational staff and administrators, and to retrain present staff. There are other *uncertain* consequences and risks because we have not anticipated them or have no way of influencing them, even if we knew of them. For example, what would be the effect on other educational institutions in the area if the center offered such a program? Where would the youth of the community receive adequate recreation services if the center reduced its services? How would the school board react to the recreation commission's acquiring an educational function?

In reviewing the criteria and objectives, we see that, in addition to being an expensive proposition, revision of center programs might not increase youth attendance. If parents are concerned about their children and center recreation programs are intended for youth and young adults, then a youth–adult facility might not meet the criteria, even if it did increase total attendance.

We apply the same analysis to the other three solutions to come up with as complete a scenario of their probable consequences as possible. A good method for analyzing the consequences of various alternatives is to pretend that the solution is already in effect or, if possible, to test the solution in the community, as suggested for newspaper publicity. Sometimes, the test itself requires the same amount of preparation as the final solution or is not easy to achieve. It is more likely the analysis or consequences, or a test of their effects, will remain conjecture.

When we have finished the evaluation (or feel it is no longer worthwhile to continue), we should have a detailed graph or list of the four solutions that we feel have the best chance of solving the problem. We can attach some weights to how closely each solution meets our main and supplementary objectives: A simple list of pros and cons, dollars and cents, and short or long-range outcomes should suffice. We should also note how closely each solution accounts for and meets the more pressing criteria.

Finally, we should have some indication of the resources needed and the changes each solution would require of those involved. What is presented to the decision maker (the problem solver at this stage) is (1) a set of solutions, (2) their known and unknown consequences, (3) the risks of undertaking each, and (4) the risks of not undertaking each. It is up to us, as the decision maker, to consider each of these before selecting the best.

References

Parnes, S. (1969). *Student workbook for creative problem-solving courses and institutes* (3rd ed.). Buffalo: State University of New York.

Osborn, A. F. (1965). *Applied imagination: Principles and procedures of creative problem-solving.* New York, NY: Charles Scribner's Sons. (Original work published 1953)

Osborn, A. F. (1979). *Applied imagination: Principles and procedures of creative problem-solving* (3rd rev. ed.). New York, NY: Scribner. (Original work published 1953)

Schnelle, K. E. (1967). *Case analysis and business problem solving.* New York, NY: McGraw-Hill.

CHAPTER 9
DECISION MAKING

Many believe decision making to be the essential task of an executive director or top level administrator. Decision making is only one of the tasks of an executive. It usually takes but a small fraction of the executive's time. But to make decisions is the specific executive task—only executives make decisions. (Drucker, 1996).

Decision making may be discussed as a skill in itself, apart from problem solving, because it may be used to reach a conclusion on a matter for which no problem analysis has been used or is needed. Many books have been devoted to decision making without any discussion of problem solving. The reverse is not possible, because a necessary step in problem solving is deciding on a solution. Many writers use decision making and problem solving (and at times policy making) interchangeably to indicate that the same skills are used in these processes. We separate decision making and problem solving in our model to indicate that they are distinctly different phases.

The separation between an administrator as a problem solver and as a decision maker appears somewhat arbitrary. Although we want to avoid a *rigid,* step-by-step approach to solving problems, for teaching purposes we must perceive the steps that an effective problem solver follows, and decision making is one of them. Separating decision making from problem solving indicates the point at which the major decision is made, though we have been making smaller decisions all along. If, as Drucker (1996) says, decision making is the *specific* executive task, selecting a solution to the problem is the *specific* administrative decision in problem solving. To make a final decision, we, as decision maker, need to know something about decision making.

At this point in the problem-solving process, we have to decide how to solve the problem. Which of the four solutions stated in the previous chapter shall be selected for final implementation? We have used a great amount of time and resources to define the problem, establish objectives, examine the blocks to problem analysis, and evaluate and reduce the possible solutions.

At this stage, we have to draw on all the available expertise and information to *decide* which of these four solutions is most likely to succeed. One of these solutions or perhaps a combination must be selected. Before discussing *how* decisions are made, we give some attention to the administrator *who* makes decisions.

People and Decisions

Research and experience have presented the pros and cons on the influence of personality on decision-making skills (Lauriola & Levin, 2001). Although we shall concentrate on the personal attributes believed necessary for making decisions, many decisions are made without a strong, personally integrated decision maker, through means of analysts or computerized programs and models. Various quantitative aids, though successful, do not meet the goal of practicality for our model. Thus, our discussion of personality is weighted because the personal idiosyncrasies of the decision maker have a greater bearing than they would if they relied more on quantitative tools. This is not to deny that behind every mathematical model or computer program, or the choice to use them, stands a person.

As the problem solver, we have primarily been a problem analyzer. As a decision maker, we go beyond problem analysis into *choice* of, *risk* in, and *responsibility* for the consequences of a solution. The skills needed for decision making are comparable to those for problem analysis, with the exception of a far greater amount of RISK.

We assume ultimate responsibility for a solution. Even if the decision is made by a group, the risk and responsibility are borne by one person, perhaps two, in the organization. In a recreation center, for example, the recreation supervisor would have final responsibility for the decision. Administrators can delegate problem analysis, but they cannot delegate decision making, no matter how democratic their methods. They can share problem solving with staff and others, but responsibility and risk are entirely with the administrator.

In many large organizations, the problem analyzer and the final decision maker often are not the same person. The problem analyzer might be responsible for defining a problem and offering specific solutions to the decision maker for final selection, and the decision maker then attempts to solve the problem by selecting one of the solutions offered by the analysts. Often, the image of a decision maker is that of an executive who delegates problem analysis, then rapidly synthesizes the information received and reaches a decision. This decision then is quickly implemented and, without fail, is a success!

Unfortunately, in many organizations, especially public service organizations, decision making and the people involved are somewhat less glorified. Regarding financial resources, for example, recreation and parks usually cannot afford separate people or groups working either as problem analyzers or as decision makers. More likely, these tasks will be performed by one person or one group working on the problem from start to finish. To separate these two functions of problem solving for recreation organizations would be expensive and somewhat arbitrary: Most staff members are involved with organizational problems and would have much to contribute to any problem resolution.

We recommend, if possible, that a group, rather than only one person, be assigned to handle problem analysis. If this task is limited to one person, there is likely to be an overburdened staff member and a poorly perceived problem. In the past, when problems were perhaps simpler to solve and the environment not so complex or dynamic, the sole problem solver/decision maker was undoubtedly effective. Such solitary action is no longer prevalent in most organizations. Even simple problems affect many people and have a multitude of consequences: We need the expertise and insights of others for effective solutions. Making decisions alone may be simpler, but the solution may not be as good as one reached cooperatively. In fact, many of the "situation variables" in measuring good decisions reflect the need for others (Trevino, 1986).

Situation Variables

1. *Rational quality requirement:* Does it make a difference which course of action is adopted?
2. *Adequacy of information:* Does the manager now have the adequate information to make a quality analysis?
3. Structure of situation: Does the manager know *exactly* what information is missing and how to get the information?
4. *Commitment requirement:* Is commitment to the solution by others critical to effective implementation?
5. *Commitment without participation:* Will they commit to a decision made by the manager without their active participation?
6. *Goal congruence:* Is there goal congruence between the subordinates and the organization?
7. *Conflict about alternatives:* Is there likely to be conflict about alternative solutions among the subordinates?
8. *Subordinate competency:* Do the personnel in the organization have the skill and know-how to implement the idea suggested?

Note: Subordinates refers to people whose information is needed or whose commitment is required for effective implementation of the solution.

The problem-solving model not only reflects today's problem environments, but also seeks to include the problems that might be encountered in the future. The decision maker will need to be able to adapt to rapid change. The future decision maker will be more dependent on others and be aware of changes in the more immediate and larger environments. An effective decision maker is well informed not only about agency concerns, but also about society and the world, especially as they affect professional decisions. Nothing is more valuable for decision making than broad, eclectic knowledge.

Our understanding of change should include a willingness to modify our own behavior and that of our organization to reflect modern realities. It is not enough to sympathize with demands for change in recreation programs, for instance; we must do something about them.

For example, we must realize that the increase in importance of recreation has brought with it a bevy of organizational, administrative, and staff problems. People have significantly more leisure, and their recreation demands must be met with a concept of recreation greater than that of the traditional use of parks, centers, and playgrounds. Recreation personnel must expand their image and abilities as leaders, offering broad, complex leisure programs. Any concept of recreation, parks, and their programs must relate to these changes.

If decisions are made that ignore psychological and social forces, within the self as well as in society, we are simply being naive about the effect of factors on decisions. All the blocks discussed in Chapter 6 rise again. Decisions are not made objectively: They are made by people, and people have varying perspectives. Emotions carry weight in decisions, no matter how rationally people view themselves or others. To be a rational decision maker is when more positive emotions are permitted to surface and more negative ones are dealt with confidently.

For instance, a park and recreation agency presented with a solution of, say, employing an athletic supervisor in the community to help with growing sports programs may respond with, "We've never needed someone to oversee our soccer and softball programs before!" This response may be rational in some contexts, but it is more likely to be an emotional response to a new idea—an unwillingness to expand beyond the agency's own group or a prejudice toward the concept itself.

On the other hand, a decision to offer active aging adult programming for local residents may be positive and enthusiastically received, but irrational as well. It may not be a need in the community if that demographic is not large or growing. It might impress friends and colleagues in the field because you are supporting trends research, but that is not what the residents need. Such a decision based on pride has no place in professional decision making.

The first step toward achieving a balance is to examine the self and others in decision making. The more time spent now on understanding the probable personal barriers to decision making, the better equipped we will be to handle objections that might arise during implementation. We do not mean a complete analysis of personalities, but a candid appraisal of the shortcomings of the decision maker and others who are bound to affect decision making.

When first setting objectives for solving the problem, we, as problem solvers, made these objectives as realistic as possible under known constraints. Decisions must be made in the same way. As decision makers, we know to some extent our own prejudices, no matter how latent, and how realistically we can deal with them. We must comprehend what personal drives, needs, and compulsions motivate us, especially when making decisions crucial not only to our professional interests, but also to the well-being of a community. An emotional response to a solution should not preclude our selecting an effective solution. As shown in Figure 9.1, an initial response to a solution might be as follows:

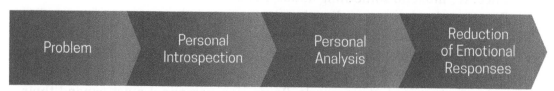

Figure 9.1. Reaction to problem solution.

In examining the emotions and drives of others, we apply the same method in an attempt to understand or reduce them. We do not pressure others with lectures on the negative influence of emotions; we simply try to find out what emotions influence us and to work with them individually and tactfully. The most important example we set is how we handle our own emotions in decision making. Our aim is to become effective, integrated decision makers. An all-around, well-adjusted person may be popular, but may lack the sharp edge of perception and criticism to make effective decisions. An effective decision maker is willing and able to take risks and to encourage others to do so. Because of the "politics" of decision making, we must consider the viewpoints of all involved in the problem. At times, our political skill may detract from our willingness to take risks. We may concentrate more on reducing conflicts and strengthening the *esprit de corps,* only to lose sight of the need to take a chance, regardless of group harmony. Sometimes, the executive staff desires to not rock the boat of the board of directors, especially when the president is at the helm. If the director is willing to speak more openly behind the scenes, but is a yes-person with the board, that may not be the best situation. Thus, it is up to the head of any organization to strive for controversy, risk, questioning, argument, and even mistrust. A harmonious group is not necessarily an effective group.

Making Decisions

As we look at the four solutions discussed in previous chapters, we know from experience that no solution is likely to be the *best* solution. It will only be best relative to the constraints we face. Any solution is a compromise of what we would like to achieve, in this case, an immediate and lasting improvement in attendance at the center and a decrease in related symptoms. What we are more likely to achieve is less dramatic growth over time, even if the decision was good. Compromise is likely, even with well-formulated solutions.

A logical question at this point might be, why were we so specific in setting objectives if we knew we couldn't meet them anyway? The need for stringency in setting objectives is important because these are what we *eventually* hope to achieve. The decision may not achieve them now, but this does not detract from the importance of *attempting* to meet them. The objectives are a continuing goal against which the solution and progress are measured. Thus, it is imperative that they not be ambiguous or overly flexible. We do not compromise on objectives, but on how likely we are to meet them with the first decision.

If, for example, there was a problem of reduced attendance at a recreation center because of lack of locker space, the simple decision would be to buy more lockers. This is a simple *corrective action,* to buy *x* number of lockers for the center. The concepts of *corrective, interim,* and *adaptive* actions are drawn from Kepner and Tregoe (1997).

Such decisions are made under conditions in which the cause of a problem and its obvious solution are known. If, however, we cannot afford to buy additional lockers, a compromise solution would be necessary. We could, for instance, decide to buy a limited amount of lockers now, with plans to buy an increased number over time, until we finally achieve the initial objective of x lockers. We have not, in this case, satisfied our initial objectives, but rather compromised on our future attainment.

The decision to buy a specific number of lockers at certain times is intentionally an *interim decision.* We plan to surpass it as soon as money is available. Interim decisions do not relinquish goals, but recognize what limitations and restraints are necessary, even with simple problems.

Whatever decision is made, we should know what options are available. These may be interim or direct actions, or *adaptive actions,* in which no decision is made. *Adaptive action* is a real *choice* because we decide to live with the problem or because the problem is insoluble. We have to adapt to a situation if there is nothing we can do about it. Whatever action is decided, we have to reassess the *consequences* of the decision. For example, the direct consequence of modifying a recreation center to include educational programs is x number of dollars in an increased budget. However, if an interim action is taken instead and only one drama specialist or an art teacher is added rather than several programs and new staff, the cost of the solution will be less.

The *decision* could be a set of decisions to take an interim action now and to follow with a corrective action later. If we decide to have an outreach worker in the neighborhood, a current staff member may perform this function as an interim action. If we believe that the decision eventually can solve the problem, we will also include a corrective action to hire a roving leader by a specific date. With such a combined decision, we may seek to reduce the cost of the solution, to give people a chance to adjust to the idea or for any variety of reasons. If we do not hope for a corrective action immediately, we compromise with a combination of actions that will allow us, over time, to find what we feel is the real cause of the problem.

Interim actions are made often before we, as the problem solver, even begin problem analysis because the problem is so pressing. This is an action to reduce more troublesome symptoms, but it is intended to be merely a stopgap to the whole problem. An interim solution at the center to reduce vandalism would be, as mentioned, a 24-hour guard.

Interim solutions are not necessarily cheap. They may be expensive, but we have little choice when facing troublesome or dangerous symptoms.

Whatever decision is made, we must operate within the organizational limits implied in the objectives and the policy values of the agency as a whole. Is it a policy (value) of the park and recreation department to contribute to the educational needs of the community? How can we rationalize the need for modifying the policy to include adult education according to its values, objectives, and criteria? We have to determine the actual effect of implementing such a decision as well as the effect for the other three solutions.

We must weigh the consequences of each solution against the risk and against the changes and costs in terms of the policies and values of the center. The problem analyst is concerned with defining as many factors and consequences as possible for each solution, whereas the decision maker has to measure and judge these consequences against each other to make a final decision. To be truly effective, a solution should have (a) the least cost, (b) with the least disadvantage, and (c) the greatest advantage to the problem. We need to judge the four solutions by how each meets these stipulations: *Which one best satisfies all three criteria?*

All four solutions will cost money, some less, some more. If the problem analyst has not specified dollar amounts for each consequence, we must determine the precise cost now. If we are seeking a quality decision, regardless of cost, and have been encouraged to do so, we will still assign specific dollar amounts to each solution, but will not indicate these as a constraint.

As we begin to reevaluate the consequences and subconsequences of each solution in view of policy constraints, we will isolate consequences not tenable within existing limitations. If we cannot, for example, spend over $200,000 for any physical changes to a facility, this will be a distinct limitation to the cost consequences of each solution. We can perhaps readjust resources. For instance, if we are limited to $200,000 for all nonpersonnel increases plus two new staff positions, we might risk converting the personnel appropriation to additional funds for a facility change if we believe the physical change of making a facility more attractive by extensive renovations is more important.

The initial weights on the consequences are the criteria for the evaluation: *Can we afford it? Will the staff be able to handle it? Do the people want it?* Analyzing each consequence against these criteria, we can visualize this process as a simple flow chart. We isolate each of the four solutions for final analysis and assign specific measures to the known or anticipated consequences. Then we measure their compatibility with the criteria. If each consequence is important, such as *It must be something we can afford* or *It must be what the people want,* we can rate each with a plus or minus for the specific criteria. (See Figure 9.2.)

Assigning a plus or minus to a consequence or applying a quantitative measurement is not a permanent evaluation. For instance, if a solution requires a $30,000 annual budget increase, we assign this consequence a + if we know the money can be readily obtained this year. However, this + might be very short range. In 4 years, it will have cost at least $120,000 for this one solution, which may be well beyond the long-range capacity. Thus, we must carefully assign weights to the various consequences, for both the shortand the longrange impact.

These weights, properly considered and applied, will aid us in making a final selection. For instance, revising the policy to add educational programs will not meet several criteria. It is not the best solution with the least disadvantage and the most advantage; it also is not what the people want, nor what we can afford because of staff limitations, cost, and improper facilities.

There is a risk in rejecting a solution as well as in selecting it. It could be that for some unknown reason an educational program would be worth inaugurating. It might develop into precisely what the people want, and the staff might easily transfer their recreational expertise and skills to adult education. So there is a risk in saying NO as well as YES.

Figure 9.2. Weighing the value of consequences.

When making a decision to alleviate the problem, we must be sure it does not create another problem greater than the original one. The following "recreation" experience illustrates this difficulty: A scenic lowland park was threatened by floodwaters from a proposed dam nearby. The problem facing those who opposed the dam and its destructive flooding was how to prevent its construction. A logical solution at the time was to take an interim action to increase public awareness of the threat to the park by an extensive publicity program. The publicity was successful, halting progress on the dam and bringing the issue into court with a suit against the builder.

Unfortunately, the publicity surrounding the dam controversy led to increased problems with traffic and vandalism by the influx of visitors who were not familiar with the park's beauty until the publicity. The damage to the park from visitors now poses an equal or greater problem than the dam construction had in the first place! In this case, an interim solution produced an additional problem in need of solving. Now the park is threatened by those for whom it was being preserved, deluged by humans, not water.

We now have to make a final decision. We have to stop when we feel we have all the information on hand, accept our own intuitions about the problem, and evaluate carefully the various consequences. To delay beyond this point is no longer fruitful for making a good decision. Viewing the four solutions, we see that the one that clearly will cost the least, achieve the most, have the fewest disadvantages, and meet the value criteria is *to employ an outreach roving recreation leader in the community.*

A roving recreation leader is generally a community-detached worker assigned to a specific area within a community for strengthening, extending, and stimulating participation of hard-to-reach youth and other community groups, as a means of engaging them in recreation programs and other activities (e.g.,

Crompton & Witt, 1997). One purpose of outreach service is to help youth use their leisure time constructively and assist them in using community resources for employment and related services.

Roving leaders, either professionals or paraprofessionals, understand the neighborhood or community in which they work and are able to meet and deal with people. Generally, the roving leader attempts to make contact with youth in an area to determine (a) what the youth visualize and use in the community in the way of services and recreation, (b) what prevents their using such services, (c) what is available to youth, (d) what needs to be made available, and (e) how to help youth obtain the resources and services needed for growth and development. Contemporary nomenclature for this work is extension work.

This solution appears best for combating lack of community involvement in the center (Baker & Witt, 2000). By employing a roving leader, we hope to reach the community on a continuing basis, at an affordable cost; obtain residents' suggestions for programs and activities at the center; and seek their participation in policy and administrative concerns. Such participation is also expected to affect the number of youth and adults using the center, to improve the community's attitude toward the center as *their* center, and to reduce the symptoms that have hurt the center's image and services.

Despite having said YES to a decision, our job as the problem solver is not over. We now have to prepare for resistance that this decision might encounter from others, especially as it entails a change in how the center previously related to the community. The staff and advisory board may resist, the recreation and park board also may refuse to fund such an idea, or the community may resent the outreach concept. If we believe this to be the best solution, we have to prepare not only to sell the idea to others, but also to formulate a plan for its implementation.

References

Baker, J. E., & Witt, P. A. (2000). Backstreet beacons: Austin's roving leaders. *Journal of Park and Recreation Administration, 18*(1), 87–105.

Crompton, J. L., & Witt, P. A. (1997). Programs that work: The roving leader program in San Antonio. *Journal of Park and Recreation Administration, 15*(2), 84–92.

Drucker, P. (1996). *The effective executive: The definitive guide to getting the right things done.* New York, NY: Harper Business.

Kepner, C. H., & Tregoe, B. B. (1997). *The new rational manager: An updated edition for a new world.* Princeton, NJ: Kepner-Tregoe.

Lauriola, M., & Levin, I. P. (2001). Personality traits and risky decision-making in a controlled experimental task: An exploratory study. *Personality and Individual Differences, 31*, 215–226.

Trevino, L. (1986). Ethical decision making in organizations: A person–situation interactionist model. *The Academy of Management Review, 11*, 601–611.

_____ CHAPTER 10 _____
STRATEGIES FOR IMPLEMENTATION

Ideas in recreation and parks are good only if they are implemented. Recreation and park professionals are usually idea people. They spend probably 95% of their time thinking up new ideas, but only 5% "selling" them to others. They are quick to suggest solutions to problems, but are not good at developing and implementing them. They seem to ignore the need for implementation, considering it an automatic part of problem solving. Or they are simply unaware of the organizational and political pressures needed to implement any idea successfully. Often, their inability to implement a solution is because they lack all the facts. In cases in which they have all the necessary facts, it is more likely an inability to plan their tactics for selling their ideas to others. That is, they are not aware of how to make their ideas acceptable. Implementation of ideas is often either troublesome or overlooked. They value the generation of ideas as a creative act in itself, but then overlook the need to put these ideas into practice, undermining the creating of the idea in the first place.

Planning for Implementation

When business firms have a product to sell, their salespeople do so by persuading or conditioning the consumer to buy it. A sale is always made in the mind of the buyer. Most books on persuasive communication in business do not confine themselves to the field of marketing. They stress that all managers, regardless of their profession, should be consumer oriented (e.g., Tillman & Kirkpatrick, 1972). Recreation and parks is a service offered or delivered to consumers, much like any commercial product. Once this analogy is recognized, recreation and park professionals will be able to use textbooks and other materials from marketing, business administration, advertising, and communications. Before they can carry out an idea, they have to plan their tactics to achieve their objective. They combine one or several of these tactics as a strategy for implementation. Planning and thinking about how to carry out an idea, whether the idea is simple or novel, are crucial to successful idea implementation. These tactics usually require several steps:
1. Informing others.
2. Persuading others.
3. Convincing others.
4. Fighting resistance to change.
5. Anticipating all blocks to acceptance of the idea.

As decided in the previous chapter, the solution we wish to use is to employ a roving recreation leader in a community. Although we are personally pleased with this idea, we should anticipate some difficulty in getting others to accept it. The enthusiasm does not come from knowing that this is the best solution, because this solution was only relatively superior to the other three that were offered. Even with its relative worth, staff enthusiasm is stimulated more by the likelihood of its solving the problem than by its superiority as an idea.

Once an idea has been selected, we need to plan how it will be presented for implementation. If we push approval for the idea without considering the attitude of others in the problem, we are likely to encounter unnecessary barriers. The question that must be answered is, how can we sell the idea of the roving recreation leader to the staff, the community, and the recreation and park board? As mentioned, we "sell" intentionally, for this is precisely what we have to do, especially if we expect resistance to the idea. Selling is conceived not as deception or pressure, but as enthusiasm for and knowledge of the "product" and the desire to sell it to others. Figure 10.1 shows, in model form, the steps in obtaining support for an idea. As is evident, it is not a simple matter.

If the previous analysis of the problem was thorough, this will benefit us in planning idea implementation. If we carefully analyzed all people and factors in the initial problem, we can draw on that information for implementation.

There is no reason to assume that the staff will agree to have a roving leader in the community, even if they participated in all of the problem solving and decision making. As discussed earlier, any change will most likely be resisted, even by those whom it is likely to benefit.

As shown in Figure 10.1, the individual needs or the desire for recognition by staff can be economic, sociological, or psychological, pertaining to, among other issues, job security, cultural pressures, or attitudes and beliefs in conflict with outreach work. These same needs and desires for recognition can be applied to all others in the problem. These needs must be anticipated and fulfilled or countered in some way or another. Ignoring them will only hinder attempts at idea implementation.

For example, if a staff member prides himself or herself on "connection" to the community, we need to anticipate their possible resentment of a special employee taking over this task. The staff member may agree to the concept of a roving leader, but plan to control anyone hired through various pressures. This person might feel he or she knows the community better than any newcomer, professional or not, and resist the perceived intrusion. We have to offset such resistance by addressing any misconceptions about the idea as well as the value of the idea itself. We have to clearly communicate the advantages of this idea to everyone in hopes of enhancing their acceptance motives.

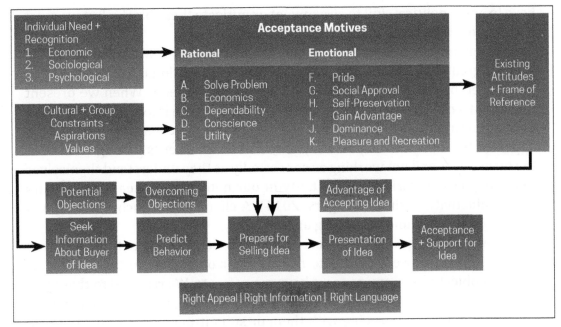

Figure 10.1. Flowchart for idea acceptance.

If the staff member is proud of his or her connection with the community, we have to sustain this pride while employing the outreach worker to do the job on a more formal basis. By appealing to the emotion of pride, and by convincing the staff member of the need to share his or her valuable insights, we may be able to not only convince this individual of the value of an outreach worker, but also gain his or her enthusiastic involvement and support. For example, "Through your great work in the community, you have convinced us of the enormous value of having a full-time community liaison worker."

Perhaps the greatest objection to outreach workers is their detachment from any apparent supervision. To offset this criticism, we have to explain the reasons for their latitude because of the type of work they are expected to do. That is, we have to summarize the activities in which roving leaders engage with community youth and other groups, and the necessity for them to be mobile and flexible. A community is not likely to relate to a liaison worker in an office. However, if the worker appears among them, on the street, at their hangouts, or in their homes, ready to help by coming to them, they might respond in kind.

We once more encounter personal and cultural blocks. There is often no way to avoid these when planning to carry out an idea, which requires approval from a diverse set of employees. In fact, we could say that they are more powerful at this phase because we are seeking a change. There is more at stake than before, and any block we encounter has the potential to be decisive, whereas previously it may have been merely annoying or frustrating. We may have to apply political skill to circumvent or mitigate these blocks, but we must prepare for them in either event.

For instance, a staff or board member may resent a worker assigned to spend a great deal of time out of the office. Most traditional work experience is bounded by specific hours, time clocks, and time sheets. When we present the idea of a roving leader, working the hours they deem important for the task in the community, and in an unorthodox manner, people may misconstrue the apparent flexibility of the job. They may feel the worker is pulling wool over the team's eyes and not working as concertedly as they understand themselves to be. We have a work-ethic mentality in our nation, with measurable hours and productivity desired (Rodgers, 2014). A change from such a tradition is bound to cause misunderstanding and difficulty.

To make the idea of a roving recreation leader acceptable to those involved with the problem, we must try to modify their objections to the concept. A person's objections to any concept have many facets. We respond to these facets by attacking them, evading or retreating from them, replacing them with a substitute objection, agreeing with them or submitting to them. One of these responses is required of us in encountering the objections of those in the problem solution.

The best way to meet such objections is to raise them ourselves, to anticipate another's objections, and to reply to them when we present our idea. If we include answers to possible objections as part of the presentation, we will achieve more than if we ignore them, hoping they will not arise. We already know many of the likely objections to our idea, and we must deal with them in detail.

The best time to meet objections is before we have to. Or, rather, we must list every conceivable objection to the idea of a roving leader before we present the idea to those essential to its implementation. We must be ready with the right appeal, with the right information, and in the right language. That is, what information will be required to translate this idea into one that fulfills identifiable needs? What words and phrases should we use to communicate so the buyer will understand the idea we are trying to sell?

What about the community? Will community members accept a roving leader? In a neighborhood where a high percentage of welfare families live, the idea of another community worker is far from new. Their need to judge a worker in terms of office hours might be minimal in contrast with the traditionalist viewpoint, but they most assuredly want the worker to achieve something while working in their community. The leader must work for the people in the community, and this raises the strongest objection: loyalty. If the roving leader works for the recreation center, to whom will the roving leader be loyal when faced with a dilemma?

There is no simple solution, but we must at least be candid with the community residents about the decisions a roving leader is likely to make. We can stress the value of the roving leader's background as comparable to theirs, but we should not define loyalty as either belonging to the community or to the center. Loyalty in this case is best framed as being loyal to the job the employee was originally hired to carry out. Because the roving leader's job is to build relations among and represent interests of the neighborhood, being loyal to the job will necessitate loyalty to the neighborhood. The question of credibility and loyalty will persist, and we should be ready for it, even if we do not know what the leader will do.

We should be sensitive to the community's ideas of how (and where) the roving leader might spend time. If we can anticipate their suggestions or objections to various activities, we can discuss them intelligently when they arise. Again, political skill is of great value. We may believe, being familiar with the concept of roving leaders, that we have the best notion of how the roving leader's time should be spent. But to be successful, the roving leader will need the acceptance and support of the entire community. If not gained, no matter how able, the leader will not succeed in solving our problem. Community understanding and openness to the idea should not be minimized.

We should explain to community representatives the goals that a roving leader seeks to achieve:

1. Helps to engage and rehabilitate disadvantaged youth by offering them constructive recreational and other outlets.
2. Salaries for community roving leaders are likely to remain in the community, thus providing income for the community.
3. Provides a means of recruiting and inspiring other youth in the community to consider training in this and related career fields.
4. Provides ways for youth to obtain services other than purely recreational, for example, education, health, employment, and so forth.
5. Attempts to alleviate some of the criticism from the poor and disadvantaged that service workers do not provide a means for them to resolve their problems by community involvement and action.

The best ways to handle objections are (a) to agree with the criticism and then to turn the objection into a selling point, (b) to ask the reason for the objection, (c) to admit the objection is valid, or (d) to deny the objection by countering it with facts.

As we proceed, we need to establish objectives for implementation. What do we want to achieve when we present this idea to those involved in the problem? We need to be specific about when we want the roving leader hired, at what salary, where the leader will work, and to whom the leader will be responsible. As we formulate these specific objectives—our WANT objectives for securing implementation—we should also be prepared to compromise on them, if necessary.

This willingness to compromise on our objectives is different from our willingness when we were establishing objectives. We were not willing then to modify our objectives, because they would remain constant whether or not we modified our means. We need to increase attendance at the center by whatever means necessary (excluding moral and ethical taboos). We are willing to compromise now on how or when we will carry out the idea, not with the need to solve the problem itself.

Our problem definition for implementation purposes is, how can we best convince the recreation and park board of the need for a roving recreation leader in the community? We confine our problem statement to selling this idea to the board, for the board members are the ones we must convince. Our WANT objectives, then, could be (a) establish a full-time position for a roving leader within a month, (b) set a salary of $38,000, and (c) have the leader responsible initially to the recreation director. Additional objectives could be to assign the matter to a study committee for further investigation or to present additional information at a specified later meeting. We should let the board know, if we encounter resistance, what other additional objectives we have in mind. We should offer the board the alternative to assign this idea to additional study; we should not leave it to them to make a decision. We may let them believe the decision for additional study was their own, but we should suggest it to them.

On the other hand, if the board recommends solutions other than ours, we may not be prepared to meet them. For instance, the board might suggest a recreation mobile be driven into the community each day, with one or two staff members, to bring the center's facilities to the neighborhood. This idea, although perhaps better or worse than using a roving leader, catches us unaware, and we are unable to respond properly. All we can do in such a situation is be honest about our reaction and request additional time to review the other solution. We should never resist an idea *because* it is not ours. What we should resist is rejecting the idea outright if we do not have immediate, substantive objections to it. It will save a lot of embarrassment and hard feelings if we give any solution courteous and considered appraisal.

Besides anticipating objections, we must consider the timeliness of presenting an idea. Consideration of the general state of affairs may go a long way to achieve our cause. For example, if we wish to submit our idea to the recreation and park board, we have to consider when it would be best to do so. If the board is short of funds or near the end of the fiscal year, we may want to wait until a new fiscal year begins. Or if advance notice for appropriations is mandatory, we may press to present our budget request as soon as possible. Some agencies, for instance, have more money near the end of a fiscal year, when they review their projects and pool surplus funds, than earlier in the year. For such an agency, we would hold our request until the end of the fiscal year.

We have to be aware of the other concerns of the board and how our request fits in with the budget and policy concerns. More than likely the board will have other equally pressing problems to handle. We should not overemphasize our request for time and money. If we neglect to acknowledge the board's preoccupation with other business, we might end up with nothing.

We see why most of the work in strategies for implementation is done before submitting the idea for consideration. This is perhaps the most intense behind-the-scenes preparation in the entire model. We have to be alert to as many contingencies as possible to meet them effectively. Our preparation indicates to others that we have given a great deal of thought to the idea and its successful implementation. Enthusiasm alone will not suffice, though it is essential. We should thoroughly understand the idea we suggest, why we suggest it, how objections to it can be countered and resolved, and how we intend to carry it out in the community. Without this preparation, we might come off as a tricky salesperson trying to sell a poor product to the seemingly uninformed.

We also should be familiar with the competitive products. Our competitive products are the three other solutions considered or any offered when we present our solution. When we introduce our idea to the board, we should summarize the other concepts rejected and why. Many of the objections the board may raise to the roving leader concept can be answered by a summary of the drawbacks to the other solutions. If we are comprehensive yet brief in our summary of the shortcomings of the other products, we can move closer to making a sale.

From sales tactics, we can infer selling tips we will need to sell an idea:
1. Make the advantages of the product obvious to the purchaser.
2. Satisfy the needs of those who should benefit from the solution.
3. Indicate the economy of the idea vis-à-vis other solutions or no solution at all.
4. Appeal to the ethical or moral concerns of those involved by showing how well tax money would be spent for this idea.
5. Enlist the support of those already in favor of the idea when presenting it.
6. Use audio-visual or other aids for selling the concept.
7. Make the change acceptable to all concerned.
8. Be convinced of your own decision before selling it to others.
9. Back up your decision with research.

If we check through the various obstacles to selling noted in sales textbooks (Russell, 1978), we also can infer the actions to avoid in our presentation:
1. Do not criticize those who object to the idea.
2. Do not get excited.
3. Do not be emotional in presenting the idea if the group becomes antagonistic or resistant.
4. Do not debate the idea, sell it.
5. Do not distort the value and effect of the solution Be realistic about what it can achieve.
6. Be ready to compromise on the implementation of objectives.
7. Avoid "empire building" by the recreation center.
8. Avoid pushing for approval Be willing to wait.

9. Be ready to change your mind about the solution Be willing to discard the idea and not make a sale if necessary.

The kind of presentation we design should reflect for whom it is intended; if we wish to convince our staff of the value of the roving leader, our presentation may not need as much background information about the concept itself as on the need for a roving leader at the center.

In the case of the community and board, however, the presentation may need more detailed background data. We can draw on our basic model when presenting the report. For instance, we could submit a detailed report on the analysis of the problem, closing with the suggestion that a roving leader is needed and how to implement the idea. By preparing a written report, we not only clarify our own thinking about implementation, but also have something to which others can refer for answers to questions prior to a formal verbal presentation. Or we could use the report as a reference document to complement the presentation. An outline for such a report could follow the steps in the model.

Presentation 1

PROBLEM SITUATION	(a discussion comparable to that presented in the case study)
BACKGROUND PROBLEM DEFINITION	(what we believe the problem to be)
PROBLEM OBJECTIVES	(what we hope to achieve by implementing this idea)
BARRIERS TO IMPLEMENTATION	(a tactful discussion of the more likely objections to be raised)
OTHER IMPLEMENTATIONS	(we can list various tactics for carrying out the idea)
SELECTED IMPLEMENTATION	(a discussion of why we have chosen a particular strategy for implementation)
DECISION	(a request for what we want from the group, for example, funds, study of the idea, and the like)
IMPLEMENTATION	(what we plan to do if the idea is approved).

This outline is one way of handling a presentation. Another example (Presentation 2) is a short summary of the problem and its solution.

Presentation 2

Problem

The Arcola Recreation Center has suffered a severe drop in attendance over the past few years. We feel that this drop originates to a great extent from a lack of participation by residents of the Arcola community. We thus have perceived our problem as, how can we involve the residents of the Arcola neighborhood in the programs of the center?

Solution

A decision was reached after much deliberation and analysis to hire a full-time roving recreation leader for the Arcola community.

Definition

A roving recreation leader is generally a community-detached worker assigned to a specific area within a community to strengthen, extend, and stimulate participation of hard-to-reach youth and other groups by engaging them in wholesome recreation programs and other activities. One purpose of this outreach service is to help the delinquency-prone, disadvantaged youth use their leisure time constructively and to assist them in using community resources for employment and related human services.

Roving leaders understand the neighborhood or community in which they work and are able to meet and deal with people, particularly youth from disadvantaged or delinquent backgrounds. Often, these leaders are from similar backgrounds, thus enhancing the personal leadership stressed by the position and by the human services profession. Generally, the roving leader attempts to make contact with youth and their parents to determine (1) what the youth use and want in the community in the way of human services and recreation, (2) what prevents them from using such services, (3) what is available to youth, (4) what should be made available, and (5) how the roving leader can help youth obtain the resources and services needed for growth and development.

Rationale

It is our belief that the roving leader is an excellent first step toward seriously involving and reflecting the community in the programs and plans of the center. By actively working in the community on a daily basis, the roving leader can elicit many ideas and suggestions from the residents that might be missed in more formal exchanges.

(This can be expanded to include as many objections as we perceive arising, or a summary, in chart form, of the advantages and disadvantages of this idea.)

We, therefore, request $38,000 for a roving leader position for the Arcola Recreation Center as a full-time worker in the Arcola community, for at least one year, effective January 1, 2018.

Whatever report style we decide to use, written or verbal, detailed or summarized, it can be complemented by illustrations, graphs, films, statements from roving leaders, statistics, and other aids. For example, we could arrange for a photographer to take pictures of the center, with evidence of poor attendance and vandalism, and then offer a comparable set of photos of a roving leader, perhaps at another center, working closely with youth in the community or in a well-maintained facility. We should never underestimate the importance of visual presentations of ideas. People retain 10% of what they hear, 35% of what they see, but 65% of what they *see and hear* (Haas, 2012).

Many ideas are rejected because they are weak. We have to anticipate such judgment of even a cherished solution. Someone other than ourselves may be better able to judge if an idea is good. We must be able to drop the idea or to hold it for another time when we feel it might be more acceptable to those whom we seek to convince. We must develop discernment to know when to stop trying to sell a solution.

Now, what is our plan if the idea is accepted? We must incorporate our plan into the written or oral presentation and begin looking for a roving leader to join the community. Based on Allio's (2005) guide to plan implementation, the following steps act as a guide for carrying out an accepted plan:

1. Keep it simple. Often, the most difficult part of implementing a "bought" idea is distilling it into something that is digestible. One of the roles of the lead on the project should be the constant refining of the idea to keep its essence without too much noise.
2. Use common language. Allio points out that words may connote different things to different people. It is crucial to develop common language across the team involved in implementation.
3. Have clear expectations. For each task needing completion during implementation, a clear party should be responsible for its completion. Furthermore, a timeline for these tasks to be completed should also be present.
4. Frequent meetings. Meet often to discuss the progress of the project. Be sure, however, to meet during planned and structured times.
5. Be flexible. In reality, the road taken to implementation will likely not be the route that was originally mapped out. This may occur for a number of reasons. It is important to practice discernment when a fork in the road appears and to know when it is appropriate to deviate from the original plan.

We should remember that many ideas fail not because a concept is weak, but because the manner in which they are presented is poor. We will never know how many bond issues have failed because of lack of forethought, good publicity, or poor planning by those responsible for the bond proposal. The same criticism applies to our attempts to attract federal and state funds for local recreation projects. For all these needs, we have to think creatively and anticipate the difficulties that we may face when we decide to carry out an idea. More and better planning by recreation personnel can yield not only better ideas, but also more effective implementation and successful solutions to everyday professional problems.

References

Allio, M. K. (2005). A short, practical guide to implementing strategy. *Journal of Business Strategy, 26*(4), 12-21.

Haas, K. B. (2012). *How to develop successful salesmen.* Whitefish, MT: Literary Licensing.

Rodgers, D. T. (2014). *The work ethic in industrial America 1850–1920.* Chicago, IL: University of Chicago Press.

Russell, F. A. (1978). *Textbook of salesmanship* (10th ed.). New York, NY: McGraw-Hill.

CASE STUDIES

INTRODUCTION

This section contains 100 case studies that represent the everyday problems facing recreation and park workers. It is recognized that individuals work in all kinds and sizes of organizations; therefore, careful consideration was given to select cases that represent problems in the areas of administration, program, personnel, finance, public relations, and human relations. The case studies provide the opportunity for students to gain an intimate understanding of the difficulties involved in the application of concepts and principles in solving everyday operational problems. They will also give students an opportunity to apply the problem-solving model discussed in the chapters. Experience has shown that use of the case-study method brings reality to the study of recreation and park work, improves students' analytical ability, and increases their potential for learning.

The reader will note that the cases have been categorized under headings that should assist the student and the instructor in selecting topics that most appropriately fit the problem-solving session. At the end of each case is a list of questions that are designed to create interest and provoke discussion about problems referred to in the case. It is not suggested that these are the only questions related to the case, for each student may perceive the case in a different way. In addition, a list of key words and phrases has been provided.

The case studies are based on actual experiences; thus, they reveal in a realistic way incidents that recreation and park workers must face. The cases have been drawn from many sources: from my own experiences while serving as superintendent of recreation in Leonia, New Jersey, and Topeka, Kansas, and while serving as chief of the Office of Recreation and Park Resources at the University of Illinois; from many practitioners in the field of recreation and parks who have willingly shared their experiences; and from many newspaper accounts of stories relating to the recreation and park field. All names have been disguised to avoid identification of organizations and individals. However, I wish to express my thanks to the many administrators, supervisors, leaders, and friends who have contributed to this section of the book. Without their assistance, this publication would not have been possible.

The Special District: Should One Be Established?

Situation

What is a special district? In general, most states define a special district as a local government that delivers a limited number of public services to a geographic area. Some of these districts include libraries, transportation, highways, schools, and fire districts, to name a few. The general public knows little about them and less about their operation and administration. Most citizens do not even know who serves on the district board. The advantages of special districts are they serve local needs, they link their costs to benefits, and they are most apt to respond to their constituents. Opponents of special districts claim these districts are subject to inefficiency, hinder regional planning, and decrease their accountability of operations and evaluation of administration. The following case study raises a number of issues concerning special districts.

You have been director of recreation and parks for the City of Olsenville for 5 years. During this time, you have found it difficult to get the mayor and council to provide enough funds to offer adequate recreation and park services. The long-range program for land acquisition and development has also suffered because of lack of funds. A number of citizens in the community recognize this deficiency and have urged the establishment of a special district that would have the power to levy a tax for the purposes of operating and maintaining recreation and park services. A separate board would be elected, and this board would control the affairs of the special district. The mayor has stated that he will lead the fight against such a district, saying, "It would saddle us with another taxing body, which once established would be next to impossible to do away with." Furthermore, his opinion is that this would not only have an immediate effect on the tax structure, but also cause the mayor and council to lose control of the recreation and park services. He cited examples of two nearby recreation and park districts in which taxes had been collected, but whose expenditures were not in proportion to the proposed budgets. He also pointed out that other districts had ignored a state law requiring all expenditures be published and filed annually with the county clerk. One councillor stated that there are already enough tax districts in the community and another would surely confuse taxpayers. Another councillor stated that for the past year efforts have been made to educate people concerning the operation of local government, hoping they would get involved in solving the city's problems. As more special tax districts are established, the more confused people become and therefore the less interested they are in citizen participation. The League of Women Voters has not taken a position, but has encouraged intensive dialogue among citizens of Olsenville concerning the issue. As director of recreation and parks, you have a particular interest in this issue, and you have been asked to express your views.

Problem

Should a special district be established? What are the advantages and disadvantages of a special district? Would it be advisable for you to publicly take a position on this issue? Why? Do special districts tend to confuse people as to government operation? On what bases do you think special districts should be established?

Suggested Key Words and Phrases for Internet Search

Citizen participation
Feasibility study
Public authorities
Funding

Municipal government
Special district
Public relations
Enabling legislation

_____ Case Study 2 _____
Admission Charge Urged at City Parks

Situation

Recreation and park services are facing a serious challenge today and in the future. Public funds and tax revenues are less available, and they will continue to decline in the future. Park and recreation administrators are constantly faced with developing new revenue resources to sustain meaningful park and recreation programs. Public officials are demanding that users of park and recreation programs pay more for services provided to them. Park and recreation executives may soon have to employ the entrepreneurial approach to develop public recreation and park services. The following case study describes this dilemma.

As the city's 238 parks are plagued by little money, inadequate maintenance, vandalism, overuse, and litter, park officials should institute an admission charge. "It is certainly conceivable," said George Monti, president of the Westchester Recreation Council, "that people would be willing to pay a nominal charge to visit a park simply to sit or picnic, if that park was clean and well maintained, if noise was controlled, and if admissions was limited to a certain number of people at one time."

Mr. Monti made his proposal yesterday at the annual meeting of the recreation council. The council is a private organization that functions as a recreation, parks, and conservation advocate. The group has just finished a report on the problems facing the city's parks and recreation department.

In a report entitled *The Prospect for Parks,* Mr. Monti said that it was recognized that the "notion of fees for the use of public parks, popular in other countries, somehow bothers the citizens of Westchester." Immediately bothered was George Bolton, director of the Westchester Parks and Recreation Department. "I am astonished," Mr. Bolton said when asked to comment, "that the council should propose such an idea. I am 100% against the proposal to have a general admission charge to any city park. This is entirely against the whole theory of city-maintained parks."

Ron Buchanan, an assistant administrator for public information, said that the legal office of the parks and recreation department asserted that the admission charge was "highly questionable from the legal point of view."

"There are admission fees to skating rinks, wading and swimming pools, and boating facilities. A $15-dollar tennis permit is required for an individual to play on city-owned courts—more for control than for revenue," Mr. Buchanan said. "But there is no cost to use the grass or for the use of a bench."

Mr. Monti's suggestion was one of four offered in the report. The others were the decentralization of the day-to-day operations of the parks, the use of streets and temporarily available space for park-related activities, and public pressure to protect parks from encroachment by "those who are looking for land for other purposes." Mr. Monti's premise was that "the prospect for the parks of our city is poor." He predicted that the city park system "as it now generally operates and exists cannot last until the end of this century. Lack of money is a major woe," he said. "It results in a loss of staff and makes all but impossible preventative maintenance and prompt repair of damaged or worn-out facilities."

Vandalism, overuse, and litter are, according to Mr. Monti, "euphemistically called 'signs' of the times." He also stated that the park system needs $3 million dollars a year for the next 10 years "just to keep the present park facilities intact and in operable condition." Yet, he said, "they would be fortunate to have $1 million dollars annually."

Problem

Should a fee be charged for the general use of the parks in Westchester? Under what conditions would you charge a fee? Is it fair to charge a fee for special facilities in the park and not for its general use? Other than increasing taxes, what can officials do to increase revenues for the parks and recreation department? Should parks be limited to a "certain number of people at any one time"? If so, how would you control this? Regarding Mr. Monti's other suggestions, what are the advantages and disadvantages of decentralizing the day-to-day operations of the parks? Is the use of the streets for recreational purposes a good idea? If so, what is the city's liability? What laws and ordinances can be created to protect the city from encroachment on parklands? Assume you are the director of parks and recreation, Mr. George Bolton. Draft a reply to the report presented by Mr. Monti and respond to the issues he has suggested.

Suggested Key Words and Phrases for Internet Search

Functions of government

Fees and charges

Public relations

Use of public parks

Local taxation

Legal responsibility

Proprietary functions

Park encroachment

Decentralization vs. centralization

Tax revenues

Municipal

Government function

Recreation streets

Disadvantages

_____ Case Study 3 _____
Alcohol Use at the Sallybrook Public Golf Course

Situation

The citizens in the Sallybrook Park District have a decision to make concerning the use of alcohol in its public parks and golf courses. The citizens of the district are evenly split on this issue. Members of the district believe that allowing alcohol on the course will create revenue and will provide the money for the needed improvements.

An analysis by the district financial officer indicated the predicted revenue from alcohol sales would be about $400,000.00 annually. It would also increase the use of the restaurant, increase golf fees and tournament play, improve the sales at the pro shop, and increase usage by the participants outside the district. It would also mean the major improvements to the course such as updating the irrigation system, expanding the cart storage facility, purchasing new golf carts, improving course landscaping, installing cart paths, and renovating the kitchen at the clubhouse.

The district financial officer also discussed the issue with a colleague in the village of Fort Ann, where a recently adopted ordinance to sell alcohol at the golf course was established. It was found that after the first three months to sell alcohol, sales lacked luster. During this period, there were $400.00 in beer sales at $3.25 per can and $350.00 in wine sales at $3.75 per glass. The manager reported those revenues were insufficient to cover the start-up cost. He did state, however, sales may increase as users become more accustomed to the new offerings.

Thomas Rodan, chair of the district, also pointed out that it makes the golf course more competitive with the six other golf courses in the area, all of which offer alcoholic beverages at their locations. Another board member stated that the game of golf is in an economic slump and will face more of a challenge from local competition.

At a recent public meeting, there was much discussion concerning the alcohol issue. George Lemory, a district activist, stated that approving the use of alcohol gives the implication of approval of drinking alcohol. He indicated that illegal alcohol use on the golf course is already the norm, which does not make it okay and does not send a good message to young people who play golf with the older adults who violate the existing ban.

Sally Sweeny, a resident of the district, stated that too much emphasis is placed on the revenue that would be generated. Sallybrook has a huge alcohol problem, and therefore, it seems that a public agency, such as the park district, should not be approving an ordinance that allows drinking at the golf course.

As the meeting was about to adjourn, Edward Chapman, attorney for Sallybrook Park District, announced that he received an e-mail from a local citizen that informed members of the board that the land where the golf course is located was the property donated to the park district by Malvina Daley in the early 1930s. Mrs. Daley was a prohibitionist who did not approve of alcohol use. She felt so strongly that the "making" and selling of alcohol would not be permitted. This condition was included in the deed that transferred her property to the district. The deed clearly restricts the making and selling of alcohol on the property that later became the golf course. Chapman also stated that for the documents Mrs. Daley signed the restrictions would no longer apply. However, two board members said the "booze policy" would not be the wishes of Mrs. Daley. It is not uncommon to hear people in the district invoke the name of Mrs. Daley, recognizing her generosity and what she would have wanted for her land donation. A number of citizens have approached the board, urging the board members not to violate the wishes of Mrs. Daley. A number of people have indicated that the issue could end up in the courts. Chair Rodan pointed out the issue of alcohol in the parks and golf course is a serious issue in the district. There have been mixed reactions by the citizens, and the issue needs further study. Board member Eileen Fleming agreed and made a motion that the district attorney and the director of the park district study the options concerning the alcohol issue and make a recommendation to the board in 6 weeks. The motion was approved unanimously.

Problem

What are the options to the board? Should the wishes of Malvina Daley be considered in the financial decision? How can the citizens of the district become actively involved in the decision-making process? Are there other options to raise money for the golf course improvements? Is too much emphasis being made on funds that will be raised for improvements? Should the issue be put on the ballot during the next election period? If alcohol becomes permissible, what rules and regulations should be established?

Suggested Key Words and Phrases for Internet Search

Land donation
Alcohol in public facilities
Golf course management

Community involvement
Competitive advantage
Alcoholic beverages – Golf course

Case Study 4
Awarding Concessions Contracts Is
Tricky Business

Awarding concessions contracts with a commercial vendor can be tricky business, particularly when it involves the public sector. For example, the National Park Service (NPS) awards concession contracts for food service, facility tours, white-water rafting, boating, and many other recreational activities as well as for amenities in more than 100 national parks. These are managed by private businesses under contract to the NPS. These services provided by more than 500 concessionaires gross more than $1 billion every year and provide jobs for more than 25,000 people during the peak season (NPS Commercial Services, 2016). This case study illustrates the need for careful planning when dealing with private vendors in contract negotiations.

Michael Williams, a top aide to Glen County Board President George Woodward, has held a sweetheart concession contract with the Glen County Park and Recreation Department for more than 25 years at a loss of millions of dollars to taxpayers according to the investigation by the *Glen Chronicle* newspaper.

Situation

Williams, a $50,000 per year administrative assistant to Woodward, has held the exclusive, no-bid contract since he wrested it from another concessionaire after a bitter court battle. The contract gives Williams and his company, Consolidated Concessions, Inc., which occupies free office space in Veteran's Field, the exclusive right to sell food, beverages, and other confections at Veteran's Field and all public parks, beaches, and golf courses south of the Hudson River. The current 3-year Consolidated contract, which expires January 31, 2016, grossed the company a record $13 million in 2013. The company is expected to set a new record for 2014 after all of the receipts are counted. Williams has won perfunctory renewal of his contract from the parks and recreation department every 3–5 years without public bidding.

In addition, the terms of the contract, which guarantee the parks and recreation department $5 million annually or 15% of revenues, whichever is greater, have remained unchanged for more than two decades. Sports complexes in other cities receive up to 42% of the revenues from concessions. The favorable treatment to Consolidated has cost the financially strapped parks and recreation department between $1 million and $2 million in revenue according to the *Glen Chronicle*. Though figures are incomplete, the loss for prior years could exceed $4 million. With the addition of the Greenjackets football games, professional soccer matches, and rock concerts, attendance has gone up and revenues have risen by more than $1 million annually. However, the parks and recreation department has not reopened negotiations on terms of the contract.

The *Glen Chronicle* investigation also found the following:

- A survey of publicly owned sports stadiums around the country disclosed that, with one exception, the parks and recreation department struck the worst bargain with its 15% of sales. For example, the sports complex in Milwaukee takes home 33.5% of revenues.
- Midwest-based concessionaires interviewed by the *Glen Chronicle* said they had never been asked to bid on the department's contract, which they regard as plum. All said they would offer 30% of sales if the bidding were open to the public.
- Because of a jurisdictional dispute between the city and the parks and recreation department, Consolidated's food and dispensing facilities, which include a cafeteria in the district's administration building, have never been inspected or licensed by the board of health. A board of health spokesperson told the *Glen Chronicle* that he believed Consolidated's mobile food trailers would not pass the board's licensing inspection. The parks and recreation department provides Consolidated with 12 free storage rooms and offices at Veteran's Field. It also picks up the tab for electricity, heat, and maintenance.
- When confronted with these findings, Williams and parks and recreation department officials said that department regulations did not require that personal service contracts, such as Consolidated's, be publicly bid.
- Nevertheless, when Consolidated took the contract away from Bob and Mary Obrine, who had held it for 12 years, Obrine filed suit in circuit court. The presiding judge suggested the bids be open to the public, saying, "This is a contract with a public body, not with a private firm or individual."

Williams, an attorney who served as an assistant under the Democratic state's attorney, defended his contract with the recreation and park board, saying he provided excellent service through the years. "We've always tried to do a good job and evidently we have because the board continues to renew our agreement," said Williams, who became president of Consolidated in 2005. "Over the years we've made heavy capital improvements at Veteran's Field and the parks, buying new refreshment stands, trucks, and dispensing machinery. We've pioneered in the business," he said.

Though he declined to reveal his salary as president of Consolidated, Williams denied the contract was lucrative. He said that Consolidated lost money during 10 years it had the agreement and that, overall, yearly company profits average only between 1% and 2% of gross sales.

He also said the cafeteria in the administration building has never made money, even though Consolidated receives a 15% credit or deduction from its gross revenues each year. Last year, Williams said the cafeteria for the parks and recreation department employees lost $45,000.00

Williams saw no conflict between his role with Consolidated and his work as an administrative assistant to Woodward. "My work with Consolidated is a weekend business. There's no need for me to be at Veteran's Field during the week," he said.

Although most area concessionaires interviewed by the *Glen Chronicle* said they have never been asked to bid on the parks and recreation department contract, some said they have attempted to bid on the work, but got "nothing but the runaround." Tony Girard, spokesperson for Interstate Corporation, one of the country's biggest concessionaires, said, "Our company has never been asked to submit a bid, but we'd love to." Interstate, which has contracts with Los Angeles Coliseum and Tampa Stadium, is remitting between 35% and 40% of gross receipts, said Girard. Another food vendor, who asked not to be identified, said, "I'd love to offer them 30%. I went to the recreation and park board 5 years ago to find out who bid on the work. I was told to come back in 2009. But when I did, I got the runaround."

George Lemory, former chief judge of the criminal courts, who now represents the park district, said he was unaware of any concessionaire being interested in the parks and recreation department contract. "If a person comes in here and demonstrates he is able to perform on the contract and comes up with a better proposal than Consolidated, I am certain the board would give the person the contract. All he has to do is submit a written letter to the recreation and park board."

Problem

What procedures should be established for awarding the concession contracts over the Glen Parks and Recreation Department? Outline these procedures in detail. What is your opinion of the involvement of Michael Williams, the administrative aide to the county board chairperson? Is this a conflict of interest? What would be a reasonable percentage of return to the park and recreation department on concession business? Give reasons for your answer. Should public bidding be required for this contract? Should Consolidated be required to pay rent for the 12 storage rooms at Veteran's Field? Should city health inspectors be required to inspect the concession stands and Veteran's Field? To what extent should financial records of Consolidated Concessions be available to the parks and recreation department?

Suggested Key Words and Phrases for Internet Search

Concessions

Contract bidding

Food service contract

Public finance

National park concessions business

Conflict of interest

Public bidding procedure

Sports complex administration

Vending machine contract

References

NPS Commercial Services. (2016). Home. Retrieved October 12, 2016, from https://concessions.nps.gov/index.htm

---

Case Study 5
Board Again in Search of a Budget Fix

Situation

Nearly one third of the nation's cities are laying off workers this year. More than half have canceled or delayed needed projects, and 2 out of 5 have raised taxes. American citizens are bracing for what they expect to be their fifth straight year of declining revenues according to a survey of city finance officers of the National League of Cities. The effects of low levels of consumer confidence and high levels of unemployment will continue to play out in cities in the future.

The park and recreation board members found themselves in a familiar spot Thursday evening as they started discussing the long-term budget fixes for the deteriorating bottom line. But this time they are doing it with the understanding that the hundreds of thousands of dollars worth of city bailouts they leaned on last year and will lean on in the coming year may not be there in the future, and with that as a backdrop, possible budget cuts or new revenue ideas that had been dismissed as too disruptive resurfaced on Thursday night. Board members kept bringing up closing recreation facilities for several hours or a full day every week, opening swimming pools later in the year, closing two recreation centers, and reducing staff, especially now as the board members start toward future budget years without a safety net.

"No idea is a bad idea," board member Paul Levack told his fellow board members as he went through how the board may avoid millions of dollars in cumulative budget deficits if it does not act. Everything is on the table after the city council last month denied the park and recreation board's request for the city to pay the board's portion of its debt through 2020.

Last month, some of the city council members had commented that they thought the park and recreation board may have dismissed alternative budget cuts too quickly. For example, charging for parking at the swimming pools, recreation centers, golf course, and ball parks should be revisited.

Barbara Rutherford, a member of the park and recreation board and the city council, said she was worried that the conservation was getting off track when members focused on new programming and facilities that would require capital expenditures. She said she would "rather focus on budget cuts. Afterall, all city functions had to undergo the process." Councillor Dorvee commented, "Yes, it's painful, but we have to emerge from some of that at the city level. We've been able to refund some of the services that were cut. So fortunes change and we have to be prepared to adapt. I don't think the park and recreation board should be in an expansion mode now." Board member Levack said, "But we already cut our staff 13%, increased fees for many of our programs, reduced operation hours at swimming pools and recreation centers, and increased fees at the golf course. I just don't know where we can go from here without significantly reducing the quality of park and recreation programs."

Nancy Moynehan, director of parks and recreation, was asked if she had comments concerning the board budget woes. Moynehan stated, "These conservations have repeated themselves for over 3 years as declining property tax revenue and ever increasing expenses keep pushing the park and recreation board into a tenuous budget situation. We have reduced staff, vacant positions have gone unfilled, maintenance of our parks has been reduced, stress levels of staff are very high, demand for our services has doubled in the last 5 years. I believe the park and recreation board and its staff have worked very hard to maintain a level of quality of the recreation and park services. However, if no solution is found soon, parks and recreation in our community will be affected negatively. I believe the council and the park and recreation board with citizen input should establish a study committee that would develop a plan of action. As director, I would closely work with this group. We can no longer put the budget issue on the back burner."

Problem

What role should the director play in dealing with the budget issue? What role should the city council play? Should a tax increase be instituted to raise revenue? Should fees and charges be increased? Would it be advisable to have a referendum asking for a tax raise for parks and recreation? What groups in the community should be involved in studying the budget issue? What role should the business community and the chamber of commerce play in finding solutions? Should the city apply for loans to meet its financial responsibilities? Are state and federal grants available?

Suggested Key Words and Phrases for Internet Search

Balancing city budgets

Cutting budgets

City budget problems

Annual operation budget

City budget shortfall

Community problems

Budget short fall

Case Study 6
The Superintendent Is Concerned With Morale

Situation

You are superintendent of recreation and parks in a community of 50,000 in the western United States. For almost a year you have noticed that the professional recreation staff has not given its full support to the programs offered by the department. You are not able to place your finger on the exact problem; however, a number of symptoms lead you to believe that your assessment of the situation is right. You have made a number of attempts to discuss this with staff members, but have found they are reluctant to do so. They tend to change the subject when you probe for insight into the situation. Realizing that you are unable to make headway on your own, you employ a management consulting firm to evaluate your personnel situation. You hope that by this firm's probing and examination you will find the crux of the problem.

Upon receiving the report from the consulting firm, you are surprised to find that the staff is unhappy with the way you are administering the department. The staff members feel that you have been completely divorced from the decision-making process and that you do not encourage them to become involved in the administration of the department. The staff members also state that you are aloof and "hard to get to know." They also feel that at the last budget meeting you did not support their salary raises, but did fight vigorously for a new car for the superintendent. One staff member said, "He is now more concerned about his new car than he is about making his staff a decent wage." The report further indicates that most staff members are looking for other employment and will leave the department as soon as they find a position.

The board of recreation and park commissioners is unaware of the personnel problem and feels the department is running smoothly. The report is submitted to you for your consideration and action.

Problem

Do you present the board with the report? Is this really an administrative matter and no concern to the board? What type of communication system could be developed that would keep you alert to staff feelings? Should the staff be involved in all administrative decisions? How much authority should the staff have in making decisions concerning the program? How would you begin to develop rapport with your staff? Should the superintendent socialize with staff members?

Suggested Key Words and Phrases for Internet Search

Human resource management
Staff morale
Personnel administration

Director–staff relations
Staff involvement
Staff communication

_____ Case Study 7 _____
Assisted Living Programs and Facilities at Jackenson Heights Health

Situation

The Jackenson Heights Health Care Center is a 206-bed facility and includes a staff of 225. Its objective is to create an environment consistent with its core values of compassion, respect, integrity, self-determination, empowerment, and flexibility and its vision for excellence. Success depends on the high quality of staff and services.

Jackenson Heights Health Care facility specializes in caring for individuals with Alzheimer's and other memory impairments. Family needs are met using the latest technologies and research in a caregiving approach. Patients enjoy the comfort of daily routines of social and recreational activities, coupled with the attention of dedicated staff. The staff provide the patient and the family with peace of mind, with 24-hour care and and an emergency call system, allowing caregivers to comfortably know the staff are attending to their loved one's every need every day.

Recently, Hogan and Associates completed an evaluation of the programs and services of the organization. The report highlighted two major deficiencies; these included (1) inadequate recreation programs for patients and (2) lack of training and knowledge of staff in dealing with individuals with Alzheimer's and dementia.

To address these issues, the director of the facility has asked you to develop a report with recommendations on how the recreation program can be improved and meet the needs of the patients and to develop a continuing in-service training program for existing staff and new employees.

Problem

What additional information do you need to undertake this assessment? What information do you need about the patients? What equipment will be needed? What budget will be required to carry out the program? How will you develop a tentative schedule for activities? How will you develop a management core philosophy for the programs? How will you identify the amount of space needed for the program? Will additional staff be required? How will you evaluate the effectiveness of the recommendations you will make? How will you gain perspective of the patients' views and staff performance? How will you involve the caregivers in program development? Design an in-service training program for part-time and full-time staff and job descriptions for people who will execute the recommended programs.

Suggested Key Words and Phrases for Internet Search

Dementia

Alzheimer's

Memory care

Caregivers

Dementia training

Case Study 8
Greenfield Village Struggles With Outsider Use of Park and Recreation Programs and Facilities

---

Situation

General tax revenue has declined during the last decade. Public officials have been stingy with providing funds to support municipal services. Recreation and park executives have wrestled with methods to increase revenue sources to offset operation costs. Increasing taxes does not seem to be an option. A question that has arisen is, should outside residents be required to pay additional fees and charges for the use of park facilities and recreation programs? There are legitimate arguments for and against the use of fees and charges for the population not living within city limits. This case study illustrates these issues.

The village of Greenfield recently enacted a policy of charging 100% higher fees to people outside the village for programs and services. This is causing misunderstanding and financial burdens to some people, according to some who expressed opinions at Tuesday's recreation and park board meeting.

The board recently decided to enforce a policy of charging people outside the village 100% more for programs than charged to village residents. John Stangle, director of Lots for Tots, a preschool day care program, said the policy will drive out some long-term users of the program because they cannot afford the extra money. Seven children from six families may be forced to drop out of the program. The enrollment in summer usually has a waiting list, but filling those vacancies in the fall and spring may be difficult.

The board agreed to consider a modified policy for the preschool program. One board member, Sue Petri, said that making an exception for only one program may not be practical. This issue has been before the board in the past, but not much has been done to enforce the policy. Because the news media are giving it more attention, community opinion has been both for and against the policy. Some taxpayers feel that it is unfair for them to carry the burden for the public recreation program: "If people outside the village want to participate in the recreation program, let them pay their fair share." Opponents of the ordinance argue that the recreation program attracts people from other communities and that this helps theirs. One citizen stated, "On weekends, over 2,000 people from outside the city go to the zoo—they spend an entire day in our community—this sure helps our economy."

Problem

Is charging double fees to citizens outside the village legitimate? What policy would you suggest to the recreation and park board? Should the citizens living in the village be responsible for paying the greater cost of the recreation program? Why or why not? What other solutions are there to this problem? Would you consider this is a fair policy if the 100% was reduced? What modified policy do you recommend? What are the possible legal problems in this policy?

Suggested Key Words and Phrases for Internet Search

Fees and charges
Budget and finance
Zero-based budgeting
Financial regulations

Recreation administration
Federal grants to local government
Fee legislation
Program fees

_____ **Case Study 9** _____
Is the Union Request Reasonable?

Situation

You are the director of parks and recreation in a city with a population of 120,000 in the southeastern United States. Five years ago, the employees of the department formed Local Union 791 and became affiliated with the American Federation of State, County, and Municipal Employees, an affiliate of AFL-CIO. During the past 4 years, you and the board have negotiated an agreeable contract. However, the demands made by the union this year will be difficult to meet. Because of a large increase in the tax rate for the school building program, and because of increased welfare costs, the mayor has restricted all city departments to a 2% general increase in budget appropriations. Your opinion is that with this restriction negotiating a contract with the union will be almost impossible. You request a meeting with the mayor to discuss the union demands to work out an equitable agreement with the following demands:

1. All employees receive a $60 per month increase. (*Note:* This represents an 8% increase in salaries and would require an overall budget increase of 12%. Union officials have indicated that this demand is not negotiable.)

2. Minimum and maximum in all classifications be increased by $60.
    3. Any employee who is presently not at the maximum of his or her rate shall receive an automatic 2.5% salary increase. However, this increase shall not exceed the dollar amount received in the first request.
    4. Any employee who is temporarily assigned to a higher paying classification shall receive the rate of pay of that classification if he or she works over 4 hours (e.g., a laborer who is temporarily assigned to equipment operation).
    5. No employee shall work on his or her birthday. If the employee's birthday falls on a Saturday, Sunday, or holiday, then another day shall be substituted.
    6. Negotiations for a new agreement shall begin 3 months prior to the end of the present agreement. (*Note:* Prior to this time, negotiations began 30 days before termination of the agreement.)
    7. The probation period for employees shall be 3 months. (*Note:* Present policy is probation for 6 months.)
    8. Any employee who is dismissed from the department shall have the right to appeal the case directly to the mayor and council. (*Note:* Present policy is that any employee who wishes to appeal his or her dismissal to the mayor and the council must request permission in writing from the director of parks and recreation within 2 weeks after dismissal.)

Employees covered in this agreement include mechanic foreman, mechanic, maintenance foreman, maintenance repairman, gardener, horticulturist, greens keeper, assistant greens keeper, equipment operator, operations foreman, forestry foreman, tree trimmer, electrical foreman, electrician, maintenance custodian, and custodian. Office personnel and supervisory personnel are not part of this contract.

Problem

What recommendations would you make to the mayor that could assist in the negotiations with the union? What compromises would you suggest? How would you approach the union officials? Do you feel that the requests made by the union are legitimate? In lieu of the present cost-of-living increase, is the $60 per month for all employees a reasonable request? Discuss the pros and cons of permitting employees to go directly to the mayor and council with their grievances. Should an employee's birthday be declared a holiday? What are the present trends regarding vacations? What do you think the union officials mean when they say "this request is not negotiable"? What requests do you feel are most negotiable? Why? Develop the plan of action you would use in negotiating this contract with union officials.

Suggested Key Words and Phrases for Internet Search

Collective bargaining – Pros and cons
Grievance procedure
Negotiation strategies
Probationary period
Union demands
Vacation
Contract

Labor relations
Personnel policies
Public relations
Unions
Successful union contracts
Preparing for union negotiations
Famous historic negotiations
Bargaining process

_____ **Case Study 10** _____
Keep Bullying Out of the Recreation Program

Situation

Bullying is fast becoming a major problem in recreation and school settings. According to the Youth Risk Behavior Surveillance (Kann et al., 2014), in 2015, just over 20% of high school students in the United States were bullied on school property during the 12 months before the survey. Each day, many students miss school for fear of being bullied. The question is, what is bullying? The answer is not as straightforward as one person shoving another person in a locker room or the recreation center. Experts define bullying in the following categories:

- Verbal bullying: This includes name calling or teasing.
- Social bullying: Conduct that results in manipulation of people's social lives or convincing others to be unfriendly in social situations.
- Physical bullying: The most common perception of bullying, which includes hitting, punching, kicking, shoving, and fights on the playground or at the recreation center.
- Cyber bullying: Using electronic forms, such as the Internet, social networks, and mobile phones, to create chaos in an individual's life.

During the past 6 months, there have been bullying situations at the recreation center and the Little League program. Bullying has become a serious concern of the Whitehall Park and Recreation Authority. Action needs to be taken. At present, the parks and recreation department has no policy relative to bullying in recreation programs. The following situations demonstrate the seriousness of the problem:

- A seventh grade boy became aware of a website that was all about him. Months later, he found that the individuals who created the website, who he thought were his friends, had been making fun of him and his family. The comments made were along the lines of him being a pedophile, gay, and dirty. The website encouraged others to be actively involved in harassing him. Also, individuals were urged to send him e-mails saying how much they dislike him.

- A group of girls stole the belongings of a fellow volleyball player. When the girl discovered that her property was missing, she reported it to the recreation center director. Later that day, she received an e-mail calling her harsh names and saying she was a tattletale. She went out with her family later that evening, and when she checked her e-mail, there were 50 threatening and intensely mean messages for her.
- One of the girls in the recreation center basketball program found a website containing terrible comments about her. Some of the comments made fun of her weight and estimated her time of death. Her mother went straight to the director of parks and recreation and the parks and recreation board asking for action to eliminate the bullying. The girl had been physically attacked twice after a recreation basketball game. Her mother and father expressed total dissatisfaction with the parks and recreation board.
- In a recent situation, a 13-year-old boy with autism was being harassed. He had a crush on a girl in his class. She pretended to like him and became friendly toward him for a time. Little did he know, she and her friends were making fun of him. She eventually sent him an e-mail telling him that she would never like a guy like him and continued to e-mail him unkind remarks. The boy was so heartbroken and humiliated that he committed suicide.

Two weeks ago, the director of parks and recreation for the Whitehall Park and Recreation Authority resigned to take a new position. The board is in the process of interviewing candidates. You have been chosen as a possible candidate and have agreed to an interview. The interview discussion was generally routine. Topics discussed were leadership style, employee evaluation, personnel, management, fund-raising, and program planning. As the interview was nearing the end, Mary O'Brien, a member of the board, asked you to address a problem that has occurred during the past 6 months at the recreation center. She pointed out that there have been a number of cases of bullying and complaints from parents expressing concerns about bullying incidents. The center director indicated that attendance has been declining. Board member O'Brien indicated that the department has no policies or procedures for dealing with bullying. She has asked two other candidates to prepare a report that indicates how the park and recreation authority should deal with the situation. She asked if you would do the same. How would you reply?

Problem

What is bullying? What are the four forms of bullying?

Organize an action plan for the Whitehall Park and Recreation Authority and establish an evaluation process to determine the effectiveness of the action program for bullying. What can be done to involve the community in the bullying crisis? What policies and regulations should be established to address the bullying problem? What staff training programs should be established to help staff deal with the existing situations? What other public officials should be involved in providing information concerning the bullying crisis? What agencies should be involved in addressing the bullying problem? Could board member O'Brien be of assistance? How can the media be used in dealing with the problem? What are the legal issues involved in the bullying situation? Do other communities have a problem with bullying? If so, how do they deal with it? What youth are at high risk to being bullied? What research is available on bullying? What local, state, and federal laws exist about bullying? What type of an environment reduces bullying behavior?

Suggested Key Words and Phrases for Internet Search

Bullying and youth
Playground bullying
Cyber bullying
Bullying prevention

Parent bullying
Bullying and harassment
Schoolyard bullies
Bullying prevention program

References

Kann, L., Kinchen, S., Shanklin, S. L., Flint, K. H., Hawkins, J., Harris, W. A., . . . Zaza, S. (2014). Youth Risk Behavior Surveillance — United States, 2013. *Morbidity and Mortality Weekly Report, 63*(4), 1–168.

—————————— **Case Study 11** ——————————
Local Recreation and the University

Situation

You have been on the job for 3 months as director of parks and recreation in a Midwestern community with a population of approximately 200,000. A state university with over 20,000 students is also located in the community. While attending a city council meeting, you hear a report by John Kilpatrick, council representative on the recreation committee. He points out the lack of adequate recreation facilities as one reason why the city's youth are roaming the streets. He also mentions that city youth are now crashing and causing a disturbance at activities held on the campus of the new state university. One of these disturbances included a riot at the student union following a dance. Over 12 youth were injured and required hospitalization, 20 were arrested, and approximately $10,000 in damage was caused at the student union. The director of the student union supports Kilpatrick's remarks and further indicates that almost all the disturbances at the student union have been caused by nonuniversity students. He further opines that the present recreation committee and the former director of parks and recreation did little to alleviate the teenage problem in the community. He notes that the recreation centers are poorly programmed and that the leadership is not effective. After a lengthy discussion by council members and citizens in the audience, most of whom agreed with the remarks of Kilpatrick and the director of the student union, the mayor asks you if you would like to comment.

Problem

What is your immediate reaction? What kind of statement would be appropriate for you to make at this public meeting? Should the student union be open to local youth who do not attend the university? What kind of relationship should exist between the student union board and the city's recreation committee? What program would you initiate to improve relations with the university community? What responsibility does the university have in providing recreation programs for the local citizenry? Write a policy statement that could be appropriately endorsed by university officials and city officials.

Suggested Key Words and Phrases for Internet Search

Community–university relations
University code of conduct
Government–university cooperation
University priorities

University office cooperative relationships
University relationship units

Case Study 12
Ridding Garbage Collection: A Social Stigma

Situation

Everyone knows that the term *garbage* was coined on the day that Adam heaved his apple core into the trash can in the Garden of Eden. Well, almost everybody. But certainly everybody knows that garbage collection and disposal has been someone else's problem ever since. Usually that "someone else" is a wiry little fellow in grimy coveralls who comes dragging through our backyards at least twice a week. His vocation (or lack of one) is one of the last really hard jobs in the United States in terms of the sheer physical strength it demands.

Keeping garbage and trash collectors motivated about their job is difficult. Because society does not recognize its role in solid waste disposal, it has attached a stigma to those who fill this role. In most studies of occupational status, the garbage collector is ranked low compared to other occupations. Most studies indicate that the public regards the garbage collector as a nonentity.

This individual is an invisible person who materializes only during times when the public perceives this person to be lax in the performance of his duty.

You have accepted the position of director of parks and recreation for Oceanville, Florida. Oceanville is on the eastern seaboard. The community has a 6-mile beach on the Atlantic Ocean with a 700-campsite development on Stern Park, which is adjacent to one of the main beaches. As in many of the communities along the shore, collecting garbage from the campgrounds and keeping the beaches clean from trash are major problems.

The parks and recreation board has made you aware of the problem. Because you will be negotiating a new union contract within a year, you have been thoroughly investigating the existing problem. You have found the morale among the garbage collectors is often low because of frequent abuse and the job's low prestige. Limited opportunities for upward job mobility and self-betterment are also to blame. To further aggravate an otherwise unhealthy situation, salary expectations stay well ahead of actual wages. Many people would not endure the physical torment of the garbage collector for 10 times the annual salary.

You also find that its not uncommon for 40% of the department's garbage collection personnel to be absent on Mondays and Tuesdays. This creates a tremendous problem, especially following the weekend when thousands of campers, picnickers, and bathers have used the campgrounds and beaches. You have also found that few workers last more than 12 weeks, and some experience difficulty in surviving the first 12 days.

Your primary problems are improving morale, reducing absenteeism, and recruiting and retaining personnel in the sanitation department. The parks and recreation board has requested you submit a report within the next 3 weeks outlining your proposal for correcting the problem.

Problem

What program would you institute that would help improve the public image of garbage collectors? What incentive program could you offer that would bring pride to the job? How would you reduce absenteeism? How would you improve morale? What recruitment methods could you establish for hiring personnel? How would you provide for upward mobility? To what extent do you think increasing the salary of garbage collectors will improve the situation? Why is on-the-job training important for garbage collectors? What mechanisms could you build into the job of the garbage collector that would increase the opportunity to be a part of the decision-making process?

Suggested Key Words and Phrases for Internet Search

Garbage collection – Performance
Problems with waste
Garbage collection issues

Garbage collection – Personnel
  problems
Adverse health problems of workers
Improve employee retention

Case Study 13
The YMCA Director Says No

Situation

As a result of a survey completed by a private planning firm, the mayor and council of a small community in northern New Jersey have decided to submit to the voters a proposal that will establish a parks and recreation district. The district would levy a tax of $0.10 per $100 per assessed valuation for operation and maintenance of a parks and recreation system. The planning firm recommends that this action be taken because the existing programs are inadequate. The firm indicated that there is a lack of sufficient programs for teenagers, senior citizens, and young adults. There are a number of clubs throughout the community; however, the membership in these clubs is small and attendance low. The firm further indicated that the summer playground offered by the board of education is poorly planned. More than 10% of the residents in the community are over 65, yet little effort has been made to ensure senior citizens adequate opportunity for recreation. Few programs are offered in the areas of art, nature, dramatics, and music, and the available opportunities can only be afforded by high-income people.

Several private agencies in the community are opposed to the formation of a parks and recreation district. These include the YMCA, the Girl Scouts, the Catholic Youth Organization, and the Baseball Federation. The director of the YMCA has been particularly vocal in his opposition to the formation of the district. He believes that if the city were to provide the YMCA with funds, it could provide the recreation and park needs in the community. The president of the chamber of commerce, who is also on the board of the YMCA, agrees with this position. The mayor, who has been a staunch supporter of the parks and recreation district, has indicated in the press that a private agency cannot and should not be expected to provide these services.

As a consultant for the state recreation commission, you have been asked to attend a public meeting during which more information concerning the issue will be presented. Both the proponents and the opponents of the proposal will be given an opportunity to speak. Your role will be to present both sides of the issue. However, you know from experience that you will probably be asked to make a recommendation.

Problem

Should a private agency be given the responsibility for public recreation and park services in a community? How do you see your role at the public meeting? Would you give a recommendation? If so, what would it be? Do you feel that personnel from the state recreation commission should influence people on how to vote on local issues? Why?

Suggested Key Words and Phrases for Internet Search

Issues with forming a park and recreation district

Public–private partnerships in parks and recreation

_____ Case Study 14 _____
No Butts About It: Not in the Park

City council will consider the Waterford Parks and Recreation Advisory Board's proposal to ban smoking and the use of other tobacco products at all Waterford Parks and Recreation playgrounds and buildings, including the ball fields and the lake at Waterford Park at Hurley School Road.

If the ban passes, Waterford would be among dozens of cities and counties in the state to prohibit cigarettes, cigars, and snuff from public parks. Waterford has 28 park properties and more than 5 miles of greenway. According to a recent survey, 73% of the county residents said they want a smoke-free playground and 79% said they do not smoke. Beverly Smith, chair of the Waterford Parks and Recreation Advisory Board, said, "The tobacco ban would prevent children's exposure to secondhand smoke, eliminate cigarette butt litter, and improve economic development." Businesses consider a community's health and quality of life when considering relocating or expanding. Paul Singleton wants to know, "Who gets the right to tell us what to do when we are outside? The wind blows the smoke away; it shouldn't bother anyone." Another citizen of Waterford stated, "The parks and recreation department has no right to tell its residents what they can and cannot put in their bodies, just another example of the government trying to dictate how people should live their lives." Sandra Carpenter, a lifetime smoker, said, "I am aghast. Banning smoking inside, I understand, but banning it outside is taking it too far. It is just one more thing we are not allowed to do." John Demero, a commissioner on the county board, stated, "I believe it would be hypocritical for the government to tax the hell out of cigarettes and then not allow smokers to smoke in public places when it is legal to smoke tobacco. I also feel it would be infringing on the rights of citizens' Fourth Amendment. They deserve their right to smoke in public, especially if the government is making such a profit on taxing tobacco sales. I also feel like it would impact business. I know that almost everyone that goes to a bar at least smokes occasionally. All of the other people who smoke would stop coming—good-bye profits, good-bye jobs."

This issue presents a major decision for the parks and recreation advisory board. It involves legal as well as moral and health issues. Assume that you are the director of parks and recreation for Waterford and you have been asked by the board to examine this issue and suggest a recommendation that would assist the board in making a decision.

Problem

Does the city council have the legal right to not allow smoking in public park and recreation areas? Would you consider submitting this question to the voters in the next election? Why or why not? To what extent do the health issues with smoking play a role in the decision? How have other communities dealt with this issue? What is your response to Commissioner John Demero's comment? If the proposed ban is adopted, what enforcement techniques would you recommend? What research can you find that supports the danger of secondhand smoke while recreating in the out of doors? Does a ban on smoking at recreation facilities increase park usage?

Suggested Key Words and Phrases for Internet Search

Smoking in public parks
Smoking related to health
Smoking – Individual rights

Laws concerning smoking
Smoking effects on children

Case Study 15
Taser Guns in the Parks: Yes or No

The Chestertown Park District in a large city in the Midwest is considering arming the park police with Taser guns while on patrol. Some citizens have expressed outrage at this possibility. Others feel arming the park police would reduce crime, particularly at special events, festivals, and major events that draw large crowds.

In a recent survey, it was found that a large segment of the population does not understand how the Taser gun works and when it is used. The question is, what is a Taser gun? A Taser gun is an electric shock weapon that emits electrical charges to subdue an antagonist target. The force is described as nonlethal and not designed to kill. Some believe that the benefits of using the Taser outweigh its dangers. Opponents of Tasers have argued that police rely on them too often. This weapon can be deadly, causing occasional seizures and exacerbating other health problems, such as cardiac arrest. Furthermore, Amnesty International has taken the stand that the ease of the Tasers amounts to "cruel, inhuman, and degrading treatment, which is prohibited by international law."

Although most Taser gun use has not caused fatalities, there is a risk of serious injury during use. According to some studies, there is a risk of serious injury. According to the Institute for Justice, in a number of cases some healthy individuals have died after encounters with Tasers. Some of the deaths were due to heart conditions or other medical ailments; however, it is not entirely known by the medical community why some cases have fatal consequences. As a result, there are concerns that the proactive of use of Tasers is not as harmless as originally thought. Opponents argue that Tasers can cause cardiovascular arrhythmia in some people, possibly leading to heart attacks or death in minutes by ventricular fibrillation.

Donald Stevens, a district police officer and president of Local 2556, said that the use of Taser guns would help officers control rowdy and intoxicated crowds at the performing arts center. The use of drugs has also become a problem. At a recent concert, the police arrested 34 people and ticketed 58 more for violations such as drug possession, underage drinking, resisting arrest, and assault. It has gotten to a point that union members have filed grievances with the park district board to establish a pilot program that would allow officers to carry Taser guns while they are on duty. This suggestion is opposed by Nancy Monahan, executive director of the arts center, who wrote a letter stating the use of Tasers is a "terrible idea."

As the city commissioner of parks and recreation, you have been asked by the mayor to prepare a report for the city council and recommend the direction to take concerning Taser use by park police.

Problem

What additional information do you need to make a recommendation? Are training programs in Taser use effective? What is the experience of the departments that are using Tasers? Would you involve the general public in your recommendations to the mayor? Under what conditions would you recommend the use of Tasers? What reasons would you state if you did not recommend the use of Tasers? Would you allow the use of Tasers in park and recreation facilities? If you approve of the use of Tasers, what training program for officers would you recommend?

Pros

- Tasers allow a police officer to subdue violent individuals without use of a gun.
- Police can use them and not worry about stray bullets that may injure or hurt someone.
- Tasers reduce suspect's injuries rather than police officers having to use dangerous weapons.
- They prevents injuries to the police officers.
- Tasers protect everyday citizens because they allow police to catch criminals.

Cons

- Tasers could lead to death.
- Police officers at times abuse their power and use Tasers when not needed.

- Innocent people could be seriously injured by being Tasered if police assume that something is done.
- Tasers could worsen serious health problems.
- If used near a flammable liquid or material, Tasers can ignite and start fires.

Suggested Key Words and Phrases for Internet Search

Tasers – Pro and cons

Police – Tasers

Health problems – Taser

Safety of Tasers

Taser injury

Taser training

_____ **Case Study 16** _____

The Center Goes to Pot

Situation

Delinquent behavior at times occurs at community recreation centers. One purpose of these centers is to give youth a positive self-image through involvement in the arts, sports, health and fitness, and instructional programs. This case study describes some of these issues.

Three recreation centers for teenagers are under your jurisdiction as superintendent of parks and recreation. During the past year, one of these centers has been the site of a number of fights and disturbances. During a dance held last Saturday night, a fight broke out that required calling the police and closing the center. As a result of these incidents, the parks and recreation board discussed this problem at length at its last meeting. The supervisory staff, the press, and the director in charge of the center were present at this meeting. During the discussion, one board member stated that he had heard that liquor flows freely, that some of the participants smoke marijuana in the center, and that many of the neighbors are complaining of rowdyism. Another board member indicated that much damage had occurred in the last 6 months and that the center had been broken into four times in 3 months. However, with all the faults, the center has the largest teenage attendance in the city. As the meeting was about to conclude, the director of the center asked if he could make a few comments. He pointed out that many of the programs are well planned and well attended. He further stated that the youth are truly involved in the operation of the center. He referred to the center attendance to support his point. He indicated that to his knowledge no drinking is occurring at the center. He admitted that he had heard that marijuana had been used there. He commented, "Though I would certainly report any of this to the authorities, I do not see anything too serious in smoking marijuana; almost all kids will try it at least once before they are 21. Maybe our attitude toward this problem should be reevaluated." Some of the board members showed their obvious displeasure with the center director's remarks.

The next day headlines in the newspaper read *Center Director Approves of Marijuana Smoking—Center Goes to "Pot"—Center Director Approves—City Recreation Approves of Marijuana—Drug Use Rampant at Center.* Your office is deluged with calls, with callers asking the meaning of the news stories. Many people are demanding the resignation of the center director. Some want *you* to resign. Others feel the center should be closed immediately. The chamber of commerce suggests an immediate investigation by the police department. Only the ministerial association has publicly urged caution and warned that hasty action should not be taken. The press is demanding that the parks and recreation board release a statement.

Problem

What statement should be released to the press? Write a press release. Then, should it be released? Should the center director be fired? Why? Should the center director be told not to speak to the press? Why? How will you deal with the police department in this matter? What follow-up would you suggest that could prevent this situation from occurring again?

Suggested Key Words and Phrases for Internet Search

Legalization of marijuana

Marijuana use reevaluated

State marijuana laws

Press relations

Marijuana recreation use

Recreation drug use

Case Study 17
Lost Tourism Revenue May Force Cuts in Washington County

Situation

Washington County is considering painful steps to deal with the lack of tourism dollars while the national park remains closed. The county's chief administrative officer said the general fund could lose about $800,000 in tourism revenue this month if the national park remains closed. He asked the board of supervisors to consider a mix of furloughs, layoffs, and closures to make up for the shutdown.

Washington's economy relies heavily on the tourists who travel on Highway 49 to the park. But now that the national park is closed, hotels and other businesses are suffering. Staff member Mary Woodward said, "There are a lot of people that are very unhappy about not getting into the park, and very disappointed, and there are a lot of cancellations."

Woodward is now helping tourism leaders promote the variety of activities in this area in hopes of attracting more visitors, but Chief Administrative Officer George Lemery is extremely concerned. Lemery said, "The major source of revenue in Washington County is the transient occupancy tax, the tax on hotel rooms, and with the National Park closed, virtually that market is drying up here in Washington County." Lemery presented several options to the board of supervisors Tuesday in front of a standing-room-only crowd. He recommended the layoffs of all extra help employees in the public works and library departments, which would essentially close the library system. He also suggested temporarily shutting down the visitor center. Several people spoke out against both of those ideas during the meeting.

One resident said, "Libraries are a lifeline for rural communities." Janet Higgins, who works at the visitor center said, "Please do not close the visitor center. We need this crucial hub now more than ever." But those are not the only options. Lemery says if the shutdown continues past November 1, the county should consider furloughing employees and equivalent pay cuts for managers and elected officials. That idea also drew criticism from residents and law enforcement leaders, who said furloughs often create more expenses than they solve.

Washington County Sheriff Edward Chapman said, "If deputies are furloughed, this would increase overtime costs significantly, and we would completely exhaust our officers, jeopardizing their safety and the public's."

Supervisors decided not to take action until November 1. They are hoping the park will be back open by then, and they will know exactly how much money they need to recoup. But if the shutdown is still going on, it could continue to cost the county hundreds of thousands of dollars each month.

Problem

What is the most effective action that the Washington County Board of Supervisors could take to solve this problem? What other agencies should be involved in the decision? What other sources of revenue could be made available to help with the situation? What responsibility does the National Park Service play? Can the community surrounding the park play a role? Have the senators and congressional representatives been contacted? What role could they play? Draft a letter that could be sent to the Washington representatives.

Suggested Key Words and Phrases for Internet Search

National park cutbacks
National parks pressing Congress
Budget cuts at national parks
Yellowstone budget cuts

Closing at national parks –
   Tourist unhappy
Economy – National parks

Case Study 18
Who Should Use University Facilities?

Situation

You have recently been appointed as director of intramurals and campus activities for State University. One of your responsibilities is to direct the administration of the use of university facilities. Under your jurisdiction are the student union, the field house, seven gymnasiums, and four swimming pools. During the past year, the chancellor and the dean of students have received an unusual number of requests for these facilities from student and local groups. The policies for the use of facilities are outdated and need revised. The chancellor sees this as a top priority for your office. He requests that this project be completed by May 12 so that your proposed changes in the policies may be submitted to the board at its regular monthly meeting.

One of your first actions to complete this project is to contact other universities in the region and determine their procedures. You also discuss the changes with your staff and encourage their comments. Following this action, you submit the following to the chancellor as your recommendation:

> The policies have been developed with the objective of encouraging the optimal use of the university's facilities and premises in the furtherance of the university's educational mission and the protection of its facilities. No attempt is made to foresee all of the types of usage that may be requested. Authority to interpret these policies and to decide upon appropriate application of them is delegated to the chancellor of the university.

I. Use of Facilities by University-Recognized Organizations

1. The term "university-recognized organizations" refers to undergraduate, graduate, professional student, or staff organizations that have been "recognized" by appropriate university officers.

2. Recognized organizations will not generally be granted permission to use university premises for events, sales, or solicitations that have the nature of a benefit activity, that is, that are intended to raise money for uses other than the expenses of the organization or the support of other university activities.

3. The chancellor (or his designated representative) may authorize specific exceptions to the preceding regulations.

4. Recognized organizations granted permission to use university premises and facilities will be held responsible for compliance with university regulations.

II. Use of Facilities by Outside Organizations

1. The term "outside organizations" refers to all organizations not included among the groups affiliated with the university but including individuals purporting to act, or in fact acting, as a representative of an outside organization.

2. Requests for the use of university premises and facilities may be approved for outside organizations if the organizations and meetings are concerned primarily with matters of educational or public significance and if the proposed use does not interfere with the work of the university. University permission for the use of premises and facilities by outside organizations implies neither approval nor disapproval of the purposes of the outside organizations nor of the events sponsored by the organizations.

3. Requests will not be granted for meetings or activities of the following types conducted by outside organizations:

   a. Meetings of such organizations scheduled on a regular basis.

   b. Meetings for the purpose of instruction that would normally be offered by or in cooperation with any unit of the university, unless the offering of the instructional program is recommended or concurred in by the appropriate university unit.

   c. Social activities, such as dances and entertainment, that are not scheduled as part of an approved meeting or activity.

   d. Sports events, unless approved or sponsored by an appropriate unit of the university or by the director of intramurals and campus activities.

   e. Meetings or events that would substantially interfere with or detract from events sponsored by the university or by university organizations.

   f. Solicitations, collections, fund drives, or any event for which an admission will be charged, even though the funds are for public benefit.

4. If the outside organization requesting the use of university space has a university-recognized local affiliate, the local organization shall participate in the arrangements for and be responsible for the use of university facilities in accordance with the university rules and regulations.

III. Procedure for Submitting and Receiving Approval of Space Requests

1. Recognized organizations seeking use of university premises shall make their requests by completing and filing the form "Request for Use of University Premises." This form must be signed by a responsible agent of the group requesting the space before any space reservation can be completed.

2. Requests by recognized organizations for business and combination meetings should be filed at least 48 hours before the space is desired.

3. Outside organizations and individuals seeking use of university premises shall make their requests by completing and filing the form "Request for Use of University Premises." This form must be signed by a responsible agent of the organization requesting the space or by the individual, as appropriate, before any space reservation can be completed.

4. Space requests for meetings or events involving visiting speakers and performers must be filed at least 10 days before the event and be approved before any contracts or commitments are made.

5. Upon receipt of request form on behalf of an organization or of an individual, all reservations offices shall act as follows:

   a. Determine the eligibility of the organization or speaker to use university premises for the proposed purpose.

   b. Notify the organization or the individual of the action taken on the request for the use of university premises or facilities.

   c. Reserve space for approved events and notify all university offices involved in the announcement, preparation, security, or conduct of the event.

Problem

Who should determine what organizations are university-recognized? The policy states that "recognized organizations will not generally be granted permission to use university premises for events, sales, or solicitations that have the nature of benefit activity," but the chancellor may authorize specific exemptions. What exceptions do you see as acceptable? Should outside groups be permitted to use university facilities only when the activity is "educational and of public significance"? Develop a priority list by function of local organizations that should be permitted use of university facilities. Should students be involved in developing policies for facility use? If yes, to what extent? Do you feel that there should be a separate policy for the student union facility?

Suggested Key Words and Phrases for Internet Search

Campus recreation
University facility use
Forms for facility use

Regulation for facility use
Granting facility use
Use of university premises

_____ **Case Study 19** _____
What Kind of a Program for Downsville?

Situation

You are presently serving as a state recreation and park consultant. You have received a request from the community of Downsville (population 31,500) asking that you assist the city's recreation committee in improving recreation opportunities. Downsville is located in the west central part of the state.

It is the center of an agricultural area about 40 miles in diameter. The economy of the area is generated in three main areas: agriculture, manufacturing, and retailing. The annual median family income is $35,000. About 20% of the population is African American. Below is a chart describing the age of the population.

Population Chart

Age	2000	%	2010	%
Under 5	4,171	9.7	4,770	9.7
5–19	11,200	26.0	12,340	25.0
20–44	13,000	30.3	16,990	34.6
45–64	8,753	20.4	8,957	18.3
65 and over	5,867	13.6	6,103	12.4

Downsville's founders were conscious of the need for open space, and they planned Laken Park and Woodworth Park in the original layout of the community. Realizing the need to maintain these park areas, Downsville citizens created the position of park director nearly 50 years ago. During this 50-year period, 11 new parks were established and park acreage increased from 10 acres to 690 acres. Other facilities in the City of Downsville include the following:

1. Municipal indoor swimming pool: Operated jointly by the city and the YMCA.
2. Lake Sagamore and Lake Vinton: Two country clubs owned by the railroad. The man-made lakes serve a large segment of the Downsville population.
3. Camp WA-NO-ME: This area is also owned by the railroad and is located across from Lake Sagamore. It is the only resident camp within 20 miles of Downsville. The camp provides an area in which school camping could be established. All buildings would need to be winterized.
4. Sun Lake: This is a small private lake built by Sun Products for its employees. The area boasts family picnicking, swimming, and playground facilities. However, presently only 200 residents of Downsville have access to it.

5. Rainbow Swim and Tennis Club: This facility is located on the south side of the community and is only open to members. Approximately 400 families pay a fee of $300 per year to use this facility.
6. Rod and Gun Club: This facility is located on 10 acres of undeveloped land 2 miles outside the city limits.
7. Downsville Country Club: This area provides an 18-hole golf course, tennis courts, and a swimming pool for its members. Family membership fees are $1,200 per year. This club serves only a few of the citizens of Downsville.
8. School facilities: Located in Downsville are 10 elementary schools, two junior high schools, and one high school.

At present, the city provides no funds for conducting a recreation program. The Downsville Citizens' Recreation Committee is concerned about this and has asked you to assist in organizing a program that could be proposed to the mayor and council for funding.

Problem

What kind of program would you recommend for the citizens of Downsville? How would you assess the needs of the community? Does the population chart reveal significant characteristics that would be helpful in planning the program? What kind of relationship should be developed with the schools? Do you think the school facilities would provide good playground locations? What staff would be required to implement your program? Would it be possible to apply for federal grants that would assist in implementing the program? What would be the total cost of implementing the recommended program? What state-enabling legislation would you recommend for administering the program? Why? How would you involve the citizens in the planning of the program? Is citizens' involvement important? Why? To what extent would you allow the citizens to become involved in the decision-making process? Be specific. What additional information would be helpful in solving this problem?

Suggested Key Words and Phrases for Internet Search

Citizen involvement
Feasibility study planning
Public–private relations

Recreation staffing
Enabling legislation
School relations

_____ **Case Study 20** _____
Who Should Be the Director of
Parks and Recreation?

Situation

At the request of the mayor, you are serving as chairperson of the search committee for the position of director of parks and recreation for Cedarville, New York. James Orcutt, the current director, will retire on December 31 after 21 years of service. Serving with you on this committee are the city's personnel officer, Tom Gaines; Tom Bolen, superintendent of parks; Nancy Ottis, a member of the department of parks and recreation advisory committee; and James Metric, a council member. The position has been advertised through the National Recreation and Park Association. To describe the position to prospective candidates, the following job description and information about the City of Cedarville were publicized in the following job announcement:

Director of Parks & Recreation
Cedarville, NY
Job Description

Under the general guidance of, and within policies, regulations, and plans set by mayor, council, and the parks and recreation board, the director of parks and recreation is responsible for planning, organizing, directing, and evaluating a comprehensive program of recreation and parks for the City of Cedarville. The director of parks and recreation serves as the chief executive officer to the department. It is further the responsibility of the director to

1. Coordinate department programs with those of other local and regional organizations.
2. Prepare and oversee the preparation of proposed actions for intermediate- and long-range recreation and park plans.
3. Keep the mayor, council, and the recreation board informed of all policy and major program matters as well as administrative and operating problems that affect the performance of the department.
4. Serve actively as the department representative within the community.
5. Direct the development of communications within the department and between it and the general public.
6. Attend and actively participate in meetings on local, state, and national levels.

The City of Cedarville, population approximately 2 million, is in central New York state. Lake Katrine forms its western boundary. The eastern and southern boundaries have no outstanding characteristics. The city covers about 75 square miles. Located in the community is a major depot of the New York Central Railroad and a newly developed airport. The New York State Thruway also covers the southwestern corner of Cedarville. Recent studies completed by County Planning Associates indicate that the population of Cedarville will increase to 2,800,000 by 2020. Both the Chrysler and Bendix Corporations have announced plans to construct two plants within the next 3 years, which will employ almost 2,000 people.

Cedarville, like thousands of other American cities, has "pockets of poverty." Racially, Cedarville's population is about 91% White. The remaining 9% is made up of minority groups, with African Americans representing about 6.5% of the total population. As in most large cities, people living in low-income areas are making their voices heard at city hall. Recently, the department of parks and recreation denied a request for the East Cedarville Civic Association to renovate the recreation center and to add recreation programs. The department reported funds were not available for these requests.

In 1928, the city charter established a strong mayor-council government. Elective offices are those of mayor, comptroller, president of the council, five council members at large, and nine district council members. The mayor prepares the budget and controls executive powers of taxation, appropriation, and confirmation. With the exception of the mayor, the president of the council and council members at large may not succeed themselves after their 4-year terms. District council members may be reelected to a second term.

The parks and recreation board is an administrative unit appointed by the mayor with the approval of the council. It has the power to employ personnel and to carry out the recreation and park services. Personnel in this unit are directly responsible to the parks and recreation board. However, the mayor has always maintained influence in recreation matters because recreation and park funds are appropriated by the mayor and council from the city's general revenue fund. The mayor and council must also approve capital improvements for recreation, land, and facilities.

For the most efficiency, the parks and recreation board has appointed a nine-member advisory council (see organization chart on p. 42). The purpose of this council is to advise the recreation and park staff in matters concerning programs and activities offered by the department.

At present, there are five senior high schools, 12 junior high schools, and 62 elementary schools. Within 2 years, the Cedarville Community College will be established; the board of education has shown great foresight in acquiring land for school development. There have been some difficulties in establishing joint use and development of school, park, and recreation sites. Recreation and park board members feel this problem exists because of the attitude by the school board that "schools are for education not recreation." However, the new superintendent is doing much to change this attitude.

Both the Democratic and Republican parties are active in Cedarville. At present, approximately 60% of the registered voters are Democrats; the remaining 40% are Republicans. Tom Landrey is the first Republican to be elected mayor in over 20 years. The coming election hinges on a number of issues. One high on the agenda is the profiling budget of the parks and recreation department. Mayor Landrey has become sensitive to these issues.

Cedarville is served by two independent newspapers, the *Times* and the *Post Star.* The *Post Star* also owns a radio station, WPAR, and WRECD-TV. The news media are always alert to problems that affect city government. The *Post Star* city hall reporter, Gene Hartman, tours the administrative offices of the city department each day looking for news. Only 2 weeks ago Gene wrote a feature story in *Post Star* pointing out the 5-year growth of the parks and recreation department. Until this appeared, many people were not aware of the budget growth of the department during the 5-year period.

The search committee has received over 75 applications for the position and has reviewed all of them. Four candidates have shown excellent potential for becoming the next director of parks and recreation. By Tuesday, your committee must submit the four potential candidates, in priority ranking, to the mayor, council, and the parks and recreation board. A brief description of the four finalists follows:

John Marrion

Present position: Assistant director of parks and recreation for Cedarville, New York, for the last 8 years

Present Responsibility: To assist the director of parks and recreation in the operation of the department

Total Years of Experience: 21

Education: BS, Recreation and Park Administration; MS, City Management

Career Goal: Has said that he would like to become director when Orcutt retires

Recommendations: All excellent

Professional Involvement: Active on New York State Recreation Society Committees, served on the curriculum review committee for Recreation Ithaca College, popular speaker at high school career days; member of the NRPA Mid-Atlantic District Council, is vice-chairperson; member of NRPA's Legislative Committee; served for 3 years on the Kennedy Foundation's Review Board for Special Olympics.

Informal Feedback: Very well-liked by present staff; has their respect and affection; well organized; may be too comfortable in the number two spot, but this may be due to serving in this position for too long; member of the Rotary Club and is now its president; held in high regard by both Democrats and

Republicans; has support from the community for becoming the next director of parks and recreation; has expressed interest in this job.

George Stein

Present Position: Assistant director of recreation and parks, Metroville, California, for 7 years

Present Responsibility: Administration of the recreation program; secretary to the park board; and acts in absence of the director of parks and recreation

Total Years of Experience: 8

Education: BS in Recreation and Park Administration, MS in City Management

Career Goal: Not stated

Recommendations: All excellent

Professional Involvement: Past president of the California State Park and Recreation Society; NRPA Legislative Committee; served as State Conference chairperson; served as the state's first professional certification chairperson; 2 years ago was named California's "most outstanding young professional."

Informal Feedback: Very well liked in his present community; is held in high regard by staff; will not "play ball" with those who want political favors; is part owner of a commercial ice rink; excellent public speaker; while in college was an All-American football player; sold insurance and real estate after graduating from college; recently became active in Republican politics as ward committee member; excellent administrator.

About Metroville, CA: Metroville is in northwestern California and has a population of about 2 million. It operates under a strong mayor-council form of government, with the mayor serving as the chief executive officer and administrator. The director of parks and recreation reports directly to the mayor and serves in his "advisory cabinet." Under the jurisdiction of the director of parks and recreation are 106 playgrounds, 4 golf courses, 33 recreation centers, 21 swimming pools, 3 national beaches, 1 botanical garden, 1 zoo, 3 marinas, 1 riding academy, 2 ice rinks, 1 tennis club, and 1 observatory. There are 75 recreation and park professionals with a staff of 630 employees. The annual operating budget is $17 million with a capital improvement budget of $3 million. Three years ago, the citizens defeated a $10 million bond issue referendum for recreation and land acquisition. Last year, the city was selected as a Gold Medal Winner for having outstanding recreation and park system for a city of its size.

Peter Stickney

Present Position: Director of recreation and parks, Ellensville, Iowa, for 3 years

Present Responsibility: Direction of the recreation and park department

Total Years of Experience: 12

Education: BS and MS in Recreation and Park Administration

Career Goal: To become a director of a large metropolitan recreation and park department

Recommendations: All excellent

Professional Involvement: Past president of State Recreation and Park Society; active on committee of the National Recreation and Park Association

Informal Feedback: Peter is an excellent administrator, good public speaker, very aggressive, works hard to accomplish his goals—a determined individual —well liked by the professionals in his state. Sometimes gets a letter about being overcommitted with responsibilities. According to one former staff member, "Sometimes does not give his staff enough credit for what they do." Probably would do excellent as a director.

About Ellensville, IA: Ellensville, Iowa, is a community of approximately 50,000. The mayor appoints an advisory board to the recreation and park department. There are four major divisions within the department: recreation center, aquatics, day camps, and maintenance. There are 12 professional staff members, with a total staff of 46 employees. Under the direction of the recreation and park department are 4 swimming pools, 6 recreation centers, 3 day camps, and over 600 acres of parkland. The annual operating budget of Ellensville is $11 million with a capital improvement budget of $2.6 million. Recreation programs are well attended and the department has a good reputation among its citizens.

Nancy Watson

Present Position: Deputy director of parks and recreation in Bennetville, New York, for the past 4 ½ years

Present Responsibility: Primarily responsible for the direction of the recreation programs

Total Years of Experience: 14

Education: BS in Recreation and Park Administration; nearly completed PhD in Political Science

Career Goal: To be chief administrator in one of the leading recreation and park departments in the U.S.

Recommendations: All excellent

Professional Involvement: Now serving as treasurer in the New York Park and Recreation Society; vice-chairperson of NRPA Mid-Atlantic Regional Council; active in legislative committee of the Municipal League; service on the board of trustees of a small women's college in upstate New York; recently appointed by the governor of New York to the state's urban problem committee.

Informal Feedback: Nancy has a great deal of energy and is very ambitious; emphasizes training and education, sometimes appears to be a little pushy; capable and knowledgeable, good administrator, gets along with the staff "most of the time"; understands the policies of city hall; a no-nonsense person; is capable of being an outstanding administrator and is highly respected by her peers.

About Bennetville, NY: Bennetville is a community of approximately 1 million people in central New York. The city operates under a strong mayoral form of government. An administrator is employed to oversee municipal functions. The director of parks and recreation reports to the mayor through the city administrator. The deputy director reports to the director of parks and recreation. The Department of Parks and Recreation is responsible for the operation of 24 recreation centers, 2 day camps and 1 resident camp, 4 golf courses, a harbor, a zoo, a museum, an ice rink, and 3 tennis facilities. There are 52 professional staff members, with a total staff of 425 employees. The total annual operating budget is $8,105,000, with a capital improvement budget of $1.5 million. The city has also been the recipient of a number of federal grants for parkland acquisition. The city has a national reputation of attempting to provide a worthwhile recreation and park program. However, like most metropolitan areas, it has had its problems—financial difficulty and racial strife.

All four candidates will be invited to Cedarville for a personal interview. What questions should be asked at the personal interview?

Problem

How would you rank the candidates for the position of director of parks and recreation in Cedarville? What criteria would you use? With the information you now have, which of the four candidates would be the best director? Why? What information about the candidates not presented would be helpful? Describe the information that is lacking.

Suggested Key Words and Phrases for Internet Search

Job interview questions
Legal consideration at job interview
Job interview preparation
Suggested interview questions

Job interview expectations
Job interview location
Employer questions at interview

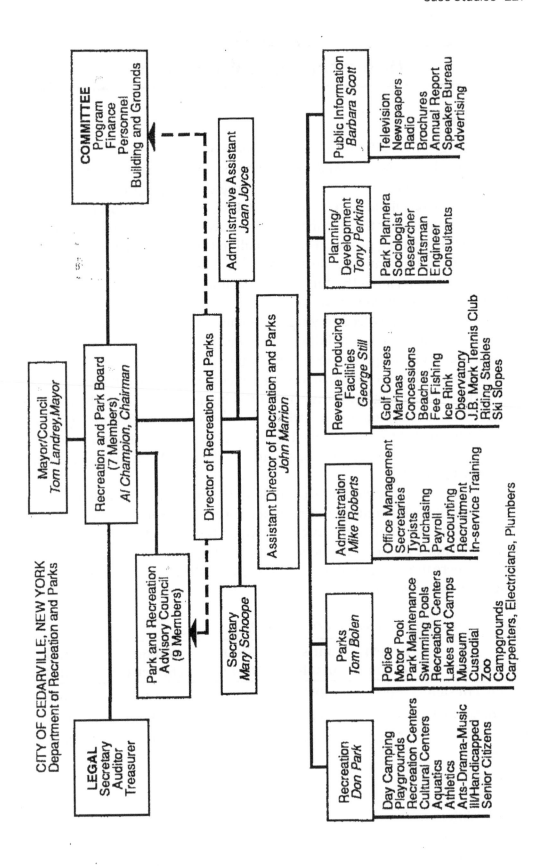

CITY OF CEDARVILLE, NEW YORK
Department of Recreation and Parks

Mayor/Council
Tom Landrey,Mayor

LEGAL
Secretary
Auditor
Treasurer

Recreation and Park Board
(7 Members)
Al Champion, Chairman

COMMITTEE
Program
Finance
Personnel
Building and Grounds

Park and Recreation Advisory Council
(9 Members)

Director of Recreation and Parks

Administrative Assistant
Joan Joyce

Secretary
Mary Schoope

Assistant Director of Recreation and Parks
John Marrion

Recreation
Don Park

Day Camping
Playgrounds
Recreation Centers
Cultural Centers
Aquatics
Athletics
Ill/Handicapped
Arts-Drama-Music
Senior Citizens

Parks
Tom Bolen

Police
Motor Pool
Park Maintenance
Swimming Pools
Recreation Centers
Lakes and Camps
Museum
Zoo
Custodial
Campgrounds
Carpenters, Electricians, Plumbers

Administration
Mike Roberts

Office Management
Secretaries
Typists
Purchasing
Payroll
Accounting
Recruitment
In-service Training

Revenue Producing Facilities
George Still

Golf Courses
Marinas
Concessions
Beaches
Fee Fishing
Ice Rink
Observatory
J.B. Mork Tennis Club
Riding Stables
Ski Slopes

Planning/Development
Tony Perkins

Park Planners
Sociologist
Researcher
Draftsman
Engineer
Consultants

Public Information
Barbara Scott

Television
Newspapers
Radio
Brochures
Annual Report
Speaker Bureau
Advertising

Case Study 21
Hiring the Consulting Firm

Situation

The village of West Bend recently passed a bond issue to allow the Village of West Bend Parks, Paths, and Recreation Department to restore an aging outdoor pool and build a recreation center on the same park property. The project has been determined to cost nearly $10,000,000. As the superintendent of parks and planning for the department, you have been tasked by the board of trustees with soliciting proposals from qualified consulting firms to lead your agency through the planning, design, and construction processes. The board requested you determine the top three consulting firms in the state and recommend one for their consideration.

You are actively involved in your state park and recreation association. A resulting benefit has been building a network of colleagues who are willing to share their knowledge and expertise. You reach out to this group to gather information on their recent construction projects and to find out their satisfaction with the consulting firms they have used in the past. You use the data you have gathered to develop and distribute a request for qualifications (RFQ) to 10 recommended consulting firms. The RFQ narrows down the competition to only firms that have successfully responded to your RFQ and meet the criteria you have requested.

Five firms emerge as potential candidates to work with your agency. As one final precaution, you contact the member services coordinator for the park and recreation association and ask if she would be willing to administer a survey to determine agency satisfaction with the five consulting firms. Over 50 park and recreation agencies are contacted, and 100% return is received. The following results are received:

Percentage of Satisfied Agencies Out of 50 Respondents

Concern	Brown & Son	Johnson Consulting	Klein Design	Walker Architecture	Hall Consulting
Original Design	50%	88%	98%	88%	95%
Cost of Service	72%	50%	88%	77%	96%
Reliability of Project Estimates	84%	56%	95%	68%	94%
Ability to Work With Contractors	66%	96%	94%	85%	92%

Concern	Brown & Son	Johnson Consulting	Klein Design	Walker Architecture	Hall Consulting
Ability to Work With Boards	44%	96%	96%	85%	92%
Supervision of Project	98%	86%	89%	87%	90%
Availability	94%	96%	90%	88%	90%
Completion of Deadline	74%	46%	95%	87%	93%
Efficiency of Design	52%	98%	95%	85%	93%
Qualified Personnel	90%	98%	95%	85%	93%
Overall Evaluation	72%	86%	94%	84%	93%

After receiving sufficient feedback from your colleagues, you compare the survey results. You decide on three consulting firms in your state to distribute your request for proposal (RFP). An RFP is a document that an agency delivers to potential vendors outlining a needed product or service. An RFP aids successful project management because it clearly outlines the project deliverables and requires the vendor to outline a plan and design to meet your needs.

The end of the day rolls around and Village President Brian Vetter pays a visit to your office. He is interested in giving you advice on consulting firm selection. President Vetter is friends with the owner of Remillard Design, a local architectural firm that has been his campaign supporter in the past. You quickly reject his suggestion knowing that Remillard Design has never worked on park and recreation construction projects, and subsequently, the company will not understand your needs. He counters with the proposition that if Remillard Design is awarded the contract, a large donation will be forthcoming for the Village of West Bend Parks, Paths, and Recreation Department. Other board members are not aware of this information. President Vetter then informs you that he has asked the owner of Remillard Design to present at the board meeting, which begins in a half an hour.

The village president sets the agenda for the board meeting and has slated Joe Remillard, owner of Remillard Design, as the first agenda item. Remillard kicks off the meeting by presenting his ideas for the pool and recreation center construction, details how his firm was left out of the RFQ process, berates the consulting firm competition, and overtly tells the board that the forthcoming RFP process is a waste of time and resources when there is a local and affordable option in Remillard Design.

Problem

Your name is on the agenda to provide an update on the selection process later that evening. Would you choose to respond to Mr. Remillard's comments at that time? If so, what would you say? Would you tell the other board members and your director about President Vetter's comments? Will you continue to support the selection process, including the RFP? Why? What firm would you recommend to the board of trustees? What is the most efficient way to select a consulting firm? What other information would you have included in the survey?

Suggested Key Words and Phrases for Internet Search

Choosing a consultant   Budgeting for consultants
Developing an RFP   Why hire consultants
How to find a consultant   Consultant - Strategic planning

_____ **Case Study 22** _____
Public Land Management

Situation

The state of Colorado is home to many significant scenic, historic, and natural wonders, which are under the jurisdiction of cooperative branches of federal, state, and local governments. One such partnership involves Elk State Park, the Columbine National Wildlife Refuge, and the City of Durango Hacienda Community Park. The two parks and refuge share borders. Many years ago, the director of Elk State Park formed a joint task force comprising leaders from each agency to develop intergovernmental policies and plans to manage the community, state, and national resources jointly. These resources include several 10,000 foot peaks, 25 miles of hiking trails, Native American dwellings and petroglyphs, a 250-site RV campground, a thriving elk herd, the endangered swift fox, and five champion trout fishing lakes.

As the executive director for the City of Durango Recreation Department, you have represented the interests of the Durango Recreation Department, Hacienda Community Park, and local residents on the joint task force for the last 10 years. You have developed outstanding relationships in this role with managers from Elk State Park and the Columbine National Wildlife Refuge. This partnership has consistently helped to protect natural resources in the area and has drawn measurable tourist dollars to a declining economy.

Despite these efforts, the City of Durango and the state of Colorado have sunk deeper into debt. In recent elections, longtime conservation effort supporters, the mayor of the Durango, and the governor of Colorado were unseated by fiscally conservative entrepreneurs. The new mayor, Nick Flood, is the retired owner of the Colorado Construction Company, and the new governor, Ben Filzen, is a past consultant to the oil and gas industry. In a few short months, Mayor Flood and Governor Filzen used their influence to secure federal, state, and local permits to erect test wells for oil and gas exploration at Hacienda Community Park, Elk State Park, and Columbine National Wildlife Refuge. You realize the wells are for show because it has been documented for years that the three parks sit on top of a substantial oil shale deposit with possible pockets of oil and natural gas. Shortly after testing commences, Mayor Flood and Governor Filzen hold a joint press conference to announce their plans for oil drilling and hydraulic fracturing (fracking) at your park. They state that the fracking process will have minimal effects on the environment and major effects on Durango and Colorado's declining economy and stagnant job market. Donations and taxes from the oil and gas companies would be used to supplement the park budgets for the City of Durango and the state of Colorado. Estimates show that it would be the first time in 10 years that both park system budgets are fully funded. Necessary maintenance projects that have been put off for years would be completed, further stimulating the economy. Mayor Flood also noted that road development into previously untouched regions of the parks and refuges will allow for increased tourist opportunities and dollars.

Prior to Mayor Flood's press conference, joint task force members voted to commission an environmental impact study on oil production and fracking in Hacienda Community Park, Columbine National Wildlife Refuge, and Elk State Park. The resulting final report highlights many concerning issues, both environmental and economic:

- Road construction will irreparably fragment wilderness, including habitat for the endangered swift fox. Noise pollution will increase from construction vehicles and the sounds of drilling, which may cause elk herds to migrate away from safer historic breeding grounds and despoil one of the regions last remnants of natural silence and solitude.
- Serious and alarming concerns are raised about water quality after the drilling and fracking begin. The five lakes within the parks are the biggest tourism draw in the region because of record trout catches. The report documents the deposition of mineral additives to near pristine water conditions and potential clarity issues resulting from runoff and groundwater changes.
- The oil and gas industry claim minimally invasive practices, but the environmental impact study outlines the need for at least 2,000 wells to deliver the stated oil production numbers.
- The impact study also highlights the increase of seismic activity in the region following the construction and implementation of the test

wells. As a result, new cracks have been found in the foundations of several historic Native American dwellings within the parks.

Problem

What is fracking? How is it different from other natural gas extraction methods? Why is there controversy surrounding fracking? Describe the concerns that some people have about fracking. What is meant by "road construction will irreparably fragment wilderness"? What is noise pollution? Can it be controlled? What is solitude? Why is it important? What is the Endangered Species Act? Would the protection of the endangered swift fox take precedence in this case? John Muir once said, "Nothing sacred is ever safe." In light of this situation, what do you think that statement means? What would you recommend as a course of action for the joint task force for the three parks? As mayor, Nick Flood is in direct authority over your position as director of the Durango Recreation Department. How can you effectively work with Mayor Flood? Do you believe there is a compromise in this situation? If you went directly to the residents of Durango with the results of the environmental impact study, what problems do you think you would encounter? What is, in your opinion, the correct decision for the City of Durango, the state of Colorado, and national interests? Direct conflict with the mayor could result in the termination of your job. Are environmental ideals worth the cost of your hard-earned career? If you side with the results of the environmental impact study, who are your allies and what resources can you use in this situation?

Suggested Key Words and Phrases for Internet Search

Bureau of Land Management

Public land management

Southern Nevada land management

Public land management strategy

Partnerships in land management

Federal land management

Case Study 23
Drinking, Drug Abuse, and Sexual Misconduct

Situation

In the past 5 years, it has been increasingly apparent to the community of Red River that it has a problem with its youth. Vandalism, drinking, and drug abuse have been on the rise. The police, park and school officials, and parents have viewed this problem with alarm. During the school year, youth have little free time. The board of education provides structured programs and, when necessary, counseling and guidance for its students. However, once summer comes, the community is faced with a different problem. The focal point of the youth changes from the school to the park.

During each summer, the citizens of Red River become concerned about youth congregating in the parks. The police department and the recreation and park department have been flooded with complaints ranging from drug trafficking to sexual misconduct. The recreation and park department feels that it can adequately plan recreation programs, but that it is not equipped to provide social services or police protection. Police department officials state that they do not have the funds to station a police officer at every park. Even if they could, this would not solve the problem, they assert.

During the winter, the Red River Youth Council worked on a plan that could solve the problem. After talking with many students at the schools, recreation and park officials, police officials, social workers, and homeowner groups, the council made a proposal to the mayor and council. The letter sent to them by the group follows:

Mr. James Farmer, Mayor
City Hall
Red River, CA 92501

Dear Mayor Farmer:

It has come to the attention of the Red River Youth Council that there was a difficult problem last summer in the parks. With the return of warm weather, the community is once again being faced with this problem. Rowdyism, drinking, vandalism, drug trafficking, and sexual misconduct are once again occurring in our parks.

This community has invested millions of dollars in its parks, yet many people feel that they can no longer use them because of the deplorable conduct of some young people. During the school year, a variety of counseling services are available to the youth of Red River, including police counselors in each of our high schools. When summer comes, these students are turned loose on the community with no provision for counseling or control. There seems to be an attitude that once school is out all youth problems simply disappear. In fact, the opposite seems to be true; with the warm weather comes a rash of vandalism, drinking, and drug offenses in our community.

We believe the city has an obligation to control and counsel these misguided youth, to enforce the law in the parks, and to make the parks safe for citizens who simply want to enjoy a wholesome recreation program without being intimidated. A youth council subcommittee was formed to look into this problem, and after meeting with police and park officials, the subcommittee submitted its report. After reviewing the report, the council voted unanimously to submit the following proposal to the mayor and council:

We propose that:

The City of Red River pay the amount of $50,000 to hire professional workers to counsel and control youth who frequent the major parks but have no interest in participating in recreational activities.

These workers be interviewed and selected by a subcommittee of the youth council. They can be trained by the heads of the police department's youth division and the recreation and park department's safety coordinator.

All major parks be patrolled 7 nights a week between 8:00 p.m. and 12:00 midnight for the 10 weeks of the summer. This would be a total of 14,000 working hours.

The program be administered and supervised by the park and recreation department's safety coordinator in cooperation with the Red River Police Department.

We would appreciate your early reply to this request.

Respectfully submitted,

George M. Bolt, Chair
Red River Youth Council

As director of recreation and parks for Red River, you have been asked by the mayor and council to prepare a recommendation for their review. You have also been requested to prepare a draft of a reply to the youth council chairperson.

Problem

Prepare a recommendation or reply for the mayor and council. Do you feel that the recreation and park department should be responsible for supervising this program? If the program is implemented, should the youth council interview and select the youth workers? What responsibility does the board of education have here? Should the city assume the full responsibility for this program? Does it seem reasonable that the main parks be "covered" from 8:00 p.m. to 12:00 midnight each night? How can you involve neighborhood groups in the solution to this problem? How would you involve staff, parents, and faculty at the school? What information is currently unavailable that would be helpful in solving this problem?

Suggested Key Words and Phrases for Internet Search

Community organization
Youth council
Police–Community relations
Outreach
Student counselors

School responsibilities
Human services – Human relations
Community involvement
Citizen associations

_____ **Case Study 24** _____
Separation of Church and Recreation

The relationship between government and religion has been debated since the founding of the United States. In 1791, the Bill of Rights was ratified by Congress and each state as an addition to the Constitution. The First Amendment was included by Congress to address the following issues: "Congress shall make no law respecting an establishment of religion, or prohibiting the free exercise thereof; or abridging the freedom of speech, or of the press; or the right of the people peaceably to assemble, and to petition the Government for a redress of grievances." More than 200 years later, the debate continues over this amendment and the separation of church and state. Over the years, lawsuits have been filed in regard to public prayers, creation versus evolution in public school textbooks, public religious music or displays, the pledge of allegiance, religious organizations' use of public facilities, and the public's use of religious facilities. Park and recreation agencies are no stranger to these controversies, including the community of Red Cedar City.

Red Cedar City, a sleepy suburb of a major metropolitan area, has been politically quiet for a numbers of years. Five years ago, the county's high profile newspaper listed Red Cedar City as the top place to live in the state because of its high quality schools, home values, and park system. Subsequently, the population of Red Cedar City has increased by leaps and bounds. The influx of new residents who have migrated from the metropolitan area has changed the political landscape, and a number of contentious debates have occurred. The following debates have specifically involved the Red Cedar City Park District.

Situation 1

Northway Park is Red Cedar City Park District's largest community park at 90 acres. One prominent feature of the park is a 1.5-mile multiuse path. The official ribbon cutting to open the park was on December 25, 1954. To celebrate the accomplishment, the park district accepted applications from community members to create their own decorative displays to coincide with a holiday light show. People came from all over the state to walk the multiuse path to see the light show and creative displays. The event was so popular that is has remained a fixture in Red Cedar City for the last 50 years and has been the highest attended event for the Red Cedar City Park District.

Recently, angry residents have been attending park district board meetings and taking to the local newspaper to complain about a number of religious-themed displays at the light show. Residents, clubs, and organizations are required to apply for a permit to create a display each December. Because the displays are on public property, opponents want the permits for religious displays to be disallowed because they feel their First Amendment rights are being violated.

Situation 2

Last year, two long-standing conservative commissioners for the Red Cedar City Park District Board of Directors lost elections to left-leaning candidates. The new board members were sworn in at the first board meeting in January 2013. The tradition of prior commissioners, staff, and attending residents was to stand and recite the pledge of allegiance at the end of each board meeting. At the close of this January meeting and subsequent meetings, the two new board members walked out during the pledge. When pressed about why they had left, the commissioners said they were taking a stand for First Amendment rights. The controversy grew when a local businesswoman pulled her support to the Red Cedar City Park Foundation over the issue. She had funded numerous program scholarships for underprivileged youth in Red Cedar City. This story soon made national news, and the Foundation for Separation of Church and State caught wind of the story. They offered to write a check to fund the scholarships.

Problem

Define *separation of church and state.* Does the First Amendment apply in these circumstances? Do residents, commissioners, and public employees have a constitutional right to put religious displays on public property or recite the pledge of allegiance at a public meeting? How should a park and recreation agency balance public needs for religious freedom and control and care over the public's resources?

Imagine you are the executive director for the Red Cedar City Park District. Do you feel it is inappropriate for your park district to allow religious displays at a public park? How would you engage constructive conversation between residents in favor of the religious displays and those against the displays? Would you remove religious displays from the holiday show? What alternative solutions are there in this situation? Would you remove the pledge of allegiance from the board meeting agenda?

There are other pressing needs in your park district, but the pledge of allegiance issue continues to grow and dominate board proceedings. What would you do to reestablish the focus of your meetings and the park district? How would you engage the commissioners who are offended by the pledge of allegiance? The local newspaper? The local businesswoman? The Foundation for Separation of Church and State? Would you accept its offer to fund the scholarships?

Suggested Key Words and Phrases for Internet Search

Lemon v. Kurtzman (1971)
The Lemon test for religious mottos
   and displays in public settings
First Amendment Center
Thomas Jefferson Wall of Separation

West Virginia State Board of
   Education v. Barnette (1943)
Bill of Rights
Pleasant Grove City, UT v. Summum
Lynch v. Donnelly (1984)
Van Orden v. Perry (2005)

_____ Case Study 25 _____
Use of Volunteers in Crisis

The history of volunteerism in America is rich and complex. Many historians believe that the earliest instances of volunteerism in America began when colonists had to form support systems to survey the many challenges that came with relocation, from forming the land to overcoming devastating illnesses. Togetherness was vital for survival. Lessons were not only learned but also remembered by future generations. Environmentalism also found its place during the 1930s when President Roosevelt raised awareness by helping the Conservation Corps plant approximately 3 million trees in a single decade. According to the Bureau of Labor Statistics (2016), 62.6 million Americans took time to volunteer one or more times between September 2014 and September 2015. That is 24.9% of all people in the United States, more women than men. The most popular age groups for volunteering are 35 to 44 and 45 to 54. The median number of hours volunteered was 52 per person, which is more than a week's worth of work.

Situation

Assume you are the director of parks and recreation in Falls, New York. Falls is a city of approximately 14,000 people. Many recreation programs are offered free of charge to citizens of Falls. The Falls Recreation Center offers public skating, hockey, and figure skating. At West Field, citizens can use a picnic pavilion, baseball stadium, and field house with locker rooms. At Christy Park, there are softball fields, basketball and tennis courts, playgrounds, and recreation trails. Sagamore Playground offers programs for younger children.

Programs are also available to senior citizens and people with disabilities. At present, Falls has an annual budget of $754,000 that is controlled by the city council. On Monday morning, you receive a phone call from Ed Stangle, mayor of Falls. He requests you meet with him at 2:00 p.m. at his office in city hall. Of course you accept his invitation. You are puzzled as to why he has called a meeting. Upon your arrival, Mayor Stangle starts his discussion by stating, "You're probably aware the city is going through some very serious financial problems, and action needs to be taken in all city departments. It will require all departments take a significant budget cut. I have discussed this action with all the council. I am now meeting with all department heads to discuss the effects of these cuts and how we can minimize the reduction of programs and how you will handle these cuts." He informs you the parks and recreation department will take a 26% cut of its budget and a reduction of four full-time staff positions. It will also have to begin to charge fees for some programs. He suggests that some of the slack may be helped by the use of volunteers. He informs you that Kingsburry and Hudson Falls support their recreation programs with volunteers for 20% of their budget. He asks, "Can we expand the volunteer program in Falls?" He requests you propose a long-range volunteer program for the parks and recreation department. The plan should include the following:

- Purpose of the volunteer program
- Methods of recruitment of volunteers
- Volunteer recognition and rewards
- Benefits for volunteers
- Background check of volunteers
- Job descriptions for volunteers
- Volunteer training
- Potential jobs in the department for volunteers
- Effects of fees and changes

All department heads are to submit their plans in 30 days. It is also suggested that citizens of Falls be urged to provide input.

Problem

What is the definition of volunteerism? What are the training skills necessary for volunteers? What policies need to be established for volunteers? What type of volunteer involvement is needed? Why do people volunteer? What issues exist with employing volunteers? What do volunteers want for their services? What are the characteristics of an effective volunteer staff? Should you ever pay volunteers? Should you purchase insurance to cover volunteers? What criteria should be used to measure the productivity of the volunteers? Should any recreation programs be eliminated? What criteria will you use in eliminating staff? Would private enterprises provide sponsorship for maintenance of facilities and some programs?

Suggested Key Words and Phrases for Internet Search

Effective use of volunteers
Volunteer management
Risk management – Volunteers

Volunteer training
Volunteer use policy
Volunteering in the public sector

References

Bureau of Labor Statistics. (2016, February). Volunteering in the United States, 2015. Retrieved from http://www.bls.gov/news.release/volun.nr0.htm

_____ Case Study 26 _____
Off-Road Vehicles: A Never Ending Debate

Situation

According to a study by the USDA Forest Service, there are 8 million registered all-terrain vehicles (ATV) and off-road motorbikes users in the United States. The snowmobile industry has determined there are currently almost 1.2 million registered snowmobile users (International Snowmobile Manufacturers Association [ISMA], n.d.). Each year, these numbers continue to grow. Off-road vehicle (ORV) industry advocacy groups also argue that ORV users account for billions of dollars in economic impact each year. Their findings support that properly regulated trails with enforcement patrols promote safe interactions between riders and the environment).

Opponents of ATVs argue that these machines and their drivers are dangerous and cause destructive and irreparable damage to public forests, open spaces, and beaches. ATVs have been found to do significant harm to vegetation, and the excessive noise may harass wildlife and visitors. Trail conditions and lax rule enforcement (excessive mud, fallen trees, etc.) may tempt riders to blaze new trails, causing erosion issues, fragmented wildlife habitat, and wilderness eyesores.

There is no better place to examine issues related to the ATV's winter counterpart, the snowmobile, than in Yellowstone National Park. Each winter, snow blankets Yellowstone National Park. The historic Grand Loop and connecting roadways turn into snowmobile trails. This opportunity brings visitors and tourist dollars to a region that would otherwise be closed for 6 months out of the year. But do the positives outweigh the negatives? Three studies by the National Park Service and Environmental Protection Agency have shown that Yellowstone's ecosystem would be "cleaner, quieter and healthier" without snowmobiles. Park rangers often wear gas masks at entrances while collecting park entrance fees because of the noxious fumes. Peace and solitude are often lost when packs of snowmobiles roar through the park like a swarm of angry bees. Snowmobiles by nature are not confined to roads, which present public safety hazards when they are used on frozen bodies of water. High-marking is also a risky game played by snowmobile riders during which each driver tries to create the high trail mark in fresh snow on steep mountainsides. High speeds and off-road capabilities also make it easy for a snowmobile to chase and harass wildlife (Yochim, 2013).

Powerful and politically active advocacy groups support and oppose ORV use on public lands. Change in political power often increases or curtails ORV access to these open spaces and forests. For a manager, it may be difficult to not take sides, especially when agency missions promote access and environmental protection. Limiting ORV access may mean a higher responsibility for your staff to enforce rules and regulations and a reduced slice of tourism dollars. Open access for ORVs may mean a poorer experience for other users and degradation of the resources you are employed to protect and preserve.

Problem

How do you balance mandates for a broad spectrum of access with your park's environmental values and mission? Would you ban or promote ORV use on public land? If you promote use, what rules and regulations would you use to govern ORV use? Would it be a fair and useful practice to develop "sacrifice" areas to try to divert ORV users from wild and scenic areas? How would you deal with proponent and opponent ORV stakeholders? If you support lowering or eliminating ORV use in your park, how will you combat pressure from opposing politicians and advocacy groups? What resources would you seek to make ORV use decisions? Is the private sector responsible for providing lands for this type of recreation?

Suggested Key Words and Phrases for Internet Search

All-terrain vehicles (ATV)
Snowmobile
Snow coach
National parks
Bureau of Land Management
Off-road vehicles (ORV)
Dirt bike

Snow machine
National forest
Off-highway vehicle (OHV)
Pollution – Noise
Four-wheeler
Wilderness

References

International Snowmobile Manufacturers Association. (n.d.). Snowmobiling statistics and facts. Retrieved October 12, 2016, from http://www.snowmobile.org/snowmobiling-statistics-and-facts.html

_____ **Case Study 27** _____
A Park Site Where History Changed Forever

Situation

Your current position is the southwest regional director for the National Park Service. The jurisdiction you oversee includes Western Texas, New Mexico, Arizona, and Southern California. Recently, a bill has been presented to the House and the Senate called the National Defense Authorization Act, which includes an amendment that authorizes the establishment of three national historic sites in Tennessee, Washington, and New Mexico. The parks will highlight the top secret development and manufacturing of the atomic bomb during World War II, better known as The Manhattan Project. You have been asked by National Park Service Director Jonathan Jarvis to chair a task force that will present a report on the viability of these historic sites of cultural significance. In the past, the House of Representatives has voted in favor of establishing these parks and the Senate has voted against their creation.

For most of your career, you have worked for the National Park Service in the southwestern United States. You have watched politicians and private organizations identify and lobby for _park_ status for many natural and cultural sites. The protection and preservation of natural and historical lands and buildings have remained important to many citizens (and the National Park Service), and the addition of _National Park_ status to any location is sure to draw development and tourism dollars. For decades, one of these identified locations of historical significance in the southwestern United States has remained in obscurity because of controversy. Several buildings on or near the Los Alamos National Laboratory played an instrumental role in the development of the atomic bomb. Supporters of the commemoration of this historical park have felt that these buildings represent an important part of the nation's history. They argue that the National Park Service is in a position to present the facts about the United States' foray into nuclear weapons objectively. Proponents argue that visits to historic sites often inspire children to become interested in history, engineering, and science. Opponents argue that the dedication of these sites as historical national parks will glorify nuclear technology and demean the National Park vision. Anti-nuclear groups feel that nuclear bombs have pushed the boundaries of science and ethics and that any recognition will put the wrong values on a pedestal. To add to the complexity, a few of the sites remain contaminated or are located at national research laboratories. Each location also has museums and interpretive centers run by private organizations. Fiscally conservative groups and politicians also argue that the current National Park System is underfunded and question from where the funds will come to support new park sites.

Problem

Would you support or oppose a historical park commemorating the role of the atomic bomb in U.S. history? How would that affect your capability to lead the task force? How will you obtain unbiased information to present in your report? How will you prepare to answer the questions or concerns of the proponents or opponents of establishing these parks? What other parks or sites commemorate other controversial historic events or locations? Can they be used to support or oppose the new historic site? How has the National Park Service dealt with controversy between stakeholders in the past? What consideration should be given to the private organizations and museums at these sites? Would the National Park Service do a better job of promoting and protecting national history? How would you deal with contamination and security issues at a national laboratory?

Suggested Key Words and Phrases for Internet Search

The Manhattan Project
Atomic bomb
Oak Ridge, Tennessee
Nuclear technology
Los Alamos National Laboratory

World War II
Hanford, Washington
National historical parks
Hiroshima
Dark tourism

Case Study 28

The Recreation and Park Commission Debate: The Value of Youth Football

Participation in youth football dropped 9.5% from 2010 to 2012 (Fainaru & Fainaru-Wada, 2013). Injuries and head concussions may bring fewer youth to programs in recreation leagues and Pop Warner football. In a recent briefing, President Obama stated, "If I had a son I'd have to think long and hard before I would let him play football." According to the data provided to "Outside the Lines," the Pop Warner program lost 23,612 players throughout the 2-year decline since the organization began keeping statistics a decade ago. In the coming months, the Pop Warner Medical Advisory Committee is expected to take up more rule changes that will eliminate some of the dangers, as parents and players continue to raise the concern and risk of youth football programs.

The following is an article by Andy Thompson at ARC Local News, who describes an actual case of concussion of youth in sport activities. Reaction to the article has been mixed:

Deb Henschel knew something was wrong with her 8-year-old son, but she was bewildered by his symptoms. In addition to feeling out or sorts, the boy was constantly tired. He was sensitive to light and had problems thinking and speaking clearly. The symptoms arose in the fall of 2011 after the boy played in a Fox Valley Pop Warner Football game.

Henschel contacted a medical helpline and was stunned to learn that her son had the classic signs of a concussion. He was taken to the doctor, who confirmed her suspicions. The doctor also noted that the boy had a previous concussion, apparently from a blow he sustained in an earlier game that season. "It was very scary," recalled Henschel of Appleton. "When we realized that we missed a concussion, it definitely scared us. It was affecting his speech and thought processes."

Henschel's recollections of her son's concussions were stirred last week with the airing on PBS of *League of Denial*, a Frontline documentary that took a crucial look at the NFL's handling and response to concussions over the years. The documentary included a feature on youth football leagues and the potentially disastrous risks to children who play the sport. "It is something that's happening, and we're starting to realize the long-term effects it can have," Henschel said.

She stressed that she doesn't blame the Pop Warner league — which has strict policies to deal swiftly with suspected or confirmed concussions — for what happened to her son. The concussions ended his season that fall, and he returned to normal in about a month after the symptoms lifted.

But the experience had a lasting impact. While her son, now 10, still enjoys playing football with his friends on the playground, he hasn't returned to organized tackle football competition. "He didn't ask if he could play again," Henschel said last week. "As an overprotective mom, had he asked to play again, I would have had to think about it." Henschel said it is up to parents to assess the level of risk associated with youth football leagues.

Situation

Assume that you are the director of parks and recreation in a small community in the Midwest. At a meeting of the parks and recreation commission, a group of parents suggests the commission sponsor a Pop Warner youth football program beginning next season. Mary Conlin, a nurse at the local hospital, reminds the people in attendance of the dangers and risks to participants in youth football. A number of parents indicate much is being done to make youth football programs safer and less risky. George Lemry stated, "What are we trying to do, eliminate high school and college football programs just because a few players get hurt?" Jack Dovee, a parent, stated, "I played high school football and it taught me a lot of important skills that helped me in later life. I want my son to play on a team so he can see the values of sportsmanship, team play, fitness, and personal discipline." Jacqueline Hamlin, an elementary school teacher, refers to the research of Dr. Robert Canta, a sport concussion expert and a professor in the Department of Neuro Surgery at Boston University. He believes that children under the age of 14 should not play tackle football because their brains and their bodies are still developing and therefore more vulnerable to serious injury. It was obvious there were strong feelings. (Both a pro and a con was that the commission should sponsor youth football.) Patric Havens, chair of the commission, will consider the comments before any decision is made and agreed more community input needs to be sought. Following the meeting, the commission asks the you to develop a report and a recommendation on youth football sponsored by the commission, to be presented at the May meeting.

Problem

What would you recommend to the commission? Would you involve the community in the process? What are major disadvantages of sponsoring youth football? What are major advantages of sponsoring youth football? What are the long-lasting effects of concussions? What risks do youth football players face? How would the decision affect other youth contact sports, such as soccer, hockey, and rugby? If you recommend the commission sponsor the program, what conditions would you suggest? What reasons would you give the commission to support your decision?

Suggested Key Words and Phrases for Internet Search

Concussions in youth sports

Concussions – Training

Concussion – Brain injury

Sports-related injury

Concussion – Causes – Symptoms

References

Fainaru, S., & Fainaru-Wada, M. (2013, November 14). Youth football participation drops. Retrieved from http://www.espn.com/espn/otl/story/_/page/popwarner/pop-warner-youth-football-participation-drops-nfl-concussion-crisis-seen-causal-factor

Case Study 29
No Tax Dollars for the Parks and Recreation Department

Situation

Three adjacent communities have recently amalgamated into one larger entity. The new city was created to reduce administrative costs and to avoid redundancy in local government. The new parks and recreation director is faced with a dilemma. She has to combine three pricing schemes into one coherent pricing strategy. The largest of the three communities offered virtually all programs free of charge, another heavily subsidized its programs, and the third offered programs at a variety of price levels.

The director has been told that she cannot offer all programs free of charge, nor is heavy subsidization an option in all cases. She must generate fees to support her programming. She is afraid that whatever option she chooses will alienate members of the community. Those who traditionally received programs free of charge will be outraged by any new fees, whereas those who are accustomed to paying higher fees may become suspicious of program quality if fee levels drop.

The director knows that this will be a public process. The new city council has given her specific instructions to establish fees that are fair and appropriate. She is not certain what this means, except that the council may blame her if complaints are made. The mayor, in particular, has made it clear that the new prices had better be well conceived. He has stated publicly that no one will be refused leisure opportunities because of the new fees and has told her privately that he will be "unhappy" if public outcry results from the new fees.

Problem

What criteria should be established for adopting a pricing policy? How can the director convince those who have never paid to begin paying for recreation programs? How can fees be charged without displacing low income members of the community? Is citizen input essential in decision making? What community groups could provide suggestions? There will likely be opposition to all suggestions. How should the director respond? What support can the mayor and council provide the parks and recreation staff? How can the department use volunteers to pick up the loss of funds? What state or federal grants are available to support the parks and recreation programs? Is it time for the department to establish a foundation? Should the business community be approached for sponsorship of selected recreation programs? Is the long-range plan in need of updating? What additional information is needed to solve this problem? Is it possible to operate the parks and recreation department without support of tax dollars? How do you think the general public will respond to the demands by the mayor? Should a consultant be employed to assist in developing the pricing plan? What community group would you invite to provide input?

Suggested Key Words and Phrases for Internet Search

Grants for recreation facilities

Funding sources – Parks and recreation

Funding options – Parks and recreation

Outdoor recreation grants

Parks and recreation – Budget cuts

Information for this case study was taken from Improving Leisure Services Through Marketing in Action *by Ron McCarville. Used with permission, Sagamore Publishing, 2002.*

Case Study 30
New Law Allows Guns in Our National Parks

Situation

Loaded guns will be allowed in Yellowstone, the Grand Canyon, and other national parks under a new law. The law lets licensed gun owners bring firearms into national parks and wildlife refuges as long as they are allowed by state law. It comes over the objections of gun control advocates who fear it will lead to increased violence in national parks. The National Rifle Association has lobbied hard to allow guns in parks and has spent millions to challenge its opponents. Guns will be allowed in all except 20 of the park services 392 locations, including some of the most iconic parks: Grand Canyon, Great Smoky Mountains, Yosemite, and Rocky Mountain National Park. Guns will not be allowed in the visitor centers or ranger offices.

Paul Helmke said, "National parks are now among the safest places in America, but that could change under the new law. Current rules severely restrict guns in national parks, generally requiring them to be locked or stored. It's sad that we've become such a paranoid society that people want to take guns pretty much everywhere. When you are at a campfire and people are getting noisy and loud, next to you, you used to have to worry about them quieting down. Now you have to worry about when they will start shooting."

Bill Wade, president of the Coalition of National Park Service Retirees, called the new law a "sad chapter in the history of park service." Wade also commented, "People go to national parks to get away from things that they face in their everyday life where the work and live. Now I think that social dynamics is really going to change." Bryan Fachner, associate director of the National Parks Conservation Association, said, "The new law will place an unfair burden on park service employees who will have to wade through a variety of state and local laws to determine if visitors are breaking this law."

A spokesperson for the National Rifle Association scoffed at the idea that parks would become more dangerous: "People have been assaulted and even murdered in our national parks." Chris Cox stated, "The common sense law will enhance the self-defense rights of law abiding Americans and also ensure uniformity of firearms laws within a state." Senator Tom Coburn (R-OKLA), who led congressional efforts to change the law, said, "Concerns about increased violence were overblown." Coburn said, "I don't expect anything major from the new law other than to restore the Second Amendment rights taken away by bureaucrats."

However, proponents of the law pointed out that in 2008 there were 3,760 major crimes, including five homicides and 37 rapes.

Problem

Should efforts be made to repeal this law? If yes, how would you convince the National Rifle Association? To what extent does the law conflict with the Second Amendment? What position has the National Recreation and Park Association taken toward the law? Are there any conditions in which guns can be allowed in national parks? What do you tell visitors who feel threatened when they go to the national parks? If guns are allowed, what rules and regulations should be established? At present, what types of guns are allowed in national parks? In what instances can an individual carry a concealed and loaded firearm along trails at Yellowstone and at the Grand Canyon?

Suggested Key Words and Phrases for Internet Search

Firearms – National parks
Guns allowed in parks
Parks – Gun regulations

National parks gun law
Pros and cons gun laws

Case Study 31
Take Every Step to Save Lake George

Situation

You take steps to protect what's most important to you. And when it comes to this region's economy, you do everything you can to protect Lake George

Earlier this month, as much as 10,000 gallons of raw sewage leaked directly into the lake from a broken pipe in a pumping station for the village's sewer treatment plant. The spill prompted officials to close three beaches in the popular Southern Basin, including Shepard Park Beach in the center of the village and the state-owned Million Dollar Beach to the east.

Had the weather not been so miserable, this spill could have a devastating economic effect. Who wants to go to a tourist area with polluted beaches? As it was, businesses lost thousands of dollars at the time of the initial spill because people simply didn't want to sit next to a beach with sewage in it. Who knows how many people avoided the lake because of the news.

Lake George is our economy. Without Lake George, we're little more than a bunch of trees and some hills that you can get at any Podunk town off any interstate in the Northeast.

Lake George is why Great Escape and the other amusement parks are here. It's why there are dozens of hotels, motels, restaurants, and businesses everywhere. It's why Americade and the other festivals come here. It's what draws boaters and fishermen and nature lovers and history buffs and kids and families to the area. It's what sustains hundreds of local businesses, pumping millions of dollars into the local economy and providing the region north of Saratoga with a reliable tourist trade generation after generation.

According to a report, *The Economic Impact of Tourism in New York State*, Warren County generated $250 million in direct and indirect labor-related income from tourism, and visitors spent more than $503 million. That's in one year. Take the lake away, and we might as well be in Franklin County.

So we applaud the efforts of the Lake George Waterkeeper, a lake protection program sponsored by the Fund for Lake George, to call for an independent review of the sewage spill. This wasn't some innocuous accident. Officials were aware of the condition of the piping, but hadn't yet addressed it. There was enough pollution from this relatively "minor" spill to close the most affected beach for three entire weeks in the heart of summer. That's even after backloaders removed the contaminated beach sand and after the lake's normal currents had three weeks to dilute the pollution.

Village officials have pledged to install an alarm in the pump house to alert officials of another leak. But why wasn't that in place already? And what good is an alarm going to do after the fact if the sewage is allowed to leak out anyway?

Not only should the state investigate the spill and recommend mitigation measures, it should also consider testing the water regularly in that area to make sure other less-obvious leaks aren't going undetected.

The state Department of Environmental Conservation, which monitors Million Dollar Beach, tests the water there for signs of pollution every week during the summer.

Rather than fine the village for the leak, as the DEC is apparently considering doing, the state should let the village keep the money and make the necessary improvements. A punitive fine in this case might be warranted to send a message to village officials. But that money would be put to better use actually addressing the problems and perhaps paying for that additional summertime testing. Remember, half of all the sales tax revenue generated by Lake George so far. But as we've seen with this spill, even a brief lapse in vigilance can lead to potentially catastrophic results.

Lake George is one resource we can't afford to turn our backs on, not even for a second.

Problem

At the present time, what is being done to eliminate the Lake George sewage problem? Is the manager of the sewer treatment plant fully informing officials of the seriousness of the social and economic impact? To what extent does closing the beaches affect the tourism industry in Warren County? Has the health department become involved in the sewage issue? To what extent has the general public been made aware of the problem? Has the chamber of commerce showed any concern about the problem? Are there any comparable situations to the Lake George issue? Is politics playing any role in not solving the problem? What specifically needs to be done to correct the situation and how much will it cost? If the situation is not corrected, what is the future of Lake George? Does a water management plan exist for Lake George?

Suggested Key Words and Phrases for Internet Search

Sewage disposal system
Lake George Health District
Lake George tourist

Lake George – Planning for future
Lake George sewage spill
Lake George sewage problems

Editorial appeared in Glen Falls Post Star *by Ken Tingley on July 24, 2009. Permission granted on April 21, 2014.*

-------- **Case Study 32** --------
Aligning Therapeutic Recreation With Culture Change Values

Situation

You have just graduated with a degree in therapeutic recreation (TR) and are excited to start your work as a therapeutic recreationist in your new job at Garden Meadows long-term care home. Garden Meadows is home to 112 older adults, the majority being 85 years of age or older. Most of the residents who live at Garden Meadows have complex, chronic health conditions, such as a musculoskeletal disorder or stroke, Alzheimer's disease or another related dementia, mental health issues, or a combination of health issues that cause significant functional challenges in being able to perform activities of daily living, such as toileting, bathing, and eating.

In the last year of your TR education, you learned about the culture change movement happening in long-term care homes in the United States, Canada, and other countries. Culture change is an ongoing, evolving process focused on moving away from the current top-down, provider-driven approaches embedded within medical and institutional models of care to approaches that are more humane, collaborative, and life-affirming guided by the following culture change values:

- Choice and self-determination
- Dignity and respect
- Nurturing body, mind, and spirit
- Knowing and focusing on the person
- Living life
- Enabling, normalizing environments
- Close interdependent relationships
- Collaborative decision making
- Flexibility

Within a medical, institutional approach, staff prescribe and provide traditional care and "treatments" to patients. There is a separation of body and mind with the primary focus on physical care and functioning and on behavior management. Patients follow facility and staff routines. Staff are viewed as the experts, have authority, and make decisions for patients. Staff provide structured activities according to a set program. Staff know patients by their diagnoses (e.g., bipolar, dementia) and are encouraged to be emotionally neutral. There is a focus on measurable outcomes.

In contrast, a person-centered or relational approach is characterized by individualized care and support that respect the unique needs and wishes of each individual. The focus is on holistic wellness in which living life to the fullest is supported and the human spirit is nurtured. Staff provide flexible care, following the individual's routine and life rhythms. Individuals have meaningful choices and make their own decisions. There is a range of planned, flexible, and spontaneous opportunities available around the clock for all. Staff know the person and his or her unique story, and rather than working for these people and their families, staff work collaboratively with them. A strong, interdisciplinary team approach is taken. Staff have close relationships with the individual and his or her family and support the individual in maintaining current relationships and in developing new relationships. Outcomes are determined by what is most meaningful to the individual and his or her present and future aspirations.

Culture change involves doing the courageous work of critically examining the language, values, assumptions, attitudes, practices, approaches, and policies embedded within an organization and working to realign these so they support a relational approach to *living* and truly reflect the culture change values.

Your supervisor was excited to hear about your understanding of culture change at your interview for the job and has asked you to help facilitate a culture change process, to ensure that the therapeutic recreation practice at Garden Meadows is more aligned with the culture change values. You pull together a culture change coalition made up of residents, family members, and other members of the recreation team, and together you decide to examine your current assessment process critically. To begin, your team members agree that it would be useful to sit in on each other's assessments and share with each other what you learned. Together you develop guiding principles so everyone feels safe during this process and so it is clear that the exercise is not about judging individuals, but about learning about your current process and imagining new ways of practicing and relating.

You begin by observing Mary who has been tasked with doing a leisure assessment on Mrs. Sally Fischer, who moved into the home recently. This is what you observe:

Therapist: Good morning, Sally. I am a recreation therapist here and would like to get some information from you. How long have you been here?

Sally: Oh, about three or four weeks, I think.

Therapist: About two, I think.

Sally (sees a person nearby painting and points at the person): My husband also did painting. We had all kinds of paintings around the house. I don't know what happened to the paintings. He died before he should have really. He had cancer. But he was really looking forward to painting before he retired. He died when he was 62. It is too bad because he waited a long time to retire. I miss him.

Therapist: While you're here, while you're living with us, we actually have bowling, we have bowling next Monday. I'll come by to get you for that. Okay, let's continue. Do you see any barriers to your leisure involvement?

Sally: Do I see any what, dear?

Therapist: Barriers to your leisure involvement.

Sally: No, just that I haven't been involved.

Therapist: In terms of social interaction, how does that make you feel, interacting with someone?

Sally: What do you mean?

Therapist: Umm, do you feel comfortable talking and initiating conversation?

Sally: Oh – (looking confused). I would talk to anybody, I do a lot of talking. That is why I miss my phone.

Therapist: I am now going to name a number of different activities and interests. When you answer, try to use this scale here. It is 1 to 5; 1 is never true, 2 is almost never true, 3 is somewhat true and 4 is often true, and 5 is always true. So what we are going to do is put one of these numbers beside each statement here. Okay, let's get started: I like to read in my free time, is that never true or always true?

Sally: No, I like to read a lot.

Therapist: So is that always true or often true?

Sally: Pardon me?

Therapist: Would you say that is always true or often true for you?

Sally: (looking confused and getting angry) I just like to read a lot.

Therapist: Ok, how about this one: I like to work with mechanical devices.

Sally: What do you mean? I can use a can opener.

Therapist: What about more leisure-based activities?

Sally: Like the lawn mower?

Therapist: Ummmmm, let's move on. I use my leisure to develop close relationships with others.

Sally: Well, I am not quite sure about that question.

Therapist: Okay, that's good. Next question: Do you regularly contribute to other organizations or activities.

Sally: Well, I never was involved, but anyone that I knew, if they needed anything, I would definitely do it for them—my husband was the same—if anyone needed help. . .

Therapist: How about, I prefer leisure activities that require social interaction. During my leisure I enjoy working with my hands in gardening, woodworking, or ceramics. Is that never true or always true?

Sally: I like woodworking, but I can't anymore because I have a bad arm here.

Therapist: You know, there is a creative arts department here; they have different shops. I should take you down there one day—just beautiful. They even have devices that have a piece of wood that is secured and you don't have to use both your hands. They make lots of things down there, and you can even sell it in the shop and make money.

Sally: That is in the past. I have no interest in that now.

Therapist: I will take you down there next week. I think you will like it.

This assessment interaction has been adapted from "Patient Focused Care: Theory and Practice," by A. Pedlar, T. Hornibrook, and B. Haasen, 2001, Therapeutic Recreation Journal, pp. 20–22.

Problem

How would you describe this assessment experience for Sally? How would you describe this assessment experience for the therapeutic recreationist conducting the assessment? What aspects of this assessment process are more aligned with the institutional, medical model of care? What other examples do you know of that reflect how typical leisure practices, policies, and procedures may be misaligned with the culture change values? What changes would you and your team make to the assessment process to align it more with the culture change values. How can you better capture Sally's story and what is most meaningful to her? With the culture change values in mind, rewrite the interaction between Sally and the therapeutic recreationist. What would you and your team do next in your culture change journey?

Suggested Key Words and Phrases for Internet Search

Culture change in workplace

Steps to culture change

Create culture change

Leisure practices with culture change

Therapeutic recreation - modalities and facilitation

Culture change - Long-term care

Case Study 33
This Land Is My Land

Situation

For the past 10 years, you have been leading the Beatty Lake Watershed Management program for the Wisconsin Department of Natural Resources. Beatty Lake is the largest lake in Wisconsin, with over 100 miles of shoreline. It is also the only freshwater resource for over 200,000 people. Several large communities hug the southern and western shores of Beatty Lake. Scott County encompasses a majority of Beatty Lake's eastern watershed, and this county has remained largely rural. Agriculture and forestry are the two main industries of the region. Large sections of the eastern shore of Beatty Lake are dotted with mansions. Most of these homes are owned by people from out of state.

Last month, the Wisconsin Department of Natural Resources imposed new sweeping regulations based on recommendations from your watershed management program. These regulations stop any new development and halt agricultural or industrial use on land within 1,000 feet of streams or rivers that feed into Beatty Lake. The ultimate goal of the watershed management program is to create a vegetative buffer that will reduce erosion and nitrogen loads, reduce sewage contamination, increase water quality, and improve the wildlife habitat of Beatty Lake.

As the director of the Beatty Lake Watershed Management program, you are required to attend county board meetings for the counties that surround Beatty Lake. The Scott County Board meeting is the first meeting you are required to attend after the regulations have been imposed.

When you arrive at the meeting, it is apparent you are walking into a hostile environment. The meeting begins with strong criticism directed at you from the supervisors of towns along Beatty Lake. Their chief complaint is that the new regulations will hurt taxpayers in the communities around Beatty Lake because the regulations will remove buildable land from their tax rolls. "Undeveloped lands around our rivers, streams, and lake are the most valuable and desired properties in our county. This regulation makes me wonder if our counties should petition to have the watershed management program disbanded since you are not serving our best interests," said Tophamville supervisor Darren Schulist. "You have never asked for input from our towns," Schulist continued. "For the past 10 years you have made rules without concern for communities in Scott County. Your rules only serve the residents on the west side of Beatty Lake." Hunter resident Randy Kessler mentioned that the watershed management program is "retroactively attempting to reverse all zoning decisions at the local level." A summer resident of Hunter who teaches at the University of Chicago was the lone supporter. "Research has shown that Beatty Lake water quality continues to decrease. This lake is the water supply for many people. Nitrogen blooms are causing declines in fish populations. The wealthy are snapping up the land along the waterways to have access to the lake. Public access is more limited now than ever before. Water contamination from neighborhood sewers will only increase with new development," stated Dr. Josh Repovsch.

The Scott County Board closed the meeting by passing a resolution requiring a representative from the Beatty Lake Watershed Management program to organize and attend public hearings in each community in Scott County over the next month.

Problem

As director for the Beatty Lake Watershed Management program, how would you work to diffuse this hostile situation? After speaking with the county board, would you still oppose any development? How would you prepare for the public hearings? Your program is coming under fire for making decisions that are not in the best interests of Scott County. What would you do to disprove these opinions? Write a position statement that describes your position regarding the relationship between environmental and development stakeholders.

Suggested Key Words and Phrases for Internet Search

http://water.epa.gov/
Eutrophication
Oxygen depletion
Algae blooms

Erosion
Sedimentation vegetative buffer
Nonpoint source pollution
Siltation

_____ **Case Study 34** _____
The Competitive Swim Team Is Too Competitive

Situation

During the past 10 years, the Kanton City Recreation Commission has been sponsoring a competitive swim team that participates in the Eastern Regional Valley Conference. Membership on this team is made up of 65 youth aged 8 to 18 years, who have the ability to excel in the various swim classifications. An active swim-team parents' organization assists the recreation commission in operating this program. Because you have recently assumed the position of superintendent of recreation in Kanton, you have only recently discovered that the parents in the organization have caused disruption in the program. On a number of occasions, they have attempted to influence the coach of the team in training methods. Some parents have frequently put a great deal of pressure on the youth to win. It has also been revealed that a large number of youth are not allowed to participate because "they are just not good enough to make the team." You have also noted that this program is costly and far exceeds the proportionate cost of other programs operated by the recreation commission. It is your opinion that the recreation commission should not sponsor highly competitive teams that serve only a few. The public recreation program should give all youth an opportunity to participate in its program, and no youth should be turned away. The sponsoring of "varsity teams" should be left to special-interest groups. You express your views to the recreation commission, and they concur with your feelings. However, they request that before any action is taken a meeting be called of parents interested in the competitive swim program so their views may be heard. Following this meeting, the recreation commission requests that you prepare a letter explaining the position of the commission that could be sent to parents of youth on the swim team. The letter follows:

Dear Parents:

At a recent meeting of the Kanton City Recreation Commission, the members reviewed its sponsorship of the competitive swim program. To arrive at a decision that would be in the best interest of all participants, the commission requested the members of the Parents' Swim Organization to attend a meeting to discuss all aspects of the program. The meeting was held on September 9 at the recreation center. Approximately 75 people were present at this meeting.

After careful thought and much consideration, the recreation commission decided the following:

1. An intramural-type competitive swim team program will be offered at all the municipal pools in the city. Every effort will be made to encourage the greatest number of youth to participate in this program. The purpose of the program will be to develop skills in the various strokes and to give each youth an opportunity to compete with people with similar skills in his or her own group.

2. The recreation commission will not sponsor a "varsity" team that will travel throughout the valley for competitive swim meets. The existing program is highly competitive; therefore, it is questionable whether or not it is desirable for the age group that it is serving. Since the program serves relatively few and requires a great deal of time, money, and effort on the part of the office staff, leadership staff, and maintenance staff, it should not be a function of the recreation commission.

3. The recreation commission will assist in the promotion of an organization that will sponsor competitive swim activities for the highly skilled individuals. The recreation commission can do this by providing facilities at a reasonable cost to the organization. It is emphasized that this organization should not in any way be officially connected with the recreation commission.

This decision was communicated to the members of the board of directors of the Parents' Swim Organization on September 21. Present at this meeting were members of the recreation commission and members of the board of directors of the Parents' Swim Organization.

At this meeting it was emphasized that the recreation commission will do all it can to assist in the formation of a strong, well-organized association to carry out the sponsorship of the varsity-team swim activities.

Sincerely,
Mike Connors, Chair
Kanton Recreation Commission

Problem

Should the recreation commission continue sponsorship of the competitive swim program? Why? Should the recreation commission sponsor highly competitive teams? What responsibility does the recreation commission have in providing for "excellence" in its program? Do you agree with the letter that is to be sent to the Parents' Swim Organization? With what points in the letter do you disagree? Is the fact that this program requires a great deal of time and effort of the staff sufficient reason to discontinue the program? What should the relationship be between the recreation commission and the Parents' Swim Organization? Offer an alternative solution.

Suggested Key Words and Phrases for Internet Search

Competitive swimming readiness
Ready for competitiveness
Parents' guide – Competitive
    swimming

Ideal swimming parent
Advice for swim parents
Association for competitive swim
    parents

_____ **Case Study 35** _____
The Public Wants Safe Parks

Situation

We are all welcoming daylight saving time and the warming weather. We have already seen park users in our communities throughout the country barbecuing, playing volleyball, playing Little League, playing tennis, and enjoying the sun and the great outdoors. The primary responsibility of park and recreation personnel is to see that parks are safe and protected from vandals. In many towns and cities, parks are the "Gem of the Community." To keep gangs and vandals from using parks as a gathering place is a priority as is making sure rules are obeyed. Should the city have a goal to ensure that the parks are safe and clean and friendly for people and visitors in the community?

Assume you are the general manager of recreation and parks in one of the nation's largest cities, and you are seriously concerned with the problem of maintaining safe parks. Police have been reporting narcotic traffic and a large number of rapes, thefts, gang fights, and other crimes. Citizens are expressing their concern; many have stated that the city parks are not safe and that they do not intend to use them. The city's largest newspaper recently surveyed readers, asking, "Do you feel safe in the city's parks?" The following is a sample of responses:

- Mary Wentworth, 17 Sagamore Street: "Not really and mainly because of inadequate lighting after dark. I always make it a policy, even during the day, to go to the park with someone. I think it would be a help to have more policemen patrolling, but I also feel that a greater asset would be more community participation in park security. After all, the parks are for the community."

- Mary Ellen McGuire, 63 Cherry Street: "Not without my dog! There should be more policemen around. To make up for this lack, I bought an Alaskan malamute. We don't have any parks where I live, so we use Lincoln Park quite a bit. And I only go there accompanied by my dog."

- George Greenvook, 19 Sands Boulevard: "I feel safe during the day, but I do a lot of jogging at night when I come home from work—and I certainly have apprehensions about doing this. You really never know what is around the corner or what dog is going to decide to run along with you. If I were a female, I wouldn't go near the parks after sundown. The parks need better lighting and more police patrols."

- Pamela Sims, 29 Fourth Street: "Considering what I read in the papers, I'd be terrified to go in the parks. Of course, during the day it doesn't frighten me so much. I guess the parks are all right."

- Allen Cutley, 78 Maple Street: "No, not really—because of what's happening everywhere these days. There should be more protection for people in the parks—policewise, but more importantly, there should be more community participation in solving this problem."

- John Stenken, 151 High Street: "I don't go near them. The kind of people that have taken them over are causing this. The parks don't have much attraction for the older person these days."

Many civic, church, and service organizations have demanded that the city and recreation and parks board take immediate action to ensure that the parks are safe. The mayor has requested that you attend a meeting and discuss what could be done.

Problem

What plan would you suggest? Should the recreation and parks department employ its own police force? Why? What relationship should exist between the recreation and parks department and the police department to bring safety to the parks? What program would begin to improve the image people have about the parks? How would you involve neighborhood groups? Would it be wise to form neighborhood "vigilante groups"? If no, why? If yes, in which ways would you support them? Who has the greatest responsibility to ensure that the parks are safe: the recreation and parks department, the police department, or the citizens in the neighborhood? Explain your answer.

Suggested Key Words and Phrases for Internet Search

Park police

Public park safety

Crime in public parks

Playground safety

Rules – Safety – Parks

Park visitor safety

_____ **Case Study 36** _____
Vandalism: A Critical Problem

Situation

Why is it important to prevent vandalism in parks? Vandalism destroys what the tax dollars have created, and it takes away from recreation programs and facilities. In some cases, it closes parks. Millions of dollars of public and private funds are wasted each year trying to cope with this unpleasant and growing problem. In the city of Baltimore, it cost the city over $251,000 in 2013. During the early morning hours in April 2010, vandals set fire to the Orems Elementary School recreation center playground at a cost of $21,000. From 2007 to 2011, the San Francisco Recreation Department spent $1.8 million repairing and replacing equipment, buildings, trees, lawns, and flowers damaged or destroyed by vandals (Gordon, 2012). Joe Padilla of the San Francisco Recreation and Park Department said, "I've seen it all. Sabotage and defacement, restrooms set fire, tennis nets cut, urinals and sinks bashed with baseball bats, toilets and water fountains intentionally clogged with sand and rubbish, roofs torn apart and their shingles tossed as frisbees, park benches yanked from their anchors, lights smashed, and graffiti throughout the park stystem."

One of the major problems in the Stitesville Park System during the last 90 days has been vandalism. This was revealed Wednesday by Frederick Hogan, president of the Stitesville Recreation and Park District, in an address to the Stitesville Exchange Club.

Hogan told club members that 25 rose bushes had been destroyed, three concrete tables had been broken ("You would have to use a sledgehammer to break them up"), and five "Keep Off the Grass" signs had been stolen from city parks.

Including these items, numerous streetlight globes have been broken by BB gunshots, lights have been damaged at the municipal pools, drinking fountains have been stolen from Sylvan Park, and doors on the shelter houses have been broken and stolen. Hogan indicated that park officials have found it almost impossible to cope with the problem.

Second in importance to the problem of vandalism is the problem of litter. "I don't know," Hogan quipped. "Maybe litter will overcome us one of these days." He noted that numerous calls from the public have been made to the park office, with callers describing incidents of picnickers throwing paper napkins on the ground rather than in the trash containers.

"Many of our recreation and park board meetings are spent trying to determine why people do these things." However, regardless of the cause, Hogan stated that such vandalism can be combated through proper design of facilities or simply by using "unbreakable" equipment. He also emphasized the need for extensive lighting of the parks and for more police patrols. He said, "Certainly the money the we are now spending on vandalism and litter could be put to better use in the park system."

Problem

Why do people vandalize parks? Why do they show little concern for litter in the parks? Is this a national problem? Do you think that by just increasing the lighting in parks and by adding police patrols vandalism and litter will be reduced? Is there such a thing as "vandalproof equipment"? What program would you suggest to reduce the vandalism and litter problem in Stitesville? How would you measure the effectiveness of this program? Brainstorm and discuss methods and techniques that would reduce vandalism and litter.

Suggested Key Words and Phrases for Internet Search

Prevent vandalism
Vandalism reduction
Park vandalism
Graffiti problems
Vandalism – City parks
State park vandalism

Littering is wrong
Littering the environment
Litter – Waste – National parks
Litter – Effects on tourism
Litter – Volunteer support
Tips – Preventing litter

References

Gordon, R. (2012, June 4). Vandals deface city's renovated parks, playgrounds. Retrieved from http://www.sfgate.com/crime/article/Vandals-deface-city-s-renovated-parks-playgrounds-3606472.php

---

Case Study 37
Atwood's Bitter Campaign

Situation

The City of Atwood is involved in one of the hottest campaigns in the last 10 years. What started out as a well-meaning proposal from a park district has now divided the town in half. The bitterness that some have expressed has been unfortunate and accomplished little. Atwood's local newspaper, *The Herald*, has done a good job in publicizing the issue—both pros and cons. All letters fit to print have found their way into the "Public Forum." The local radio station has given equal time to the proponents and opponents of the issue. Two letters that seem to point to the critical issue of the campaign follow:

Letter 1

Editor: *The Herald*

Recently, we all sat back and listened to and read about all the nice things we need for the City of Atwood, how our children and the people of Atwood need swimming pools and parks, flowers, trees, and many things that make a city worth living in. I was born and raised in Atwood and now have three boys of my own to bring up. I see that what this city needs is more industries, not pools and flowers. If the city fathers, councilmen, Chamber of Commerce, and the Jaycees would spend a little more time and energy to entice the new industries to this town, to assure us that our children aren't swimming on empty stomachs, a lot of these nice things wouldn't be so hard to pay for.

Someone should go over to the high schools and ask the graduates where they are going to work, or ask the men who were laid off at L-O-F if they will have time this year to take their children swimming when they are not out of town looking for work.

Let's all stop wasting our time and money trying for the luxuries and spend a little more time assuring our young people that they will have, in the future, a place to work in Atwood, instead of a place to spend their spare time—because there will be plenty of spare time for all if we don't wake up.

Donald Hogan

Letter 2

Editor: *The Herald*

There presently is a movement to create a park district for the City of Atwood and its immediate environs. This movement has been characterized as a progressive one for our community. No one is against so-called progress in a general sense, but progress for the sake of progress at the expense of the taxpayer is not progress at all but rather regression, pure and simple.

One need only consider the critical educational needs and requirements of this community. To have available a faculty and facilities needed to acquire a well-rounded education is a need far superior to the need of a place within which to recreate.

All real-estate owners are only too familiar with the continuing pattern of sharply increasing real-estate taxes. Tenants, too, are affected, since taxes are a cost of operation and are reflected in rents. A large portion of the tax increases in recent years has resulted in necessary construction of school facilities to meet ever expanding population needs. Moreover, those who support and maintain the parochial education facilities of this community have been and will continue to be called upon for substantially increased sums to properly operate and maintain such parochial systems in addition to paying their regular real-estate and other taxes.

The argument is heard that our city cannot grow without a park district. This is without merit. New industry or newcomers first look to the quality and quantity of schools, whether public or parochial; the presence or absence of modern and complete hospital facilities; and the availability of well-improved, maintained, and easily accessible streets and thoroughfares.

Paying for a park district can only be done at the expense of sacrificing and taking away funds from basic education and health needs. I say vote "no" for the park district and let's spend money where it counts—for education.

Kenneth O'Connor
Attorney

Problem: Letter 1

To what degree does a prospective industry consider park and recreation facilities in the selection of a site? Would the establishment of a recreation and park system increase or decrease the assessed valuation of property in Atwood? Does the lack of recreation and park facilities have any relationship to the unemployment rate? What effects would a good recreation and park system have on the youth who are graduating from high school? What role will these facilities play in their future? What reply would you give Hogan when he states that recreation is just a luxury?

Problem: Letter 2

How do you reply to an individual who insists that education, health, and welfare needs must take precedence over recreation needs? How important is a sound recreation and park system to the orderly and progressive growth of a community? Is it fair to assume that tax rates will automatically increase because a recreation and park system is established?

As chair of the committee that is promoting the establishment of a recreation and park system in Atwood, write replies to the letters from Hogan and O'Connor.

Suggested Key Words and Phrases for Internet Search

Parks and recreation - Value to community

Parks and recreation - Essential to public services

Why parks are important

Economic benefits - Public parks and recreation

Parks and recreation values

Economic value of urban parks

_____ **Case Study 38** _____
Is 26% Representative?

Situation

Planno Associates has recently completed an attitude, interest, and opinion survey in your community, which has a population of 13,000. The purpose of the survey was to determine the scope of opportunities available for use in the community, the recreational activities in which adults and youth participate, the recommendations of adults and youth for additional park facilities and programs, and the sufficiency of programs and facilities according to adults and youth. A systematic random stratified sample of all adults and junior and senior high school students was employed for this survey. Questionnaires were delivered to 600 homes, and 417 were returned. This represents a 70.16% response. Questionnaires were distributed to 1,000 junior and senior high school student, with 679 returned. This represents a 67.9% response.

As a result of the survey, the recreation and park board is submitting to the voters a referendum that will decide if the board will build an indoor–outdoor swimming pool facility. You and the board feel that this issue will receive a favorable response because over 26% of those surveyed indicated the desire for such a facility when asked, "What recreation facilities and programs do you feel are needed in the community?" You have been quoted in the newspaper saying that this 26% is a "significant response" and that the citizens will support the construction of a swimming pool.

While attending a public meeting, a number of citizens who are vigorously opposed to the passage of the referendum make the following comments:

- "It is not possible for only 417 adults and 679 youth to be representative of the entire community."
- "How do we know that those surveyed came from a cross section of the community?"
- "The percentage of 26 is not 'significant' and represents only a few people in the community."
- "It is impossible to get a representative sample."
- "If 26% were a fair reading of community support, they still represent a resoundingly unimpressive minority."

Problem

What is a systematic random stratified sample? Is it possible to get a representative sample? Is 26% significant in predicting the community interest for the construction of a swimming pool? Did Planno Associates give all people in the community an opportunity to fill out the questionnaire? Are the percentages of 70.16 for adults and 67.9 for youth high or low returns? What is the normal return for surveys like the one conducted in your community? What would be the best way for you to explain to the community the meaning and interpretation of the survey figures? Write a press release that could clarify the questions raised at the public meeting.

Suggested Key Words and Phrases for Internet Search

Survey research
Random stratified sample
Survey design

Survey research methods
Questionnaire surveys
Statistics data analysis

_____ **Case Study 39** _____
Testing Will Tell the Story

Situation

As the director of a large recreation and park department, you see the needs for establishing a training program for your 40 supervisors. On a number of occasions they have mentioned to you that training in human relations is desperately needed if they are to perform their jobs effectively. Because the local university has many of the resources available, you contact Professor Strump for assistance in planning the program. You inform him that the purpose of the program is to help your supervisors better understand the attitudes and goals of community groups and their relationship to the recreation and park department.

After a number of planning sessions, Professor Strump and you agree that the following topics should be included in the training program: philosophy and administration of community relations, the role of citizen action organizations in the community, successful programs in other cities, ethnic group relations, referral process and referral sources, and recreation program planning. You have determined that the cost of conducting the program will be $20,000. As presently planned, the training program will be conducted in 4-hour sessions twice a week over 3 months. Before implementing the program, you must first submit it to your board for approval.

Upon your request for the funds and approval of the program, some board members object and indicate that the program is expensive, no way has been developed to determine its effectiveness, and it is not known if it will help supervisors. Another board member, the personnel director for the Jafco Corporation, states, "I have seen supervisors down at the plant who return from these so-called training programs and make very few changes in their operation." The board chair agrees with these statements; however, he is in favor of trying the program if you will incorporate testing procedures to determine the effectiveness of the program. Those who object to your program agree that this is an acceptable compromise, and they are willing to vote in favor of the program under these conditions. The board instructs you to return to the meeting next month with the testing procedure for review.

Problem

How will you determine the effectiveness of the training program? What testing procedures will you use? What problems will you encounter in setting up your testing procedure? Do you feel that all your training programs should be evaluated? Why?

Suggested Key Words and Phrases for Internet Search

Recreation program effectiveness
Program effectiveness
Outcome effectiveness – Recreation
Evaluation – Recreation programs

Planning program evaluation
Research – Recreation – Park – Sport – Tourism

_____ **Case Study 40** _____
The Bomb Threat

Situation

A popular activity at the recreation center is the roller-skating program held each Friday night. Approximately 450 youth turn out for this event. For the center director, this is the busiest night of the week.

On Friday evening, November 17, about 8 p.m., Salle Midas, a junior leader, answered the phone and a voice asked to speak with the center director. When the center director answered, the voice said, "Within the next 15 minutes a bomb will go off in the main rink area. That will teach you to be too strict with the teenagers." The caller then hung up. The director realized that he had to take quick action. Over 400 youth were in the rink area, and they were wearing skates. To clear the building would cause a problem and be somewhat of a safety hazard. This was the first bomb threat, and no procedure had been developed for evacuation of the building.

The director went to the public address system and announced that all participants should leave the building immediately through the fire exits and should take positions at least 50 yards from the building. When someone asked the reason for the evacuation, Salle Midas blurted out, "I think a bomb will go off." This information spread like wildfire throughout the crowd. Several younger children began to panic and cause a problem. However, within 15 minutes the center was evacuated.

Everyone waited anxiously to see if the caller's threat would come true. Police Chief Shirley and the bomb crew were called to examine the building—no bomb was found. The youth returned to the center and resumed roller skating. Shortly after 9:30 p.m., the caller phoned again and said, "I hope that was good practice because the real thing will happen within the next 2 months."

Problem

Did the center director properly announce the evacuation of the building to the participants? Should he have permitted the participants to return after no bomb was found? When should the police have been notified? How could the director have prevented Salle from blurting out the rumor? What would be the most effective evacuation procedure when the roller-skating program is held? (Use a center with which you are familiar.) How long should it take to evacuate the building? What other agencies in the community could assist you in developing a procedure for evacuation in the event of a bomb threat? How would you plan for the threat "this will happen within the next 2 months"? Would you inform the participants of this threat? The parents? The newspapers? How would you attempt to determine who made the call?

Suggested Key Words and Phrases for Internet Search

Bomb threat checklist

Bomb threat – Emergency

Bomb threat by phone

Bomb threat letter

Handling bomb threats

Homeland Security – Bomb alerts

Preparedness

Case Study 41

Don't Store Oil Tankers in Park

Situation

We want Saratoga & North Creek Railway to figure out ways to make money, but creating a toxic waste site in the heart of the Adirondack Park wasn't what we had in mind.

The railway's president, Ed Ellis, told Warren County political leaders on Tuesday the railway intends to store hundreds of tanker cars on miles of rail sidings it owns along the remote rail line that runs to Tahawus, in the town of Newcomb.

Tahawus was the site of a huge mine, now closed. Heaps of tailings — waste from the mines — are still at the site, and rail company officials have worked to find customers for that waste.

We support the effort to move tailings out of Tahawus by rail and sell them. That benefits the environment, and if the company can make a profit from it, all the better.

But we cannot support a plan to move toxic waste into the Adirondack Park, even in small amounts in the bottom of tankers and even if the arrangement is temporary.

The problem with temporary arrangements is they often become permanent by default. Ellis assured county leaders that the rail tankers are valuable as scrap, so they would not be left on the rail spurs indefinitely.

But moving the rail cars from the remote spurs and getting them to a place where they can be sold for scrap will have a cost, and that cost — combined with the inertia that affects all human affairs — could keep the tankers parked in the mountains.

Ellis has said the cars may be cleaned, but wouldn't guarantee it. At least some of them are likely to have oil sludge in the bottom. The longer they are left parked out in the woods, the more likely they are to leak.

They should not be parked in the woods at all. This is a privately owned rail line, but we do not believe that means it can be used for anything at all.

One of the problems with the crude oil being carried east by rail from the Bakken shale in the western U.S. is its volatility. We have seen the results of that volatility in dangerous tanker explosions and fires.

New federal regulations to make tanker cars safer have made some of the older cars obsolete, which has created the market for storage that Saratoga & North Creek Railway intends to exploit. So any residue in these tankers is likely to be that volatile crude oil. Not only is this an argument against storage in the Adirondack Park, it is an argument against movement of the cars through settled areas, such as Corinth and Lake Luzerne.

This is one of those projects that can't be confirmed as an obviously bad idea until a disaster occurs. Perhaps hundreds of tankers that were used to carry toxic crude can be moved into the heart of the Adirondack wilderness, left there for a time, and moved out again, with no unfortunate consequences.

But the project raises too many scary what if questions.

Saratoga and North Creek Railway is struggling financially. What happens if its parent company — Iowa Pacific Holdings — sells the railway after it has parked all those tankers in the woods?

We appreciate Mr. Ellis' candor in bringing this project to the attention of local political leaders. Now those leaders should do everything they can to stop it.

You have been employed by the Adirondack Association of Towns and Villages to study the toxic waste issue presented by the railway company and to recommend how the association should proceed with the proposal. You should submit the final report to the association within 90 days.

Problem

Should the railway company be allowed to store toxic waste tankers in the Adirondack Park? If no, what can be done to stop this action? If yes, under what conditions should it be done? What are the dangers to the environment if it is allowed? Because the railway company is in financial difficulty, should this be a factor in if the company is allowed to store the toxic waste? Why? Is this proposal compatible with the county's long-range plan? How much residual oil will be left in the trains? Will local municipalities be compensated for the risks? If allowed, will it set a precedent for the storage of additional hazardous materials within the Adirondack Park? Can the railway company guarantee there will be no oil leaks? If it can, how can they support this statement? What safeguard will the railway take to prevent leaks? Has the governor been made aware of the situation? Does the railway company have the legal right to proceed with the oil storage project? What solution would be acceptable to the county, surrounding communities, the association, and the railway? Is the railway required to obtain a permit to proceed with the oil storage project? The railway claims the oil tank project is not subject to state review or approval. Is this true?

Suggested Key Words and Phrases for Internet Search

Oil tanker storage – Adirondack explorer

What to do with railroad tanker cars

Adirondack council – Oil tank storage

Tourism railroad – Oil tanker problem

Oil by rail – Industry bullies

Adirondack oil storage plan

From "Don't Store Oil Tankers in Park," The Post-Star, July 31, 2015, p. A4. Article reprinted with permission from the Glen Falls Post-Star by Ken Tingley, Editor, on October 2, 2015.

—————————— Case Study 42 ——————————
The Layoff Dilemma

Situation

You are superintendent of recreation and parks in a large Midwestern city. During the past year, a number of projects were completed that cost the city taxpayers large sums of money. The mayor has informed all department heads that budgets must be cut by 30%. He recognizes that needs exist and that increases rather than decreases are needed if public demands are to be met. However, this is an election year, and increases in the tax rate could prove disastrous for the mayor and two councillors who are running for reelection. The mayor indicates that he will leave the budget cuts entirely to the discretion of the department heads.

You summon your four supervisors to your office to discuss the budget situation. It is generally agreed that each supervisor must lay off a certain number of personnel to meet the mayor's demand. Naturally, each supervisor raises the question, who should be laid off? After full discussion, it is agreed that each supervisor shall be responsible for determining the policy of who should be laid off in his or her section.

Jim Stolk, who heads the maintenance division, returns to the garage and calls his staff together. He states, "The mayor is requiring all departments to reduce by 30%. This means a layoff by January 1. I have been asked by the superintendent to lay off three people. I do not like to do it, but it is out of my control. Those who are laid off will be told before the day ends. My selection will be based partly on seniority and partly on ability."

Dave Jones, supervisor of the recreation centers, calls his staff together and says, "The mayor has given the word—30% of the operation must go. Of course this means that four assistant center directors will have to be laid off. I have decided to lay off strictly on the basis of seniority. This will be the only fair procedure."

Mary Stein, supervisor of the aquatics program, simply puts a notice on the bulletin board listing the names of the five lifeguards whose employment is being terminated. The announcement indicates that if there are questions, they may make an appointment to see her.

George Stone, office manager, is upset that he has to lay off seven typists. In the past when crises such as this occurred, the staff became upset and it affected the morale of other typists. He decides that the best way to notify the individuals of the layoff is to put a notice in their pay envelopes. This should cause the least embarrassment and gossip.

Problem

What are the unique differences in each layoff procedure? How do you think employees would react to each procedure? Do you think that each supervisor should have the responsibility for his or her own layoff procedure? Why? If these procedures are not acceptable, what procedures would be better? Should there be a general department procedure concerning layoff? If yes, what should it be? How would you prepare employees for being laid off? What do you tell people who will be remaining with the organization? What method will you use to notify the people to be laid off?

Suggested Key Words and Phrases for Internet Search

Layoff – Downsizing

Layoff policy

Layoff – Employee rights

Layoff resource guide

Reduction in workforce

Best practices in layoff policies

Case Study 43
Will Your Agency "Cell" Out?

Situation

At their last meeting, the village trustees of Goodreau rejected a plan to build a 125-foot cell phone tower at Goody Park. The dissenting officials said voting against the tower would possibly expose the village to lawsuits and "leave revenue on the table."

Unfortunately, the naysayers were correct. The national wireless carrier filed a federal lawsuit against the village shortly after the meeting seeking to overturn the trustees' decision and force the construction of its cell phone tower. The federal lawsuit states that the wireless provider met all of the village's requirements by agreeing to make every effort possible to limit impediments to the scenery and natural beauty of Goody Park. The lawsuit also claims that the village has allowed television stations to build similar sized towers in other parks in Goodreau. Wind turbines have also been built at Julie Park to provide energy for the park and recreation administration office. The turbine stands at 75 feet tall, but it is significantly wider than the proposed cell tower.

The attorney for the cellular provider filed a lengthy litigation asking for the village of Goodreau to issue permits for constructing the tower. The lawsuit also demanded the village pay for all the legal costs associated with the lawsuit.

The village attorney, Zoe Jake, who was the most outspoken supporter of the cell tower plan, said she is not surprised, but does not see the lawsuit as problematic.

Jake plans to call to question the trustees' actions at a special closed session of the next board meeting. Jake stated that legal fees alone to fight this court case could amount to more than $25,000.

What spurred the trustees to resist the cell phone company's tower construction application? Roughly 250 residents from the Goody Park neighborhood submitted written and verbal complaints to the trustees saying the height of the tower would visibly obscure scenic views, obstruct bird migration patterns to marshes and natural areas in Goody Park, and destroy the open space in the park. Many of these residents effectively argue the tower is not needed because they have never experienced issues with service as users of the cell phone provider in question.

The lawsuit claims the tower would mitigate the largest gap in regional cellular coverage in the area.

The Goodreau Park and Recreation Division, which is in charge of managing Goody Park, is in favor of the tower proposal. The park and recreation division stands to make $50,000 per year on fees for rights to use the space in Goody Park. "We should think twice about turning down additional revenue streams. Fifty thousand dollars would provide our community with funds for programming and staffing. It would have a direct impact on jobs," stated Goodreau Park and Recreation Director Antonia Flores.

Problem

Imagine you are the superintendent of natural areas of the Goodreau Park and Recreation Division. In this position, your mission is to create sustainable landscapes, to protect and enhance the natural resources in your community, and to promote massive recreation opportunities. What are your recommendations? Your director has shown support for the cell tower. How does that affect your recommendations? Should there be a policy concerning this issue? What roles and rights should neighboring residents have in Goody Park? What compromise can be reached to make all stakeholders happy? What networks or resources would you seek to speak out against or to support the cell phone tower?

Suggested Key Words and Phrases for Internet Search

Telecommunications Act of 1996

Cell phone tower disguises

Clear skylines

Adirondack Park review of telecommunications towers and other tall structures

Adirondack Park cell tower substantially invisible

Effects of cell towers on property values

American Cancer Society cell tower facts

Avian mortality at communication towers

Case Study 44
Coyote Situation Getting Ugly

Situation

Meredith Barnes was walking her usual route around Steve Camp Park. It was dusk, and she was walking her two dogs, Bella and Abbie. Then she saw the shadow of a large animal lurking in a small coppice of trees.

Her dogs began to growl, and she noticed the hair on the back of their necks stand up. Before she could stop the 6- and 10-pound Yorkshire terriers from running, she heard a yelp, and Bella was gone.

The coyote attack on Barnes' dog was the first of two recent coyote attacks in the town of Makenna. Three weeks ago, a small dog was attacked in a fenced yard near Steve Camp Park. Its owner intervened in the attack and possibly saved the dog from being carried away.

"Up until the drought hit, coyotes have only been a small nuisance at times," said Makenna Park District Director Gail Tab. "It's the time of year when pups are born and the drought has made food scarce."

The incident has left Barnes and the residents of Steve Camp Park neighborhood uneasy. "I'm distraught over the tragic death of my pet," she said.

Another resident said, "I have a young daughter that plays in this park all the time. Now I have to think twice about where I let her play. You can see their footprints everywhere in the park. It's not like it's a squirrel or rabbit eating my plants. They're meat-eaters and they want to take a bite out of anything! I won't feel safe until the coyotes are removed."

Up until this point, the town of Makenna has taken action by sending out postcards notifying area residents to take the following coyote precautions:

- The town ordinance requires all dogs be walked on a leash. The leash must not be longer than 6 feet and needs to be under direct control of the owner at all times. Dogs are viewed as a threat or as a food source for coyotes.
- Do not leave your pet unattended in the yard and keep them indoors at night. When it is necessary to let them outside at night, keep the yard well lit.
- Do not feed coyotes. Feeding coyotes will cause them to lose their fear of humans and cause them to become more aggressive.
- Protect all your food sources. Keep water dishes and food for your pets inside. Make sure your grills and barbecues are clean. Cover and secure compost pits and garbage/recycling bins.

"Your interaction with coyotes makes all the difference," stated Tab. "Negative reinforcements keep coyotes from developing aggressive behaviors with humans and pets. Be cautious, but confident. Be loud by clapping your hands and yelling. Don't run. If you encounter an aggressive coyote, throw sticks, rocks, or clumps of dirt in its direction."

The park district has a policy that allows for trapping or culling of nuisance animals, but has never acted on this policy. Despite recent support for removing coyotes, Tab noted that in the attacks, the dogs were not on leashes. She encouraged residents to keep a watchful eye on their pets and scare the coyotes when they display aggressive behavior.

"They're coming back to the town of Makenna for a reason. Most of the time, they're coming back because someone's feeding them or they have easy access to food. Other parks in our district have had coyote dens for years without incident," said Tab.

Barnes plans to fight the park district on removing the coyotes from Steve Camp Park. "We have the right to walk in our neighborhood park without fear for our pets' and children's safety."

Problem

Do you agree with the policy set forth by the administrators of the Makenna Park District? Why or why not? How would you respond to the concerns of Meredith Barnes? What are the advantages and disadvantages to removing the coyotes? Assume that you are the manager of parks and recreation for the Makenna Park District. The *Evening Star* blog allows you the opportunity to clarify the park district's position on coyote management. Write a blog post for the next day's edition.

Suggested Key Words and Phrases for Internet Search

Urban coyote research
Coyotes and pets
Park district coyote policies

Learning to live with coyotes in
  metropolitan areas
Coexisting with coyotes
Coyote attack

Case Study 45
Development Threatens Community Resources

Situation

You have been hired by the Fish Creek Board of Trustees to provide counsel on a potential commercial recreation project. Fish Creek has a population of around 5,500 and is nestled in a scenic valley between Stone Mountain and Tall Peak. The Arapaho National Forest shapes the western border of Fish Creek, and the interstate defines the northern border. Despite a 2-hour proximity to Denver, Fish Creek has remained relatively quiet.

Mayor Brian Vetter, the person who recommended your consulting firm to advise the board of trustees on a sports complex development, says he remembers the town before the days of McDonald's and Wal-Mart. Nearly 25 years ago, Vetter was elected as the town's first mayor. His own home served as his office, and he held public meetings in his living room.

"It was quintessential small-town America here," he tells you. "Before the Internet revolution, everyone knew each other from spending time in the great outdoors together. Kids in our neighborhood used to organize street soccer games, or they would walk to the local ski hill. Businesses used to close early on days with nice weather so employees could bike or hike or fish or ski. These days, everyone wants to be entertained, and we have to learn to roll with the punches or get knocked out of the way. Our tax income has decreased lately, and our community really needs to figure out some new revenue streams."

Right now, a stagnant economy may be the biggest challenge for Fish Creek. However, Fish Creek is a scenic wonderland with amazing outdoor recreation opportunities. The Wondra family would like to capitalize on these assets by building a regional sports complex, which would possibly double Fish Creek's tax revenue. Tom Wondra has proposed to develop 1,500 acres of private land into a sports complex, which would include a water theme park, black diamond ski runs, hiking and biking trails, resort hotel, condominiums, 18-hole golf course, IMAX movie theater, go-cart track, and an indoor sports complex, which would feature four basketball courts, half-mile walking track, fitness center, Olympic-sized swimming pool, space to accommodate indoor football and baseball, and a spa.

The chamber of commerce unanimously approved the Wondra family's plan last fall, stating the project would be "a much needed shot in the arm for the local economy." The chamber of commerce hopes that the Wondra's plan will ultimately turn Fish Creek into a world-class resort town on par with Breckinridge and Vail.

Fish Creek residents recently passed a tax increase to pay for the construction of a modest public recreation center that houses a basketball court, lap pool, and fitness center. A local philanthropist has offered to fund an addition, but she has broken off conversations with Fish Creek after being courted by the Wondra family to fund parts of their project.

To add fuel to the fire, most residents currently purchase season passes to Beckmann Hill, a quiet, low capacity ski hill. Everyone in the Beckmann family works at the ski hill, and the family is well liked and well known in the community. The Beckmanns groom the cross-country ski trails in Fish Creek at no cost and often plow the driveways of residents in need for free. Any new competition in town would certainly put this community icon out of business.

Local environmental groups also bemoan the loss of the greatest asset in Fish Creek: its natural beauty. "We are very concerned about what this means for the scenic beauty of our community and state," said Robbie Jansen, the leader of the local Audubon Society. "The proposed construction site is located in prime wilderness right next to the Arapaho National Forest. The land is private property, but the sports complex will affect the water supply, wildlife, scenery, heritage, and way of life in Fish Creek. We've fought hard to weave preservation in the fabric of our community. Four thousand people signed a petition opposing the project. The Wondra's may own the property, but it belongs to everyone in our community."

Mayor Vetter dismissed the claims of the opposition, citing that the petition was signed by a "large number of tourists." He also claimed the Wondra project will have little effect on the environment and will use green technology in the new construction. Jansen acknowledges this claim, but suggests that Fish Creek should not deny the voice of its current tourism base that is already visiting Fish Creek and spending money. "An alternative plan should be created to cater to the current tourists. We are leaving a lot of money on the table that could make up budget shortfalls without a big construction project damaging our landscape," Jansen said.

Problem

What would you recommend to the board of trustees and Mayor Vetter? Is Mayor Vetter realistic about how little environmental damage this project will cause? Who should have the right to determine the fate of the scenic land: the owner or the public? What should Fish Creek do about the conflict of interest between its own recreation center, the pending sports complex, and the potential donor? How will this development affect Beckmann Hill and the Beckmann's role in the community? Should the Beckmann's interests be considered? Could the town better market its current assets rather than seek to bring in new attractions? Devise a marketing strategy to do this. Assume you are being paid by the mayor and council. How does this influence your decision on whether you recommend the project; how does it influence how you word your presentation?

Suggested Key Words and Phrases for Internet Search

Chamber of commerce
Commercial recreation
Green space
Wilderness
Outdoor recreation
Rural development

Tourism
Consulting
Environmental impact
Public land
Special interest groups

Case Study 46
Use of Stadium for Demonstration

Situation

You have accepted the position of director of parks and recreation in a small suburban community in the Midwest. You have been on the job for 1 week. Under your jurisdiction is a 25-acre park that includes a stadium with a seating capacity of 3,000.

When you open the morning's mail, you find a letter from Nora Sullivan, the president of the student council at the local junior college. She requests the junior college be permitted to use the stadium for a demonstration. She indicates that students from all high schools in the area will be asked to participate along with students from Dundee Junior College. Total attendance at the demonstration will include about 2,500 people.

In checking further about the groups who will attend the demonstration, you find that many of the students in Dundee Junior College were active in the demonstrations in the past. You learn that 12 of these students were arrested and fined for disturbing the peace. The chief of police has informed you that "if you give permission to students from Dundee, you are sure to have trouble."

He advises against the use of the stadium. When you check with the mayor, he informs you that a request for the stadium for this purpose has not occurred before and that there is no policy concerning it. The city attorney informs you that if you feel that allowing the use of the stadium could in any way cause a disturbance in the community, you have a right to deny the request. The local *Evening Post* has complicated the matter by publishing a copy of the request. It received a copy of the letter from the student council secretary. An editorial in the paper supports the use of the stadium for the demonstration.

Problem

Would you permit the stadium to be used for the demonstration? If you do, would you permit the students from Dundee Junior College to attend? If permission was granted, what action would you take to maintain security? If you permit use, how do you think this will affect your relationship with the chief of police? What groups should be permitted to use public facilities? Write a policy statement concerning the use of public facilities by outside groups.

Suggested Key Words and Phrases for Internet Search

Organizing public demonstrations
Protest demonstration

Demonstration – Marches – Rallies
Right of assembly

_____ Case Study 47 _____
Cast as Safe Havens, Some Rec Centers Must Deal With Violence

Situation

Last October, amid a spate of shootings in and around some of Philadelphia's public recreation centers — the most recent one involving an 18-month-old who was critically wounded by an errant bullet — former city recreation commissioner Victor Richard III offered this statement to the *Philadelphia Daily News*: "The rec centers are not unsafe; it's disheartening that inner-city children are caught up in this nonsense."

The statement is perplexing, if not outright contradictory. It also illustrates a mindset shared by the many recreation providers who not only see their facilities as refuges from gun-related violence, but who also are faced with the painful evidence from around the country that belies that notion.

As of this writing, the family of a 19-year-old Long Island, N.Y., man who was shot to death this Memorial Day during an informal party at a recreation center was pleading for witnesses to come forth. Meanwhile, in Yuba City, Calif., a 22-year-old man was headed to trial for allegedly opening fire with an Uzi semiautomatic weapon at a youth-and-community center, wounding three people attending a March concert. Philadelphia has been hit especially hard by crime spreading from the streets into its parks and recreation centers. According to a June report in the *Daily News*, 16 people were shot, five fatally, within or on the grounds of city recreation property since January 2007.

To be sure, such anecdotal evidence doesn't necessarily represent a national trend. But as Asheville (N.C.) Parks and Recreation Department director Roderick Simmons points out, it is the very suddenness and unpredictability of these incidents that should resonate with all recreation providers. Simmons knows firsthand the damage that can be caused by unforeseen violent crime.

While there may be no way to completely prevent violent crime at rec centers, there are some easy-to-implement strategies for combating it, suggests Harry Erickson, of Long Beach, Calif.-based CPTED Security Consultants, a firm specializing in "crime prevention through environmental design," a multidisciplinary approach to deterring criminal activity.

"At a public space such as a recreation center, we always recommend that people entering the building have to check in, so there is a record," says Erickson. "If your facility is already built and you don't have the funds to move your check-in desk, it's important to have a live body there, a person with a position of authority who people coming into the facility have to pass by."

Simmons says many of Asheville's neighborhood recreation centers are small, converted schools that are capable of serving only the surrounding residents, who, prior to last year's shooting, could come and go freely. After a thorough review of the department's security procedures, involving extensive input from local police and fire officials, Asheville's rec centers now not only enforce a check-in/sign-out system, but also benefit from increased staff and police presence.

In order to quell anxiety in the surrounding neighborhood, Simmons' department also worked closely with police to inform residents and facility users of security and policy changes, as well as to provide them some specifics about the incident itself. "We basically shared as much information with the public as we could to let them know what was going on," says Simmons. "But situations like this are tough. It's not like you can just go into martial law and start shaking everyone down; then people are not going to want to use your facility."

That way of thinking appears to also exist in Philadelphia, despite that "the brazen daylight shootings, stabbings and murders on the rec-center grounds seem to have handcuffed the department as it struggles to maintain its programs," wrote *Daily News* reporter Damon C. Williams last October, adding, "Philadelphia's gun violence permeates the safest of safe havens."

The city has since launched an interdepartmental and multifaceted initiative that goes well beyond just bolstering security. "There is a lack of consistent programs," Sue Slawson, who was promoted in June from the police ranks to head the rec department, commented, "A big crime-fighting tool is programs."

Erickson, who regularly works with municipalities to create cost-effective crime-prevention measures at their facilities, agrees that the mere presence of more "legitimate" users and facility staff members will make those who might perpetrate a crime take pause. "You want more sets of eyes," he says. "If legitimate users feel safe because of openness, visibility and lighting, then chances are that the illegitimate users will feel at risk."

Erickson also fully subscribes to the "broken windows" theory — which asserts that seemingly minor problems, such as the presence of graffiti, will ultimately lead to more serious problems — as it applies to rec centers. "If the municipality doesn't pay enough attention to that graffiti, then law-abiding citizens are going to feel afraid, like they're in a bad area," he says. "If people are allowed to sit on a park bench and drink beer — something that is probably illegal in most jurisdictions — it may seem minor. People might say, 'We need to focus on the bigger things. We just had a homicide.' But the problem is if you don't focus on those little things, they're going to lead to larger things."

Erickson acknowledges that there is no firm guarantee against gun-related violence in rec centers or any public building, for that matter, even with a comprehensive security plan that may include locks, security patrols, education, ordinances, alarm systems, surveillance cameras and a range of other target-hardening devices, as well as CPTED strategies. But he urges recreation providers to consider measures to make their facilities seem off-limits in potential criminals' minds. "Most crimes are crimes of opportunity," he says. "Whether they consciously make the decision or not, there's a decision-making process going on when a suspect chooses a location to commit a crime, and the environment plays into that."

While Asheville's parks and recreation department has been careful to review and update all of its policies and procedures for emergency situations, and enhanced security has been implemented, Simmons says that to suggest that any rec center is perfectly safeguarded against a violent crime such as a shooting would be naïve. "Always keep in the back of your mind that we are providing public facilities, and these things could always happen," he says. "Just have a plan in place for when they do."

But even the most pragmatic thinker has a difficult time coping with an apparently random and violent crime.

Problem

What should the relationship be between the police department and the recreation department? Should police officers be employed at recreation centers? Should cameras be installed in strategic areas of recreation centers? What regulations could be established to reduce and possibly eliminate crime at recreation centers? What can be done to make participants feel safe? Develop a training program for recreation personnel that would address the crime issue. What federal funds are available to address this issue?

Suggested Key Words and Phrases for Internet Search

Neighborhood crime

Crime prevention council

Crime – Recreation prevention

Crime prevention control

Crime prevention programs

Youth crime prevention

From "Cast As Safe Havens, Some Rec Centers Must Deal With Violence," by N. Brown, 2008, Athletic Business. *Reprinted with permission of* Athletic Business.

_____ **Case Study 48** _____

No More Snow Party Fun: Recreation Agencies Ban Sledding Over Liability Concerns

Situation

It is winter in the North, which means that countless numbers of children and their parents are excited to engage in that timeless pursuit of youthful seasonal pleasure: sledding. Many who grew up in cooler climates have gone sledding at least once or twice. Yes, it is sometimes dangerous, but so are many other activities in which youth engage. That is part of being a child. A number of cities reportedly have placed limitations on sledding in public streets and municipal parks or banned the activity altogether because of liability concerns. The city council in Ft. Ann, New York, recently banned sledding on all but two streets, citing a $2 million lawsuit brought against other cities in the area. The most sobering statistic was to learn that a 13-year-old boy was killed in January when the plastic sled he was riding during a winter festival sent him sliding into a metal ski, causing massive trauma. Another city council had to pay out $12 million in 2011 to a sledder who collided with a concrete cube at the bottom of the hill.

The Consumer Product Safety Commission reported that approximately 10,000 sledding-related injuries in children under the age of 14 were treated in hospital emergency departments in 2012. At a recent council meeting in Foley, New Jersey, a sledding discussion ensued concerning if sledding should be allowed on city streets and in public parks. David Donovan, a local attorney, stated that the legal liability should be a factor in any decision. Mary Conlin, a parent of an 8-year-old girl and 15-year-old boy, stated, "My family has been sledding on Wing Street for over 20 years. Sure, there have been some injuries over the years, but none serious in nature. Sledding in the winter is one recreational activity every kid looks forward to. I would hope the council would find a way to continue this activity." John Phillips, a local IGA store manager, said, "Since there is a possibility of injury, maybe we should eliminate football, soccer, field hockey, gymnastics, rock climbing, wrestling, cycling, lacrosse. There is risk in almost everything we do." Joe Sherman wanted to know, "Where am

I going to park my car if the streets are closed? I have no garage and my property is too small."

In the City of Belville, New York, the director of recreation and parks informs Mayor Bob Folley that sledding on public streets and parks is going to be a "hot" issue at the next council meeting. The mayor immediately directs you to study the sledding issue and recommend how the council should proceed. He also indicates that the city attorney will be available for counsel.

Problem Solving

Should sledding on public streets be allowed? If sledding is permitted, what rules, regulations, and conditions should be established? Who should be involved in studying the sledding issue? How would you involve the general public in the decision process? What city agencies should provide input? What are the pros and cons of allowing sledding on public streets? What information do you need to make a decision? What role should the police department play in the decision process?

Suggested Key Words and Phrases for Internet Search

Sledding on public streets
Sledding injuries
Sledding – Tubing safety

Streets – Legal – Sledding
Sledding injury prevention
Snow sledding

_____ Case Study 49 _____
Does Metal Attract the Wrong Crowd?

Special events include any event limited in duration on public or private property open to the public, held on a one-time, occasional, or annual basis including festivals, block parties, rallies, dances, shows, carnivals, circuses, concerts, running events, and similar activities. Most recreation and park departments provide their communities with special events. Special events have become an important part of recreation programming. For example, the City of Longmoat, Colorado, offers 25 special events each year. The City of Clinton, Missouri, provides six special events each year. The City of Anacortes, Washington, offers 13, and the Chicago Park District offers numerous special events at 14 of its city parks. Special events have obviously become a major function for recreation and park departments. Special events can raise awareness on programs offering fund-raising costs of service delivery. Making the decision to have an event involves certain risks. Not planning ahead may have a huge effect on your agency's reputation and financial stability. Media coverage of your special event will raise the profile of your recreation agency and increase the awareness of the services and the programs. It will also help to spread the word to potential participants in your program.

Situation

You are the public arena manager in a city of 50,000. For years, your 40,000-seat arena has been used for circuses, country music shows, and sporting events. The arena has rarely been more than half filled, and in recent years, it has lost considerable money. Concert promoters Grant & West believe that you could make a fortune from heavy metal concerts. The company claims that such shows would bring many people into town and would help the sagging economy of the town, not to mention the financial condition of the arena.

Police Chief Johnson also thinks it would bring many people into town, but he calls it a bad idea. He claims the additional visitors will mean that he will need additional personnel. He suspects that brawls will likely erupt and questions if there is enough jail space for individuals. He points out that the extra people coming into town could cause severe traffic jams. When Grant & West point out that people may come throughout the day rather than all at once, he argues that crowd control could become a problem.

Maggie Marple, representing the senior center in town, is also against the proposed concert. She claims that the heavy metal concerts will bring undesirables to town. She says that the concerts would indeed revive the town's economy, but adds, "Who wants to sell their soul?" She suspects that the concert would attract drug users and rowdiness, and she asks the city council to please keep such people out of town. Of course, the downtown business community is supportive of the idea.

Problem

How would you answer each of Chief Johnson's objections? Is it possible to overcome each of these practical considerations? If so, suggest how. Is one problem he suggested dominant over all the others? Should the concert promoters be expected to "chip in" to help start the project? Should the financial goal of a public arena be to make money, break even, or lose money? How do you answer each of Maggie Marple's concerns and fears? Is she objecting for security reasons? What can you do to "bridge the generation gap"? What, if anything, would be unacceptable for presentation in a public arena?

Suggested Key Words and Phrases for Internet Search

Planning special events
Recreation special events
Special event crowd control

Event planning
Creating special events

————————————— **Case Study 50** —————————————
Boys and Girls Clubs Faces Budget Dilemma

The Boys and Girls Clubs of America is an important youth organization in several communities. Its mission is to "enable all young people, especially those who need us most, to reach their full potential as productive, caring, responsible citizens" (Boys and Girls Clubs of America, n.d., para. 1). For over 150 years, the Boys and Girls Clubs has been helping youth reach their full potential. Its membership and community outreach span over 4,100 club facilities throughout the country and U.S. military institutions. In 2014, Boys and Girls Club youth development programs affected nearly 4 million youth (Boys and Girls Club, 2015).

Situation

For the fourth time this decade, the Nutonville Boys and Girls Club is appealing to the community to help keep its doors open. The club will not be able to offer its popular summer program for children and teens unless it raises about $40,000 by June 1 and another $75,000 by July 1. "We're in a cash crunch," said the executive director. "The club could be closing for good if we do not get more support. People do not understand that the Boys and Girls Club only survives off of benevolent giving. We're not a state-funded agency," said the executive director.

The club has faced similar problems in previous years. The club relies heavily on community support, including $157,000 from the United Way. The recession, state budget woes, and competition from the county YMCA's capital-fund drive have made funding scarce. Meanwhile, demand for the club's programs has continued to rise, with attendance doubling in the last 5 or 6 years.

Average daily attendance in the club's after-school program rose from 121 in 2013 to 137 in 2014. For the summer program, average attendance grew from 141 to 167 in that span. The club charges a $5 membership fee per child, plus additional fees in the summer. "The product is there. The parents want our services more so than ever. It's a constant drain on our resources," said the executive director.

The club has been open for over 20 years, but funds are simply not available. Mrs. Dolan, a single parent of four children, said, "I'm very upset and angry. My kids attend the after-school program at the club. It keeps them in a locally run program and in constructive activities." George Rozell, a club attendee, said, "The club is my life. They taught me math, reading, literature, and science. They help me with my homework." Richard Clancy, the county sheriff, said, "I worry about the juvenile crime escalating this summer. Local teens need a positive outlet like the Boys and Girls Club."

The club recently sent out mailings to 3,000 homes and businesses seeking financial help. It has relied increasingly on fund-raising to pay for its operations in recent years, but donations have been "sluggish" the last few months. Overall, income is 9% behind projections, or as much as 14% if grants and other restricted funds are not counted. Expenses are also down 13%, to about $897,000.

The revenue goal for this year was about $500,000, but less than half of that has been raised. The state also owes the club $15,000 in reimbursements from a $62,000 program grant. The club has not received a payment from the state since December.

The idea was to move away from temporary grants and labor-intensive special events and find investors to fund the ongoing operations of the club. Grants have become more restrictive and are targeted mainly toward new programs and some events.

The club has a line of credit up to $200,000 from a local bank, but it does not want to borrow any more money, as that can be "a recipe for disaster." The organization has little wiggle room. There is not enough money to pay the staff unless the community comes through. Board members are making plans to secure the long-term future of the club, including pursuing a sizable endowment. But for now, they are working to spread the word about the immediate need.

To try to contain costs, the director froze hiring several years ago, though the club won a grant this year for a program director, a job that had gone empty for several years. Administrators have gone without raises for 3 years, and board members funded modest Christmas bonuses out of their own pockets.

To squeeze out more savings, the following adjustments have been instituted: adjust insurance coverage every year, participate in cooperative energy programs, freeze some spending, postpone staff training, and limit program hours.

Problem

What options do the staff and board have in keeping the Nutonville Boys and Girls Club open? What grants are available that could reduce the financial rises? Should membership fees be increased? What reply do you have for Mrs. Dolan? What potential donors could provide funds? Is it possible to name the Boys and Girls Club after a major donor? Should the United Way be approached for support? How will you evaluate the effectiveness of the infusion of the new money? Does a job description exist for the director of the club? What other information do you need to solve this budget problem?

Suggested Key Words and Phrases for Internet Search

Fund-raising – Boys and Girls Club
Boys and Girls Club – Federal grants
Special events – Fund-raisers
Fund-raising guide

Fund-raising ideas
Donation – Boys and Girls Club
Boys and Girls Club – Volunteers

References

Boys and Girls Clubs of America. (n.d.). Our mission. Retrieved from http://www.bgca.org/whoweare/pages/mission.aspx

Boys and Girls Clubs of America. (2015). *2014 annual report.* Retrieved from http://www.bgca.org/whoweare/Pages/AnnualReport.aspx

_____ **Case Study 51** _____
Should Floatplanes for People With Disabilities Be Allowed in a Wilderness Area?

Situation

The *Adirondack Explorer* is a nonprofit news magazine "devoted to the protection and enjoyment of the Adirondack Park." Found in the *Explorer* was an article by Phil Brown (2012) titled "Should Floatplanes Be Allowed on Lake Lila?" The focus of the article was that the state attorney general was asking a federal judge to dismiss a lawsuit that demanded people with disabilities be allowed to use floatplanes to fly into remote lakes in regions of Adirondack Park that are classified as wilderness, where motorized access is prohibited.

Five men with disabilities filed the suit to access the wilderness areas by floatplane because they were unable to visit on foot. The plaintiffs filed the suit in U.S. District Court, claiming the regulations that prohibit the use of floatplanes for access to the wilderness areas violate the Americans With Disabilities Act (ADA). There are 860 lakes and ponds in the protected wilderness area, and the plaintiffs' suit seeks permission to fly to the 38 of them that are large enough to accommodate a floatplane. Lake Lila is the largest lake in Adirondack Park and is a popular destination for paddlers.

The ADA prohibits discrimination against people with disabilities. It is a mandate that recreation facilities open to the public be accessible to all people. The ADA is often referred to as "the civil rights act for people with disabilities" because of its intent to have people with disabilities exercise their right to access every aspect of society.

Reactions to the *Adirondack Explorer* article were mixed, with some opposing the suit, others supporting it, and still others suggesting some compromise be reached. Of those opposed, one indicated, "It seems to me it should be no. It's a wilderness—no motorized access." A second wrote, "As we all know, only a fraction of Adirondack Waters are off-limits to motors. People with disabilities can enjoy all the waters that are open to motors. It's not a wilderness experience if you encounter floatplanes, so if you need a motor to visit it, you might as well just go where motors are already permitted." Still another stated, "So this disabled guy wants to climb into and out of a floatplane, paddle to a wilderness lake with no motor, presumably camp, pitch tents, sleep in bags, etc., but he can't walk less than half a mile to the lake? This is clearly just an attack on wilderness land classifications NOT a real disability case." A final individual speaking against the suit brought up the point that within the Wilderness Act, Congress indicated "no agency is required to provide any form of special treatment or accommodations, or to construct any facilities or modify any conditions of lands within a wilderness area in order to facilitate such use." This individual did have to admit, however, "Granted, the Wilderness Act is federal and doesn't apply to the Adirondacks. Still, the intent of Congress seems pretty clear: 'no special treatment.'"

Others voiced strong support for the suit. One wrote: "As a native 'adirondacker' I firmly believe that float planes should be allowed into all of those lakes for everyone to enjoy. We all pay taxes and support N.Y.S. Instead of closing off these lakes and putting more and more pressure on a dwindling number of flyable water they should open those lakes listed. Not everyone has the time or capabilty to paddle in." Another indicated that people with disabilities were fully capable of using the wilderness. He wrote, "We have photographic evidence of, and people willing to testify to, how disabled people in wheelchairs are able to use floatplanes to access the wilderness lakes and their shorelines." Still another exclaimed, "I don't like the idea [of floatplanes] either, but isn't it the right thing to do to ensure all people are able to enjoy what we do?"

A third group suggested a compromise be reached. One advances the idea that there could be a policy to "limit the days of the week for landing and taking off." This person went on to propose it would be "better to identify one particular lake with handicap-accessible landing and take-off." Another seeking compromise wrote, "I say yes, but requirements would be [to] fill out an application and submit it to approval from some sort of board."

Problem

What is your opinion regarding the plaintiffs' suit? Should people with disabilities be allowed motorized access to wilderness areas via floatplanes because under the Americans With Disabilities Act it is their right? Is it not their right to have access to all recreation facilities open to the public? Wilderness areas are, by their nature, places that are to be left natural, without any special treatment or accommodations. Shouldn't wilderness areas be protected from the use of motorized means of transportation? Should the sound and sight of floatplanes landing and taking off disrupt the wilderness experiences of those paddling the lakes? Or should some compromise be reached? Could a compromise be designating access by floatplanes to a limited number of lakes?

Suggested Key Words and Phrases for Internet Search

Adirondack Park
Americans With Disabilities Act
 (ADA)

Floatplanes on Lake Lila
Wilderness areas

References

Brown, P. (2012). Should floatplanes be allowed on Lake Lila? *Adirondack Explorer.* Retrieved from http://www.adirondackexplorer.org/outtakes/disabled-seek-access-to-38-wilderness-lakes

This case study was submitted by David Austin.

<hr>

Case Study 52
The Image of the Park and Recreation Department Needs an Overhaul

<hr>

Joan Vanier has recently been appointed director of the park and recreation department for Wilsonville, Utah. The population of Wilsonville is 125,000. As the director, she directs and manages all parks, parkways, and green spaces that belong to the city. This includes improvements to those properties and the management of many others assigned under her authority by the mayor and council. Her duty is also to approve and direct new improvements and maintenance of these properties. She also oversees the supervision and recreation of all the recreation programs and activities. Upon her arrival as the new director, she observed that her department had a reputation of being second best to the private recreation agencies. This troubles her for two reasons. First, she believes the perceptions by the community are incorrect. The department offers some of the finest programs in the area. Citizens are assuming that the private sector is able to offer better quality than the public sector. Community members are paying premium-level fees for private offerings and missing out on quality public programs provided for free. Second, she knows she will need widespread community support each year she returns to the city council for funds to support the department programs. She feels that the political will to support the department programs will diminish unless she can show clearly that the entire community benefits from the department programs. As a result, she knows that without change in attitudes, the department programs will clearly be in jeopardy.

Problem

What are the most pressing perceptual issues for the director? What additional information do you need to deal with this case, and where do you find it? What technique can be used to change community views of the park and recreation department? How can electronic media be used to market the recreation program? What major special events can be offered that could draw the attention to department activities? How can local organizations become involved in improving the image of the park and recreation department? How can program participants become involved in image building? What techniques can the staff use to improve the image of the department? Should a consultant be hired to review the department marketing plan? Is the existing staff aware of the department image problem? The mayor asks you to prepare a marketing program that will improve the image of the department.

Suggested Key Words and Phrases for Internet Search

Benefits of parks and recreation
Public health benefits of recreation
Economic benefits of recreation

Health – Recreation
Importance of play
Marketing and management

_____ **Case Study 53** _____
Builders Say No to Dedicated Parkland

Situation

The youth in Craven South Subdivision are playing in the streets today, their neighborhood park existing only as a hope.

Corinth's recreation and park superintendent, George Malone, says that negotiations with Dauncy Builders for donating 5 acres for a park in the subdivision have come to a standstill. "They have indicated that they're absolutely not going to give up any property for a park," Malone says. "So we're just sitting—we have no authority to do anything—now it's up to the city fathers."

Dauncy Builders, developers of the Craven Subdivision, requested last month that the Corinth Plan Commission approve plans for a new subdivision north of Craven South. But the plan commission put off approval when the Craven Homeowners Association president, Walt Conrad, demanded that land be donated for a park there. The recreation and park department said it would be glad to recommend the acquisition of 5 acres, but the builders said they would not give up the 5 acres. "We need this park badly," says Malone. "We need 5 acres of land in Craven South so the children won't have to cross Sagemore Road." Crossing a major street like that defeats the whole purpose of a neighborhood park.

Malone says that under the city code, the recreation and park department can advise the plan commission that the proposed subdivision does not meet department requirements. He says the recreation and park board will meet next Thursday to consider what advice it will give the commission.

The problem for the plan commission is that there is no clear law or precedent requiring subdivision builders to provide parkland in the state. In the early 1970s according to the city subdivision code, developers were required to provide an acre of parkland for every 60 residential buildings. But that ordinance was repealed in 2001 with the adoption of an entirely new subdivision code. The new code provides that school and recreation authorities can only advise the plan commission that a proposed subdivision does not meet their requirements for future land use.

In this case, the official map of the city does not show the recreation and park department's intentions for a park at Craven South. Fred Meroni, city manager, says the recreation and park department had requested a parcel of land to be shown on the official map of the county, but that it was never transferred to the city map. Park officials thought that if it was shown on the county map, it would automatically be on the city map.

Problem

As the director of recreation and parks, what recommendation would you have for your board at Thursday's meeting? Does a city have a right to require builders to dedicate a portion of subdivision property for park purposes? Is that legal? Have any cities adopted this action? What information would you seek from the Craven Homeowners Association? Could state officials assist in this case? Assuming that you would recommend the city to adopt an ordinance to require dedicated parkland by builders, what procedures would you recommend? What standards would you use? What enforcement techniques would you suggest?

Suggested Key Words and Phrases for Internet Search

Land use
Land dedication
Standards
Land legislation
Real estate
Playgrounds

Open space preservation
Community planning
Plan commission
Zoning board
City planning
Public lands

Case Study 54
It's a BIRD, It's a PLANE, NO It's a Drone

What is a drone? It is an unmanned aerial vehicle. Essentially, a drone is a flying robot. It is often associated with the military for surveillance activity. A number of experts predict that drone technology is going to soar when commercial and security applications are available. Drones come in all shapes and sizes for many uses. It is easy today to find a small drone for personal use that a person can fly, much along the same lines as traditional model airplanes and helicopters. Some police departments are considering using drones to help cut down on crime, but some people believe there is great potential for misuse of this technology. A strong monitoring program needs to be in place so individual privacy is not violated.

The sudden use of flying devices around sports stadiums and other outdoor recreation facilities presents new problems for police and recreation agencies. This is becoming a serious concern for many cities and counties throughout the nation. At present, the California legislature is considering banning the use of flying drones. Drones at events, such as athletic contests, festivals, concerts, football and soccer games, track meets, and flea markets, cause safety problems. A good example of this is a game between the University of Illinois and the University of Wisconsin, when a drone was sighted over the Camp Randall Stadium and frightened the people in the student section. In another Midwestern city, a group of teenagers was harassing young soccer players during play. In September 2014, a booster club sponsored a cookout fund-raiser for a high school basketball team. A drone was being used to deliver styrofoam food containers of barbecue to fans in the crowd. Most drones have a wingspan of less than 4 feet, and their speed can be hazardous at 50 miles per hour. Experts say that in a crowded area, it can be an accident waiting to happen. The Federal Aviation Administration expects U.S. airspace to be crowded with 8,000 commercial drones within the next 5 years. These do not include estimates on local hobbyists flying drones in neighborhoods and over parks during the summertime concert and festival season. Chances are, the next time you are at a large outdoor recreation event, there will probably be people (most likely amateurs) flying their drones. Recently, the Cleveland Metro Park System announced it will use drones to provide photographs and produce maps that are far more detailed than what is available from satellite images. Park officials say the detailed photos will help the park system to document native and invasive plant species and will allow resource managers to make better decisions about managing natural areas.

Situation

Jack Daley has been appointed the director of the park and recreation department in Hillsville, Idaho. Hillsville has a population of 100,000. John Phillips, mayor, has indicated that the use of drones should be considered for the park and recreation department, for example, in delivery of food from concession stands, in lining athletic fields, and in mowing parkland. He says their use should save money by reducing staff and equipment costs and would be more efficient. He also informs you that three council members are opposed to the use of drones in any department within the city. Council member Norma Sullivan says, "We don't want drones in our parks where we could watch people picnicking or playing tennis. Some people come to our parks for private time." Council member Hellen Stright states, "We don't need big brother watching over us." Chief of Police Eugene Brodeur states, "We might make an exception for crowd control, particularly for youth concerts. We have a responsibility to protect people's safety and privacy. I think we need more study of this issue before we take any action. Certainly the police department has a real interest in this issue, and we would like to be involved in any study that is done." The chief of police will meet with Daley and Phillips to discuss the issue in more depth.

Problem

What are the positive uses of drones? What are the negative uses of drones? How can park and recreation agencies use drones? What conditions need to be established if drones are permitted? How can individual privacy be maintained? Should individuals who have drones for recreational use be required to have licenses? Should the citizens of Hillsville be involved in any study undertaken? What kind of liability does a drone user incur? Should special training be required for drone users? What are the privacy concerns of allowing the general public to use drones? Where does an agency go to obtain advice concerning the positive and negative uses of drones? What information do you not have to make an effective decision? Should you even consider recreational use of drones, or should you limit it to commercial use with licenses, proof of insurance, and so forth? If you permit drones in the parks, do you need signage warning other park users that drones may be in use? Would you have to create a floor by which you would not permit to fly drones lower than? How would you police that? Is there a right to privacy issue in a park? If park space is rented for an event, such as a private wedding, can that area be a "no-fly zone" so people do not take video or photos without consent? If a drone is damaged by an errant baseball or some other item, who takes the responsibility or blame? Should the use of drones be restricted based on the size of the park and activities in the park? Perhaps allowing drones in a passive park is okay, but does their presence hurt the visiting experience of others? If you choose to employ drone use (e.g., for security surveillance), are park users required to be notified that they are in use? If drones are used in a park with nearby residential or commercial areas, do you need to be concerned about the effects this will have on the surrounding community? Should recreational use be limited based on age? Are only adults allowed to fly the drones in parks?

Suggested Key Words and Phrases for Internet Search

Aircraft and drones
Drones – Banned in national parks
Flying drones
Stadiums

Drones – Privacy problems
Drones – Safety
Drones – Positive – Negative

Don Decker, director of parks and recreation in Weston, Florida, contributed to the development of this case study.

Case Study 55
All-Terrain Vehicles: A Dilemma for Park Administrators

Situation

Many believe all-terrain vehicles (ATVs) can provide the ultimate outdoor experience, but with the ever increasing growth of this sport, adverse effects to the environment and landowners are also on the rise. Specifically, the actions of a few riders have resulted in negative situations, such as destroyed vegetation, increased erosion, damage to wetlands, saltation of soil, dust, and other particles into lakes and streams, damage to fish and wildlife, and impact on water supply sources, much of which occurs on private property. This occurrence has now become a concern of state governments. If the trend does not change for the better, this sport will become highly regulated or banned in many areas. In Hackensack, New Jersey, wild trails among the trees show it clearly. ATVs are illegally roaming the protected forest. This was at one time a simple little trail. Now there are four lanes. George Lemory, who oversees the maintenance of the New Jersey trails says, "Things aren't getting better, but worse." To deal with the situation, the state legislator drew up a bill signed into law. The law aims to deter illegal off-road recreation by setting large penalties. Fines are now $75–$100 and registration fees are higher. While the state tries to pass a new bill that will be accepted by the legislator, a debate between conservationist and ATV enthusiasts continues.

Several problems have been created by the increased use of ATVs on public lands. They can be damaging, disruptive, and in some places, potentially dangerous. Two complaints against them are that they make noise and leave odors foreign to the natural environment, offensive to many people, especially when encountered in remote areas.

ATVs can be dangerous, and in 2012, an estimated 100,000 individuals were treated in hospital emergency rooms for ATV-related injuries, and 353 deaths were reported in 2012 (CPSC Blogger, n.d.). About 25% of the injuries treated in emergency rooms were children under 16, and of the deaths from 2001–2008, 144 were kids and 568 were adults (CPSC Blogger, n.d.)

On steep, narrow trails, motorized vehicles may be dangerous, not only to horses, riders, and hikers, but also to their own users. They frequently cause erosion if used improperly on or off trails, as well as frequently damage vegetation, including timber and forage, and leave unsightly scars. They sometimes ruin some recreational experiences and disturb wildlife. The vehicles also contribute to heavy use of some attractive, popular backcountry areas, and their users can contribute to difficult sanitation problems and to excessive harvesting of game and fish.

In the state of Vermont, a number of residents have expressed outrage at the Department of Natural Resources and recommended that it oppose the use of ATVs on state land. Malvina Lagault, a citizen of Rutland, Vermont, said in a letter to the governor, "I find the moose do more damage to the trails than ATVs." Marie More never knew her son was riding an ATV until the call came to tell her that her 14-year-old son had been in an accident and was being rushed to the hospital. Her son died before she and her husband arrived. It was reported that he was an amateur riding a 700-lb ATV and crashed into a tree. "More and more families are devastated by deaths and injuries caused by ATVs. A new report shows more of the same continues. High death and injury rates among children on ATVs are increasing," said American Academy of Pediatrics President David Tayloe.

Snowmobiles are unique because they are used when the ground is snow covered and often frozen. They also can be used to travel frozen waterways. Their potential to cause erosion is minimal, but in avalanche country and on frozen waterways, they present special public safety problems. In addition, vegetation not covered by snow may be damaged by snowmobiles and wildlife may be harassed.

As the director of state parks, you have been besieged by groups who either support the use of these vehicles or contend that they are destroying the landscape and add to the noise and air pollution. The governor's office has asked you to recommend a policy concerning the use of these vehicles on state-owned land.

Problem

Should these vehicles be banned from state-owned land? Should their use be allowed and promoted? If allowed, what laws should govern them? What operating procedures should be established? How would you deal with the proponents and opponents? What resources would you seek to make this decision? Is the private sector responsible for providing this type of recreation? What role should the many facts of ATVs play in the use of ATVs? What training should be available to ATV riders? Who should provide it? What gear should be worn by ATV riders? What roles should local state government play in maintaining safety for ATV users?

Suggested Key Words and Phrases for Internet Search

Recreational vehicles

All-terrain vehicles

Snowmobiles

Ski-Doo

National parks

Environment

Pollution – Air – Noise

Legislation for ATVs

Wilderness

Motor vehicles

Parks

Trail bikes

References

CPSC Blogger. (n.d.). CPSC infographic: Big real rough tough deadly ATV statistics. Retrieved October 12, 2016, from http://onsafety.cpsc.gov/blog/2014/05/22/cpsc-infographic-big-real-rough-tough-deadly-atv-statistics/

_____ **Case Study 56** _____
The Park District Warns the Fall Programs Are in Jeopardy

Situation

As property taxes continue to rise throughout the country, citizens are asking what they are receiving in return for their dollars. Any program that combines the resources of government agencies to provide services will enhance each agency's public image. Many park districts throughout the nation are trying to meet the need for recreation by providing cooperative ventures with school districts, city governments, and park districts. The combination of two tax-supported agencies combining their services to provide a needed community service is a way to show taxpayers they are receiving something of value for their tax dollars.

All public recreation facilities and grounds, either owned by the school district or the park district, should benefit and be used by youth, adults, and families to the maximum extent. The park district and the school district have mutual interest in helping young people learn and develop recreational skills and in providing opportunities for people of all ages to participate in recreational activities. It is incumbent on the park district and the school district to develop a unified approach to serving the community recreational needs and to maintain park district and school district facilities cooperatively.

The school district and park district of Cherry Hills are presently dealing with this situation. Park district officials say they are prepared to shut down the fall athletic programs if an intergovernmental agreement cannot be reached with the local school district. The park board plans to meet next week with the school district and grounds committee to discuss the agreement and hopefully come to a consensus. School district members reiterate at their meeting with the park district that the park district cannot afford the fees that would be charged under the proposed agreement. The school district requests the park district begin paying a rental fee for use of school gyms for its adult leagues and share the cost of maintenance of gyms and ball fields used by the park district. "I don't mind paying one fee and one fee only," said park board member John Singleton. "But to have to pay these little fees going on here and there and all that? I say no."

The school district requests the park district pay a building rental fee of $300.00 per program, per use of school district gyms for adult activities. Under this arrangement per week, a 6-week adult basketball league would cost the park district more than $1,500. The school district also proposes in its written intergovernmental agreement the park district pay three payments of an unspecified amount per year for wear and tear on school facilities. According to Hellen Trobey, chair of the park district, "It would put us out of business."

Problem

How should the park district respond to the school district's proposed agreement? What issues are most important in settling the agreement? What additional information do you need to complete the agreement? Would it be possible for the superintendent and the director of parks and recreation to hammer out a new agreement and submit it to the respective boards? Would it be appropriate to solicit input of the general public concerning this issue? What areas should be covered in the agreement? Should legal counsel of both parties be involved in constructing the new contract? Develop a model contract between a school district and a park district. Should the park district shut down the fall athletic programs if an intergovernmental agreement cannot be reached? Do the fees proposed by the school district seem reasonable? If an agreement is reached, how long should it be in effect? If an agreement cannot be reached, who should be the go-between for the gridlock?

Suggested Key Words and Phrases for Internet Search

Agreement – Park district –
   School district
Negotiation – Agreements –
   Recreation – Parks

Intergovernmental agreements
Agencies – Work together
Agency – Partnerships
School district – Facility leasing

_____ **Case Study 57** _____
Controlling Halloween Disturbances

Situation

Local officials and community leaders hope to prevent a reprise of last year's Halloween trouble. The action came a year following the worst Halloween the Village of Fort Ann has ever seen. "Our goal this year is to make this Halloween a fun, safe event," said Mayor Marcy McArthur.

Last year, mobs of several young people broke store windows and threw rocks, bricks, and bottles at police in a repeat of traditional Halloween nights. At least 25 people were arrested according to Police Chief Lawrence O'Hara. O'Hara said most of the troublemakers appeared to be 16 years old to early 20s.

Assume you are the director of parks and recreation in the City of Fort Ann, and the population is 50,000. Many of the young people have established a tradition of going out to the city bars dressed up in Halloween costumes. This has grown in popularity and attracts thousands of masked people into town. When the bars close at 1 a.m., many are not ready to retire for the evening and leave the festive atmosphere behind. So most of the masqueraders linger in the streets with nothing to do. A few people seeking entertainment begin to block traffic in the street and rock cars. The resulting traffic jam attracts not only an even larger crowd, but also the police. When the vandals refuse to disperse upon request from the police, a small-scale riot begins. Police bring out riot sticks and dogs. Young people reply with bottle and can throwing and verbal abuse. Before the area is cleared, a substantial amount of vandalism has occurred, several minor injuries have occurred to young people and police officers, and 10 to 20 people have been arrested. This confrontation between young people and police has been repeated for the last 2 years.

A special communitywide committee of recreation programmers and administrators has been formed to discuss the problem. The decision has been made to plan a special nighttime program that will preserve the festive ritual of dressing up, but will avoid another police confrontation. You and your staff are responsible for creating a challenging program that will provide activities for the Halloween enthusiasts.

Problem

What do you think are the main causes of the Halloween disturbances? Outline your idea for the programmed activities for the evening, and be ready to present this plan to the committee. Do you feel that scheduled activities alone can solve the problem? What extent of police patrol would you recommend for the evening? What special arrangements could you make with the town businesses? Do you feel it will be necessary to close off the streets? Why or why not?

Suggested Key Words and Phrases for Internet Search

Halloween disturbances

Halloween vandalism

Halloween riots

Halloween command center

Halloween preparation

Halloween history

Case Study 58
The Adventure Playground: The Junkyard of Play

Situation

Mary Thompson is in her second year at the Bedford Park and Recreation Department as the supervisor of centers and playgrounds. The department serves the entire population of Bedford, an eastern city with a population of 50,000.

A large area of prairie land was donated 2 years ago to the city. It is located three blocks from an influential upper class subdivision of the city, Airshire Estates.

In the first year after the city acquired the land, the park and recreation department began many new programs on the site. These included nature day camps, garden clubs, environmental classes, and an adventure playground. By far the most popular and successful was the adventure playground. An adventure playground is an area where children are allowed and encouraged to create their own play environment under nonrestrictive adult supervision. The land is left in its virginal state, with building materials, such as wood, cardboard boxes, logs, planks, and bricks, provided for the children to build almost anything they desire. Building a house, planting a garden, digging a tunnel, cooking a meal, swinging on ropes from trees, or anything children enjoy that does not endanger them or others is permitted.

Mary started the adventure playground during her first year as supervisor for the Bedford Park and Recreation Department. She had worked as an adventure playground leader in the small town where she went to college. Mary considered it to be a challenging, innovative, and successful program. In the first year of the program, it was considered a huge success. Children from the lower, middle, and upper classes participated.

By the second year, enrollment had doubled, and more space in the prairie was provided for the program. However, George Stark, the director of the Bedford Park and Recreation Department, began receiving phone calls from Airshire Estates complaining about the "junkyard" being built "practically in their own backyard." Three weeks later, he received a personal visit from Dr. Georgine Erwin, a resident of Airshire Estates. She had a petition with 1,200 names of residents and nonresidents of Airshire Estates demanding the entire playground be razed from the site. George talked to Mary about it, but Mary feels strongly about the importance of the program. George plans to call an emergency park and recreation board meeting to discuss the situation. Two members of the board live in Airshire Estates. You know that one is in favor of continuing the program and the other is one of the signers of the petition to abolish it.

Problem

What recommendations would you make to the board? Do you think the petitioners have a right to demand the playground be eliminated? Are 1,200 names a sufficient number of names to abolish the program? What would you argue to support the board's decision if it is in favor of abolishing the program, or what would you argue to defend what you believe is a worthwhile and needed program? What would you tell the residents of Airshire Estates? How would you deal with the one board member who is opposed to the program? What would you say to the parents of the children who have participated in the program during the past 2 years? What would you say to the children? What rights do the citizens in Airshire Estates have in this situation?

Suggested Key Words and Phrases for Internet Search

Adventure playgrounds

Playground full of junk

Adventure playground and ideas

Junkyard play

Adventure play safety

Adventure playground rules

Case Study 59

Community Group Wants the Park District to Take Over Private Facility

---

Situation

Toronto, Illinois, is home to several indoor and outdoor aquatic facilities. Some are privately owned and operated, and others are part of the local university or belong to the parks and recreation department. One of these local facilities, the Jay Aquatic Center, is a large indoor pool and fitness center built in the early 1900s. The center has gone through many renovations over the years, and much of the structure is original, but the pools and other amenities were added in the 1970s and 1980s when the building functioned as a YMCA. The YMCA moved out of the facility 5 years ago, citing significant maintenance and structural concerns, and built a new multimillion-dollar facility on the outskirts of town. A private real-estate investor purchased the Jay Aquatic Center from the YMCA for approximately $500,000 and after some minor repairs attempted to operate it as a private, members-only fitness and aquatic center.

The main draw of the Jay Aquatic Center is its quiet, adult atmosphere and the only deep, warm-water therapy pool in the area. Many of the center members are adults over the age of 65, and a large proportion of them have health problems or mobility issues that are aided by the use of the deep, warm-water pool. Despite pricey membership dues and a small but dedicated group of users, the facility has been unable to attract a large enough membership base to become financially viable, and it has been operating at a $5,000 per month loss since it opened. The facility's owner, John Solis, has recently announced that the facility will close within months.

As facility closure becomes imminent, several Jay Aquatic Center members approach the Toronto Parks and Recreation Department and ask the department to consider either partnering with Solis to share operational costs and potential profits or purchasing the facility outright from Solis so the community will continue to have access to the unique features of the center. The Toronto Parks and Recreation Department currently owns and operates one seasonal outdoor pool, but it does not have an indoor pool. Solis offers to sell the facility for $2 million (his initial purchase price was $500,000). In response to requests from center members, the parks and recreation staff meet with Solis to tour the facility and come away with serious concerns about structural viability, operational standards, aging equipment, ADA accessibility, safety, and overall usability of the space. The parks and recreation department hires an architect to evaluate the facility and provide an estimate for what it would cost to renovate the facility to meet codes, create a safe environment, and add features that will attract more members. The department also asks the architect to compare these costs and considerations to those associated with building a brand new aquatic center on undeveloped land.

The community as a whole is mostly not involved in the issue, but approximately 30 Jay Aquatic Center members attend a parks and recreation department public meeting to ask the department to keep the facility going. The members are passionate about the warm-water therapy pool and are adamant that no other facility like it exists within 100 miles. The department receives several letters and petitions from center members in support of taking over the center, but the community at large does not seem engaged with the issue.

As the architect continues to work on his plans, the state health department inspects the center and finds so many violations, particularly in the pool area, that it threatens to close the facility if improvements are not made soon. The violations are substantial, and the work and expense to correct them would be significant. Solis has made a few minor repairs since he took over the facility, but he is not an experienced aquatics operator and does not have the funds required to make necessary repairs or upgrade failing equipment. Shortly thereafter, the architect reports that it will cost an estimated $8,000,000 to renovate the facility, add necessary attractive features, and bring it up to code. The cost to build a new facility on undeveloped land is approximately $12,000,000. Staff estimates also indicate that annual costs (revenue minus direct expenses) to operate either the Jay Aquatic Center or a new center will be approximately $100,000 to $250,000 in new expense for the department. This amount is not currently accounted for in the department budget.

Problem

You are the executive director for the Toronto Parks and Recreation Department, and you must decide whether you will purchase or co-operate the Jay Aquatic Center, pursue the construction of a new indoor aquatic center, or do neither. Do you believe that offering indoor aquatics is in the best interest of your community? What do you need to know to make that decision? Is an indoor aquatic center worth $100,000–$250,000 in new annual expenses for your organization? Is it better to renovate an older facility and have less choice in features but also spend less money or to build a new facility to your specifications but spend more money to do so? If you decide to move forward with an indoor aquatic center, how will you pay for it assuming no one in the community will simply donate the funds each year? How do you prioritize your programs and services? How do you decide that a community interest group is large enough to warrant changes in the way you operate your organization? Indoor pools almost never make money and cost a lot to operate, but the same could be said of many of parks and recreation functions to varying degrees. Does the potential to generate revenue affect your decisions? If so, how? What is the role of public opinion in your decision? You did not hear from your community either way in this case. What do you think that means? What may be the long-term effects of your decision either way? What other information would you want before making your decision? What other creative solutions are there to solving this problem? What are the pros and cons of each?

Suggested Key Words and Phrases for Internet Search

Cost to operate indoor pool
Cooperative agreements
Pool construction
ADA
Model aquatic health code
Indoor pool

Public–private partnership
Aquatics
Renovation costs
New construction costs
Budget priorities

_____ Case Study 60 _____
Park Visitors Warm to Winter Wonderland

Situation

You are the chief naturalist for the Forest Service at a large national park located in the heart of Wyoming. Winter has fallen on the park, and many problems associated with summer tourists are gone. However, recent national newscasts have promoted the winter beauty of the park, and tourists have begun to flock to the park despite it being January.

The tourists are not prepared for what they encounter. Although the 6 feet of snow is beautiful to see, the tourists are ill prepared to cross it. The parks department has special snowcoaches, similar to snowmobiles but with an enclosed cab, but the park shuttle service is having trouble keeping up with the demand. In addition, animals have a limited amount of food, and the extra human population is destroying their food supply. The animals also have limited energy, and many have literally been scared to death by tourists hot-rodding on snowmobiles.

One afternoon, the program director calls a special meeting of all ranking park personnel. He explains that access to citizens is important, but so is preservation. He asks for feedback on how to best handle the situation.

Problem

What do you suggest? What kind of access should people have? Who should determine who can have access to the park? Does a public park have the right to deny access to anyone wanting to use the public land? What guidelines should be established to preserve the winter experience? Who should enforce these guidelines, and what sort of penalties should be administered? Draft sample guidelines. What is the primary goal of a national park: conservation, education, research, or recreation? Why is this goal the most important? Does is make a difference that this is wilderness management instead of forest management? If so, why? What is the purpose of preserving a wilderness? What techniques are used to preserve the wilderness? What is the naturalist's role in promoting the wilderness?

Suggested Key Words and Phrases for Internet Search

Wilderness in winter

Winter backcountry

Winter use plan

Effects of winter on recreation

Wildlife winter problems

Yellowstone winter use plan

_____ Case Study 61 _____
School District Wants to Build a High School on Park District Land

Situation

The school district in Empire, Illinois, needs to build a new centrally located high school because the current high school is at capacity and the school's athletic programs share many off-site athletic fields with another older high school in the district. After a difficult 8-year process, the Empire School District buys 80 acres of land in a large shopping area on the outskirts of town. The school district announces its intention to build the new school on these 80 acres. The community is unhappy with the proposed site, in particular its remote location, and in response to criticism, the school district states that the only alternative site it will consider for the new high school is 70 acres of land that is currently part of a 100-acre sports park owned by Empire Park District.

The school district prefers this site because it is more centrally located and adjacent to the local community college, which may provide opportunities for classes, collaborations, and further student development.

After mounting community pressure, the school district superintendent sends a formal written request to the Empire Park District asking the it to swap 70 of the 100 acres that make up Kelly Sports Park in exchange for an unspecified amount of the school district's newly purchased acreage on the outer limits of town. The school district also suggests that it will pay for some of the costs related to relocating key features at Kelly Sports Park, such as ball fields, soccer fields, and other amenities.

The park board denies the request, citing the popularity and importance of the sports park, and instead offers the school district 40 acres at an older centrally located park site that is in a transitional phase of development. As the months and weeks pass, community interest in the school site issue grows and the issue becomes a frequent topic of discussion in local media outlets; on social media; and in churches, coffee shops, and workplaces all over town. The Empire School District, in reaction to mounting public pressure, issues another formal written request to the Empire Park District, this time requesting 50 of the 100 acres of parkland that make up Kelly Sports Park. After this second request, the park board chooses to hold a public forum to learn more about the proposed land swap and to hear from the community about the issue. In the buildup to this public forum, community interest is high and the local media feature daily stories about the issue. The park board and school district receive frequent communications from the public during this time, including letters, phone calls, and in some cases, Freedom of Information Act (FOIA) requests. In working to gather information for one particular FOIA request, a park district staff member discovers a new complication to the land swap plan. A decades-old walking trail that traverses Kelly Sports Park was built with a Land and Water Conservation Fund (LWCF) grant, and as a result, the entire park is now restricted to open space and recreational uses. A process exists to lift those restrictions, but it is time consuming and complicated, will cost a lot of staff hours, and will require final approval from the National Park Service. Also as a result of this restriction, the park district learns that any potential land swap would need to be approved by four out of the five park board members. Most park board decisions require three out of the five, so this supermajority requirement presents an additional obstacle to the school district's plan.

Kelly Sports Park is also home to many "memorial trees," trees purchased by community members and planted by the park district in recognition of deceased family members. The families who purchased these trees begin to speak publicly about their strong desire to leave the park as a park because constructing a new high school on the site would require the removal of their memorial trees.

To further complicate matters, Kelly Sports Park is named after Robert Kelly, a past park board member who gave over 30 years of service to the park district, and the Kelly family does not want to see the park used as anything but a park. Like the families who planted memorial trees, the Kelly family begins to speak to the media and attends community meetings to voice their opposition to using the park as a site for the new high school.

Interest in this issue continues to grow, and local media cover the story daily. Community members write letters to the editor and post online comments with increasing frequency. There is passion on both sides of the issue. The following comments appear in the media and in letters to park board members:

- "I am writing in support of putting the new high school in Kelly Sports Park. Locating the high school next to the community college will provide students with expanded educational opportunities including access to technical training, college prep classes, shared athletic spaces, and training in the trades. This kind of collaboration could be a model for high school education nationwide."

- "I do not want to see anything happen to Kelly Sports Park. My son died unexpectedly when he was just 25 years old. He played Empire Park District soccer at Kelly Sports Park for years. When he died, we planted a Memorial Tree in the park. We visit it year-round, rain or shine. It's not the tree that's most important to us, it's the soccer fields. The tree is just a symbol that reminds us of his passing. The fields remind us of his life. We like to sit by his tree on Saturday mornings and watch the soccer games and point out kids who look like him."

- "This issue has become a battle between the school district and the park district, and I don't like that at all. Both agencies get my tax dollars, and while they may have their own designated pieces of the pie, it's still one pie, so they should work together when the community has a need. I'd like to see the school district and the park district work together to put a new high school at Kelly Sports Park. They could share athletic facilities and show the community that, in hard economic times, public agencies are willing to band together to maximize tax dollars."

- "Some people are saying that putting a new high school next to a community college is a good idea because it will give high school students access to services and opportunities that they wouldn't get at a normal school. That may be true, but I don't think it's right to mix high school and community college students. Community college students are adults — and in fact many are quite a bit older than high school students. Their lifestyles, interests, and behaviors may not be appropriate for sharing spaces with high school students. Community colleges also provide an important pathway for people who are putting their lives back together after tough times — whether that be criminal activity or late life career changes. Is that really an appropriate environment for high school kids? I don't think it is, so I'm asking the Park District to reject the School District's request for land at Kelly Sports Park."

- "I don't think the Park District should have to give the school district land just because the School District didn't plan ahead for growth. The park district has done a great job banking land for future needs, making sure that it has parks in all areas of town, and looking ahead to future park needs. The school district did not bank any land even when it knew that the high school was getting too old and too small. Why should the park district have to give up its spaces to bail out the School District? I pay taxes to the park district to provide parks and programs, and I pay taxes to the school district to provide schools. They should stick to their missions and one should not be expected to bail out the other. I do not want to see a high school go in at Kelly Sports Park."

- "Kelly Sports Park is a perfect site for a new school because it's centrally located, it's on existing bus routes, and it would be safe for kids who walk and bike to school. The land that the school district bought on the outskirts of town is in a shopping area where traffic is bad already, there aren't enough intersections or other improvements, and kids really couldn't walk or bike to school. I'd like to see the new high school at Kelly Sports Park instead."

The local newspaper, the school district, and some community groups are putting pressure on the park board to give the land to the school district, and other organizations and community groups are demanding the opposite. The day of the public forum arrives, and community interest and public participation are high. Nearly 30 of the many community members in the audience that night choose to speak publicly about their views, and the majority who speak do not want Kelly Sports Park to be used as a site for the new high school. Nevertheless, there is no clear unified public opinion on the topic, and the park board is presented with the difficult task of making a decision that will shape the community for decades.

Problem

You are an elected member of the park board, and you must decide if you will vote to allow a swap of 50 acres of Kelly Sports Park for 50 acres of school district land on the outskirts of town. How could the proposed land swap help or hinder the park district mission to provide exceptional recreational and park services to the community? To what extent should the park district mission factor into your decision-making process? What should be the role of public opinion in the park board's decision? Are you elected to do what you think is best for the community regardless of public opinion, or are you elected to implement public opinion regardless of your personal views? To what extent do tax-funded community organizations, such as the school district and the park district, have an obligation to work together to address community needs? What assurances do you want from the school district before you would be comfortable approving the land swap? If the land swap proceeds, what are the financial obligations for the school district and the park district? How do the memorial trees and/or the Kelly family's opinions affect your decision? How does the LWCF restriction affect your decision? Is it the park board's job to decide if Kelly Sports Park is the best place for a school, or should you limit yourselves to deciding if it will be an option, but leave the final site selection up to the school board? What may be the long-term effects of your decision? What other information would you want before making your decision?

Suggested Key Words and Phrases for Internet Search

Conversion of land use
Land development
Public schools
Intergovernmental property transfer

Land and Water Conservation Fund
Park district
Land swap
Intergovernmental cooperation

Case Study 62
Learned Helplessness in a Senior Living Facility

Situation

The Yellowwood Senior Living Facility provides seniors all levels of care including assisted living services, skilled nursing care, and Alzheimer's care. The warm, friendly staff is made up of registered nurses who are on-site 24 hours a day as well as physical, occupational, speech, and recreational therapists. Facilities include a large dining room, a spacious recreation room with a large-screen television, an arts and crafts room, a small library, a common sitting room, a bistro, and a beauty/barber shop. Additionally, there is an enclosed courtyard, an outdoor porch with rocking chairs and benches, an outdoor courtyard with a seating area that has a table with an umbrella for shade and chairs, and a garden area with walking paths.

The recreational therapist (RT) is nationally certified, but she is a recent graduate and new to the job. She desires to create a welcoming, optimistic atmosphere and to offer individually tailored programs for residents because she sees each resident as being unique. But apparently, because of her relative inexperience, she seems self-concerned, perhaps more worried about herself and about appearing competent than about focusing on the outcomes residents could derive from their experiences while participating in recreational activities. In short, the novice RT seems unable to recognize and acknowledge that self-doubts and anxiety are common among practitioners at her stage of professional development. Her anxiety is to the point that it is overwhelming and is affecting her functioning.

To complicate the situation, a systematic assessment of resident satisfaction was conducted before the new RT began her work. This satisfaction survey found that a number of residents saw themselves as being socially isolated and felt they had little control within the environment of the senior living facility. They stated that aside from occasions when they were eating together they had few opportunities for social interactions. Scheduled recreational activities were few in number. Those that did occur offered little in the way of residents having opportunities for choosing what they wanted to do and generally were not stimulating. Furthermore, the residents complained they had limited opportunities to interact with friends or family members in social activities. Some residents complained the isolation and lack of control had brought on feelings of depression. A psychologist may arrive at the conclusion that the residents were encountering a sense of learned helplessness, a condition caused by a controlling environment in which people feel they lack a sense of control and have little responsibility for what occurs in the environment in which they live.

To deal with the situation, the program manager of the Yellowwood Senior Living Facility has asked you to recommend steps the RT can take to lessen the residents' complaints of isolation and lack of control and to reduce the residents' current feelings of helplessness and depression.

Problem

What information do you need to understand the situation? What do you need to know about the residents' complaints? What actions can be taken within the recreational therapy program to give residents more control and responsibility? How can the recreational therapy program be structured in ways to bring about greater socialization? How will you approach your task? What will you report to the program manager? What can you do to make the young RT feel more comfortable in her new position? What training can be provided to the RT so she understands the situation and can design interventions to counter feelings of learned helplessness?

Suggested Key Words and Phrases for Internet Search

Senior living facility
Social isolation
Lack of control

Lack of responsibility
Institutional environment
Learned helplessness

—————————— **Case Study 63** ——————————
Maryland-National Capital Park and Planning Commission Department of Parks and Recreation, Prince George's County, Riverdale, MD

Situation

The department of parks and recreation in Prince George's County in the Maryland suburbs of Washington, D.C., is one of the two entities that makes up the Maryland-National Capital Park and Planning Commission (M-NCPPC). Created in 1927, M-NCPPC embodied the vision of forward-looking community leaders who saw the need to plan for orderly development and protection of the natural resources in the two suburban counties bordering the District of Columbia. In Prince George's County, M-NCPPC includes the department of parks and recreation and since the mid-1970s, has been a consistent nationwide leader in access for and inclusion of people with disabilities. This case study identifies some of the factors responsible for this positioning and how the department has addressed challenges in this area.

Prince George's County is unique. With almost 1,000,000 residents, it is a diverse urban community. Its proximity to Washington, D.C., makes it an attractive community for business, political, and nonprofit thought leaders. Home to the University of Maryland campus in College Park, it is philosophically progressive.

The department's mission statement is integral to this discussion:

In partnership with our citizens, the Department of Parks and Recreation provides comprehensive park and recreation programs, facilities, and services, which respond to changing needs within our communities. We strive to preserve, enhance and protect our open spaces to enrich the quality of life for present and future generations in a safe and secure environment. (Prince George's County Department of Parks and Recreation, n.d., para. 1)

The visibility of people with disabilities has changed greatly since the 1970s. The rights of people with disabilities have changed greatly since 1992, the year in which the comprehensive Americans With Disabilities Act (ADA) became effective for 89,004 units of state and local government. The incidence of disability in Prince George's County has risen significantly every decade.

Recognizing the increased visibility, the civil rights, and the rising incidence of people with disabilities, the department launched two key initiatives to address infrastructure and recreation services. In the mid-1990s, the department committed to providing supports for people with disabilities that enabled recreation participation alongside people without disabilities. Commonly known as recreation inclusion, this approach is mandated by the ADA. At times in the 1990s, there was more demand for inclusion than there were resources. Recognizing the importance of compliance with the ADA, the department reallocated funds from other areas to support inclusion.

That continues today, and the department is recognized nationally as a leader in inclusion. It shares that experience with others and was instrumental in developing practical curricula regarding inclusion in public park and recreation agencies.

In another area of ADA compliance, the department succeeded where others have not. In 2011, it retained Recreation Accessibility Consultants LLC (RAC), an Illinois firm specializing in ADA compliance, to train department staff. The RAC experts conducted access audits of 40 department sites. The sites chosen were diverse so the department staff, who would later complete audits of more than 400 other sites, would have experienced virtually every park and recreation asset.

This capacity building approach worked well, with RAC finishing its work in late 2012. The department staff finished their audits of sites and facilities. Today, the department has completed Phase 1 of its transition plan based on the access audits by RAC and department staff and is actively finalizing Phase 2.

Your employer, a large park and recreation agency, wants to address access and inclusion mandates. You have been asked to evaluate the approach taken by the department of parks and recreation in Prince George's County and determine if it could work within your agency.

Problem

What is the problem or decision? Is it to comply with the standards of ADA for physical accessibility, is it to develop a transition plan, or is to decide to hire an external consultant or attempt to use internal staff to complete audits and transition plans? Benchmarking by comparative analysis is certainly one way to establish best practices. What additional information do you need to undertake this evaluation? What risk arises if your agency does not evaluate existing sites and facilities for accessibility? What are the advantages and disadvantages to your agency retaining a contractor to evaluate your sites and facilities? What staff qualifications are best to support inclusive recreation? What risk arises if your agency does not support inclusive recreation?

Suggested Key Words and Phrases for Internet Search

Americans With Disabilities Act –
  Title II
ADA most integrated setting

Recreation accessibility consultants
U.S. Department of Justice ADA office
ADA transition plans

References

Prince George's County Department of Parks and Recreation. (n.d.). Mission and vision statements. Retrieved from http://www.pgparks.com/About-Parks-and-Recreation/Mission_and_Vision_Statements.htm

_____ **Case Study 64** _____
Corporate Sponsorship of Public Parks and Recreation Facilities

Situation

For spectator sports, sponsorship dollars are growing exponentially. By 2018, revenue is projected to reach $17.5 billion. It is almost double the sponsorship dollars produced in 2006!

Park and recreation facilities are generally funded by taxpayer dollars, but an accelerated effort has occurred this millennium to cultivate sponsorship support from caring corporate citizens. City fathers and governmental agencies, under whom aging park and recreation programs fall, have essentially given this undertaking their inferred approval.

Hamstrung by limited taxpayer budgets, park and recreation facility administrators are banking on the support of corporations to grow park programs and in some cases do no more than maintain aging facilities.

Sizable San Diego County (n.d.), for example, has a well-organized sponsorship and naming rights program for its park and recreation facilities. The program is detailed in a booklet, the title of which is striking, _A Campaign for the Future of Our Parks!_ The booklet includes an explicit rate card. From signage at swimming pools to naming rights at athletic fields, specific costs for sponsorships and advertising are spelled out.

In sparsely populated Cheyenne, Wyoming, Charter Communications donated $10,000 toward constructing a universally accessible playground at Cahill Park. In Lansing, Michigan, corporations are solicited for a Concert in the Park series. It is positioned as "Give Back to the Community."

In 2006, Scottsdale Healthcare agreed to give the City of Scottsdale $150,000 for equipment that it needed at its 4,000-square-foot recreation facility. As part of the commitment, Scottsdale Healthcare was allowed to stamp its logo on the facility for 3 years and to use the building to conduct medical wellness programs and health education seminars.

To comply with a self-supporting mandate in the 1990s, New Hampshire accepted a single beverage provider, offering the company advertising rights and product resale in its parks. Soon after, Washington State Parks made a 5-year vendor deal for $2.1 million. The deal included a _can't alter public policy clause._

In Houston, where the menu of sponsorships includes Tree Lighting festivities, a full-time staff sells corporate partnerships. In Modesto, California, the sponsorship effort is organized. A committee keys into the community, identifying the who's who of spenders. Like other municipalities, Modesto is aware of prospects that have a stake in the local park infrastructure, and management strategically elicits their financial support.

Naming rights are not limited to corporations. In Fairfax, Virginia, Geraldine Sherwood donated $5 million to a community center on behalf of her late husband, Stacy (The Stacy C. Sherwood Center). The agreement does not prohibit other donors to sponsor affiliated trails, ball fields, and trees.

The American public is generally receptive. A Penn State survey in 2012, conducted in cooperation with Fairfax County, Virginia, indicates that 74% of Americans are supportive of sponsorship and advertising at parks after only 53% felt as such in 1998. Complete naming rights, though, are taking longer to gain acceptance. The same 2012 survey indicated that only 45% approve of naming rights at athletic fields. The study also showed public concern for overcommercialization at playing fields.

There is uneasiness. As the old adage goes, "The one who pays the fiddler calls the tunes." If and when park management contemplates unpopular decisions, such as closures, parking policies, or traffic restrictions, it has to weigh the lingering if not the parallel effect on sponsor perception. When decision making affects the public, park management feels compelled to consider sponsor ramifications. After all, sponsors in many cases commit hefty and indispensable dollars.

States and park agencies set rules of engagement. In California, for instance, park sponsors must protect the environment and be sensitive to historical practices. They must also promote healthy living, diverse cultures, and quality products.

Problem

Is it fair to ask park and recreation facility management to raise money to support programs? Should these administrators be graded on the amount of money they drum up? If corporate partnership is a serious business at park and recreation facilities, should selling be outsourced to a professional third party that specializes in sponsorship sales? What restrictions would you put on sponsorships and partnerships? If Pepsi, for example, wants to put up a tennis court in a public park, should it receive exclusive pouring rights as part of the deal if it requests it as part of the program? What policies should govern the sponsorships? For instance, should lotteries and beer advertising be allowed? If it is beer advertising, should the brewery be forced to include a message on drunk driving? Are sponsorships at parks creative funding or commercial exploitation? How would you compare sponsorship of recreational areas to corporate sponsorship of stretches of American highways? What are the dangers in counting on corporate sponsorships? What should these parks and facilities do during economic downturns when companies' budgets are depleted? For this reason, should park operations remain exclusively a governmental obligation? Should parks leverage relationships with vendors who provide equipment? Should these corporations be compelled to sponsor activities at the park (e.g., sporting goods retailers and manufacturers)? Other than pure cash, what else can a sponsor do to help parks and facilities? What other promotional undertakings would help promote attendance? Shouldn't parks be named for the pioneers or politicians who helped create them? In the case of Charter Communications in Cheyenne, did it make a contribution to the park to protect its cable franchise in Cheyenne? Does the donation create too chummy a relationship? If you were selling, how would you strengthen the sales story of park sponsorship to a sponsor? If you were a sponsor, how would you evaluate your investment?

Through the years, Mark Dunlap (2014) of Dunlap Grantworks has raised over $25 million in grants for parks. This is his view on the subject:

> This is a slippery slope that we need to climb with our eyes wide open. I support advertising fees at facilities, such as signs on the outfield fences at ball diamonds and corporate sponsors for special events and programs. It's easy to change when the sponsor withdraws its funding. But cities should not let the quest for additional dollars make them lose focus on their parks and recreation priorities. Parks are a sacred trust we must maintain in order to pass them on to future generations. (Selling the Naming Rights of Parks, para. 1)

How do you feel about Dunlap's View?

Suggested Key Words and Phrases for Internet Search

Sponsorship of public parks

Overcommercialization at athletic fields

Donations to athletic facilities

Naming rights at public parks

Parks and corporate sponsorship

Should parks accept sponsorships?

Contribute to parks

References

Dunlap, M. (2014, May 21). Public parks, poor funding, corporate sponsorship [Blog post]. Retrieved from http://blog.ecivis.com/bid/206415/Public-Parks-Poor-Funding-Corporate-Sponsorship

County of San Diego Parks and Recreation. (n.d.). *A campaign for the future of our parks.* Retrieved from http://www.sandiegocounty.gov/content/dam/sdc/parks/NamingRights/NamingRightOpportunitiesBooklet.pdf

This case study was submitted by David Halberstam, Principal Halby Group.

Case Study 65
Language and Disabilities: What Is Right?

Situation

Disabilities are caused by impairments that substantially limit one or more major life activities. There are many disabilities that may affect a person's hearing, vision, movement, thinking, remembering, learning, communication, mental health, and social relationships. Disabilities affect a large number of Americans, perhaps one fifth of the population. Park, recreation, and tourism students, when they become practitioners, are going to provide services to all citizens, and as such, they need to develop fundamental knowledge about interacting with people with disabilities. A basic part of this knowledge is how to refer to those with disabilities. This, however, may be more difficult than it initially seems.

Most students have probably heard about using politically correct terminology in describing people with disabilities. What is politically correct is using what has been termed *preferred terminology* or *person-first* language. Rather than the term *disability* or the name of a disability coming first as an adjective, the word *person* is placed first so the phrase would be *person with a disability* instead of *disabled person* or *person with a visual impairment* instead of *blind person*. The idea is to emphasize the individual is a person first, because people with disabilities are, first and foremost, people. A disability is like ethnicity or any trait. It is simply a characteristic of being a human. In fact, as people age, most develop one or more disabilities.

According to those favoring person-first language, it avoids stereotypes and is more respectful of individuals with disabilities and is more positive. Examples are saying *people with disabilities,* not *the handicapped* or *the disabled,* and avoiding terms such as *afflicted with, suffers from, a victim of, cripple, psycho, retarded, wheelchair bound,* or *confined to a wheelchair.*

Some in the disabled community, however, object to person-first language. They see it as being imposed on them by politically correct professionals. Terms such as *individuals who are differently abled* or *people with special needs* are resented by those to whom they are sometimes applied. Even person-first terms are not accepted by those within certain disability groups, such as those who would term themselves as *blind people, deaf people,* or *autistic people.* They reject person-first language for many reasons. For example, they view separating the disability from the person as an effort to dissociate the person from the disability, as if it were something negative rather than another way of being. Furthermore, expressions such as *person with autism* suggest that even if autism is a part of a person, it is not an important part. They ask why it is acceptable to apply race or nationality in identifying someone (e.g., Black man or Mexican woman) but not a disability? They say, for example, that they call themselves blind and not a person with blindness. Others object to person-first language because it is cumbersome, not crisp, accurate prose. As such, it goes against normal English usage. Their position is that person-first language simply takes too long to say. Why not just say blind people and get to the point?

It therefore can be a dilemma as to what terminology should be employed. Should you refer to people with disabilities or disabled people? When writing for publication person-first language may be required, as many professional journals have adopted it. Putting aside the publication issue, what is the right thing to do in terms of referring to people with disabilities or disabled people? Develop and support a rationale for how you think the issue should be handled.

Problem

What additional information do you require to come to a rationale for which you can make a case? In fact, can you arrive at a firm conclusion? Are there simply two sides to the issue that create a dilemma that cannot be solved?

Suggested Key Words and Phrases for Internet Search

Person-first language
People-first language
Preferred terminology

Against person-first language
Disability language

This case study was submitted by David Austin, Indiana University.

_____ **Case Study 66** _____

Sharing Client Information: What Is Essential to Inclusive Programming?

As health care expands from the doctor's office and hospitals to community-based services, more agencies and professionals are becoming members of health and human service teams. This shift from a medical approach to a biopsychosocial approach is grounded in an ecological approach. Program delivery is influenced by interrelationships among participants and their communities. Program planners consider each person's capacities and resources as they design programs. Professionals are concerned not only with removing deficiencies, but also with enhancing individual assets that contribute to quality of life.

Initially, inclusion referred to supporting people in appropriate programs. Presently, inclusive concepts encompass individuals with disabilities, illnesses, and differences; their communities; and their experiences related to health, functional status, and ability to perform in life situations. This paradigm extends services to a broader clientele and expands program opportunities and the outcomes desired from participation.

Best Practices

Researchers have investigated and reported effective inclusive practices for enabling increasing numbers of individuals with disabilities to engage in community recreation services with individuals without disabilities. This evidence-based information is foundational to delivering programs to individuals experiencing health issues who are living in the community.

Two case scenarios are presented. Successful inclusion relies on communication and collaboration among professionals in therapeutic recreation (CTRS) and recreation agencies to provide the inclusive opportunities. Family members, professionals in related disciplines, and the community at large also have valuable information and resources to support inclusion. Several best practices relate to professional responsibilities and the significance of communication among team members as inclusive opportunities are designed and implemented.

Management Best Practices

- An agencywide mission statement articulates inclusive practices and promotes a welcoming culture.
- Agencies employ qualified (CTRS credential) professionals to facilitate and coordinate inclusive services.
- Staff training on principles and practices of inclusive service delivery is offered agencywide and involves all staff, volunteers, people without disabilities, and companions.
- Networking, communication, and collaboration among professionals, caregivers, and community agencies and schools through, for example, advisory groups create greater awareness, information sharing, and service promotion.
- Marketing materials, print and electronic, use inclusive language, target people with disabilities, and include official welcoming statements.
- Caregiver support for inclusion is considered, with appropriate strategies used to promote caregiver acceptance and alleviate their concerns.

Program Best Practices

- The APIE process is used to design and deliver programs:

Assessments:

- Assessments are completed on individual, activity, and the environment to identify strengths and supports for successful engagements.

Planning:

- Information from assessments and activity analyses is used to prepare participant and accommodation plans.

Implementation:

- Adaptations occur with equipment/materials, activities, environments, participants, and instruction.
- Inclusion support staff are used to increase staff-to-participant ratios when individual assistance facilitates participant success.
- Qualified staff provide technical support on specific accommodations for individual participants.

Evaluation:

- Program evaluation measures participant satisfaction and outcomes, the inclusion process, and staff training needs.

Situation 1

Dylan is a 6-year-old boy who has been diagnosed with ADHD (attention deficit hyperactivity disorder) and sensory processing dysfunction, displays characteristics associated with autism, and displays mood swings. He is verbal and can read above his grade level, but struggles in math. Dylan appears to be well liked by his peers, and he socializes appropriately during free time and on the playground in the after-school program in which he is registered. Unfortunately, the after-school program staff have heard negative things about his behavior and his family, and the reputation that follows him is negative. Teachers and staff are expressing concerns even prior to meeting Dylan. He uses a support staff/inclusion companion, deemed necessary by the CTRS for him to be successful. He also has an individual inclusion plan with other techniques for staff to use based on prior parent meetings and discussion with his teacher to help address the behaviors that he has displayed in the past (i.e., violent to self, others, and property).

One afternoon, the CTRS receives a phone call from the supervisor of the after-school program, who informs her Dylan has been removed from all programs for an incident in another program over the weekend. The CTRS asks for more details because she was unaware that Dylan was registered for other programs except the after-school program and says he must not have had accommodations in the weekend program. The program supervisor informs the

CTRS that Dylan hit a staff member during a tantrum because he was put in a timeout. This incident was the last straw for the park and recreation agency and resulted in his suspension from its programs indefinitely.

Fast forward 1 year: Dylan's mom wants to register him for programs with the park and recreation agency.

Situation 2

Anna is 4 years old and has cerebral palsy. She has the biggest, brightest smile you have ever seen. She loves to be around the other kids, art, and music. Anna uses a wheelchair for mobility and is working on her core strength. She attends preschool in the afternoons. The CTRS completed an intake to gain crucial information on how staff can support her in the program. Her dad says that she is nonverbal, but can communicate with her eyes and some noises; she is in pull-ups and needs full assist in the bathroom and with other daily living skills (feeding, dressing, etc.). On her first day, the CTRS is present to introduce Anna to the inclusion companion and recreation staff and to answer questions and respond to concerns. The CTRS shows the staff how to transfer Anna out of the chair and onto the ground or a beanbag chair so she can play next to her peers.

Everything seems to be going fine, and it has been a month since Anna started the program. The CTRS begins to receive phone calls from the companions and recreation staff stating that Anna keeps throwing up shortly after lunchtime and always seems to be running a fever. The policy of the recreation agency is that a child is sent home that day and cannot come back until there is no fever for 24 hours. Anna has been sent home four times within 2 weeks. The parents e-mail the CTRS complaining about the amount of times that Anna has been sent home, saying it is becoming a burden for their family because they need to work.

A parent meeting was set up during the intake to consider how Anna's health could affect her program participation, yet documentation regarding the fever, throwing up due to acid reflux, and types of food she should not be eating was not reported.

Problem Situation 1

What communication or information did or did not happen to cause Dylan to be dismissed from the agency programs indefinitely? What policies and procedures emanating from the agency mission could guide staff responses? What can happen to assist his mother to improve the situation? What type of training is needed on what topic? What information could the CTRS, recreation agency, and mother exchange to change the situation? What information should be presented in program marketing materials about agency programs? What can the mother, Dylan, CTRS, and agency do to prepare for the next experience? What technical assistance or adaptions may be helpful?

Problem Situation 2

What communication or information did or did not happen to cause Anna to be sent home? What information from an assessment would be helpful? What can happen to assist Anna's parents to improve the situation? What strategies can the agency and the CTRS employ to support Anna's parents? How can the CTRS, recreation agency, and parents share information to change the situation? What additional information should the parents present? What can the parents, Anna, CTRS, and agency do to prepare for the next experience? How could a program evaluation help improve future experiences?

Suggested Key Words and Phrases for Internet Search

Client confidential

Disclosure – Sharing client information

Legal issue – Client confidentiality

Maintaining client confidentiality

Privacy clients rights

Ethics – Client confidentiality

Marcia Carter, Western Illinois University, and Heather Andersen, Fox Valley Special Recreation provided information for this case study.

_____ Case Study 67 _____
Time for ATVs in Shawnee National Forest?

Situation

A few weeks ago, Keith Benefield and some of his friends were riding their ATVs on Horse Creek Trail in the Shawnee National Forest.

They were stopped by a forest ranger, and his two friends were ticketed and their ATVs impounded. Benefield now wants to push the issue of allowing ATV use on some trails in the national forest, noting that it is a recreational pursuit for some people and can lead the state to a great burst in revenue.

"We ride, and there is no place for us to ride (in national forests) in the state of Illinois," Benefield said. "No place, really, legally."

Currently, the use of all-terrain vehicles (ATVs) in Shawnee National Forest is only available through a disability permit program, spokeswoman Amanda Patrick said. Benefield and some of his friends took their concern to U.S. Rep. Mike Bost, R-Murphysboro, when he made a stop in Cairo a few weeks ago. A spokesman for Bost said the representative is beginning to look into the issue.

Environmentalists, such as Barbara McKasson of the Sierra Club Shawnee Group, are opposed to any thought of allowing ATV use in the national forest.

While Benefield and his friends might be responsible people, not everyone who uses an ATV is, McKasson said.

"Not all ATVers are responsible, and if you look at other areas where ATVs are allowed, they denude the greenery, they just make a mud hole out of places that they use," she said.

What if the ATVers had a special area, away from horseback riders, bicyclists and other pedestrians just out to enjoy a bit of nature?

"Why should we have to sacrifice an area in Illinois for the ATVers coming down here?" she asked.

Even though Benefield proposes that the national forest could make money by allowing recreational ATV use, McKasson said the Forest Service is ill-equipped to patrol and police the area.

She points to an incident in which she and others were on a Sierra Club–hosted outing and found themselves harassed by two men on ATVs in the forest. As a man in her group attempted to photograph the two ATV riders, one of them tried to remove the man's camera from his neck, she said. The two men were charged with assault, but they were not found guilty in a subsequent trial, she said.

"Illinois is about No. 48 or 49, way low down on the list, on the amount of public land that we have in this state, and we really need to protect what little that we have," McKasson said. "There is less than 2% that is protected (land)."

Unmanaged use of recreational activities, such as ATV use, is one of four cited threats to the national forests, according to the USDA Forest Service. National forests can have such varying laws regarding ATV/OHV use because they have different types of land and soil, said Ken Arbogast, public information officer for Michigan's Huron-Manistee National Forests. That forest has set aside 450 miles of trail for ATV use.

Benefield points to some national figures to support his point, noting that national forests in surrounding states have trails for ATV and OHV use.

For instance, Kentucky's Land Between the Lakes, a 17,280-acre national recreation area also managed by the Forest Service, allows ATV use on the 100-mile Turkey Bay Trail.

Tennessee's 650,000-acre Cherokee National Forest relegates ATV use to the 12-mile stretch of its Buffalo Mountain Trail No. 29.

He points to what other neighboring states do: Michigan's three national forests all allow OHV use on selected trains. Indiana's Hoosier National Forest does not allow OHV recreational use on its trails.

Another area he has driven on is West Virginia's Hatfield-McCoy Trail, home of the annual Hatfield-McCoy National TrailFest. A report completed this past July indicated that the trail generated more than $22 million income for the state.

"People will come to places like that and spend their money for the weekend or week of vacation and ride and just have fun with their families and friends," Benefield said.

Environmental groups will complain but, as is too often the case, these protests will only serve to conceal the real complaint. These debates almost always boil down to a monopoly of the correct way to experience the outdoors. It's a myopic view that works against the future of all-important public holdings. The more people who enjoy the wilderness, the more who will understand the value in public ownership.

Problem

Should ATVs be used in Shawnee National Forest? Do you agree with Barbara McKasson, a member of the Sierra Club, who says her group is opposed to any thought of allowing ATV use in the Shawnee National Forest? Should sectioned areas of the national forest be available to ATVs? If they are permitted, what condition and regulations should exist? Is it possible to set aside a portion of the park for ATV only? To what point does increased revenue play into the decision of ATV use? What roll should groups, such as the Sierra Club and companion organizations, play in the decision-making process? How can these groups become involved? How can the general public become involved? Is it fair to allow the environmental groups to have a monopoly on what use should be made in national parks? What legitimate compromise is there to this problem?

Suggested Key Words and Phrases for Internet Search

ATV regulations
ATV off-roading
Environmentalist – ATV

Off-road ATV – Shawnee Forest
ATV dangerous
ATV – National parks

"Time for ATVs in Shawnee National Forest?" by S. Esters, 2015, The Southern Illinoisan. *Reprinted with permission.*

_____ Case Study 68 _____
Rock Festival More of a Picnic
Than a Musical Show

Situation

The following is a typical example of the problems facing recreation and park directors nationwide. They frequently receive requests from groups to use public facilities. As a result, problems arise and many questions need answers.

The "good vibrations" of a freaky weekend picnic were turning on more young people on Saturday than the music at the Sound Storm rock festival. Some 15,000 youth turned out Saturday afternoon for the second day of the 3-day event. By 8 p.m., the crowd had grown to about 25,000. The crowd was quiet during the midmorning 2-hour break that separated the end of Friday's music and the beginning of the Saturday show. The small clusters of fans looked as if they were enjoying their own private party.

The sense of isolation bothered some of the fans. Chris Tilley, 21, said he enjoyed last year's huge festival in New Orleans. The feeling of togetherness "was stronger there because it was more of a survival situation," he said.

The New Orleans event, the first rock festival to attract nationwide attention, faced weather, food, and water problems during the 3-day span, but no fights or arguments were reported.

"The vibes are good here," said John Davis of Chicago, who was also in New Orleans. "But it's impossible to have the same amount of feeling because there's not 200,000 people here."

Davis, coordinator of the Mifflin Street Cooperative food project, said, "The bands haven't got any good response from the people. But then again, the bands here are mostly local bands. The bands in New Orleans were the best in the country." The Mifflin Street Cooperative, a Madison store, early Saturday cooked some $500 worth of donated food and distributed it free.

But the crowd could come together at crucial moments. About noon Saturday, three more fires broke out at the hot, dry periphery of the festival site. As soon as the fires were spotted, hundreds rushed to help put them out with blankets, jackets, and shovels. All of the fires were quickly doused, despite high winds. There were no injuries. Spectators were urged not to light campfires during the day and to guard them closely at night.

Potential trouble was avoided early Saturday night when a motorcycle gang leader from Chicago, according to the legend on his jacket, and others in his gang burned two U.S. flags that had been displayed. The leader then grabbed the microphone and lectured the fans on their lack of patriotism.

Donald K. Bobo, a vice president of the sponsoring Golden Freak Enterprises, in turn sharply criticized the motorcycle gang leader. "Anybody who tries to ruin my thing is going to get strung up," said Bobo, whereupon the motorcycle gang leader climbed back on stage. However, the two shook hands and peace was maintained.

For many hip youth, good "dope" and good music go together. By Saturday night, the medical station had treated about 20 people for "bad trips"—feelings of depression, confusion, and hopelessness. Another 20 or so had been treated for minor cuts and burns, and four people had been taken to hospitals, but none for drug use.

Despite the high ingestion of drugs, bad trips were not considered serious. "We try to talk them down," said Bruce Adams, a volunteer worker who is a medical student at the University of Minnesota. Adams is part of an "acid rescue" squad formed by the Mifflin Street group to help youth with drug problems.

County Sheriff Vernon Golz said Saturday that the patrons were unexpectedly cooperative and that there had been only two arrests on charges of destroying a no-parking sign.

Problem

Should public facilities be open to all groups and organizations? If so, in what conditions is this an acceptable practice? If not, why? Write a policy statement for the use of facilities by outside groups. What are the roles and responsibilities of the park and recreation staff? What other agencies need to be involved in controlling behavior at the rock festival? What is the role of the city police department? What is the role of the festival sponsor? To what extent is the entertainment responsible for controlling behavior? Draw up a sample contract between the park and recreation department and the rock festival promoters. What is acceptable rock concert behavior? What agencies should be involved in security? Should alcohol be sold or permitted at the festival?

Suggested Key Words and Phrases for Internet Search

Rock festivals
Park safety
Commercial use of parks
Park administration

Band concerts
Public administration
Drug problems

_____ Case Study 69 _____

Special Parks for Sidewalk "Surfers"

Situation

Those kids in cutoffs have a lot of courage. They coast down the sidewalks on their skateboards without a trace of worry. Arms spread for balance, lower body leaning to maneuver, they talk as they skate. Skateboarding is a popular recreational activity among youth. The capability of attaining speeds up to 40 miles per hour and the possibility of performing tricks have added a thrill factor to this sport. Its inherent instability adds to the excitement of skateboarding. There is little wonder that a range of injuries is seen with skateboarding. Is the skateboard really dangerous? Is the call to ban really justifiable?

Despite its negative image among the medical fraternity, skateboarding does not appear to be a dangerous sport, with a low incidence of injuries, most not severe. Skateboarding should be restricted to supervised skateboard parks, and skateboarders should wear protective gear. These measures would reduce the number of skateboarders injured in motor vehicle collisions, reduce personal injuries among skateboarders, and reduce the number of pedestrians injured in collisions with skateboarders. Because skateboarding is the third most popular recreational activity for youth between 6 and 18 years old, it could be assumed there are skate parks all across the country. There are baseball fields, soccer pitches, jogging paths, and plenty of other places for people to be active. Yet there are few skate parks! It is time to address the needs of today's recreational youth.

Skateboarding is still dangerous. Enough youth are bowling over shopping carts and dogs, thudding on the pavement, or sliding in front of cars of concerned parents and pedestrians. Sidewalks and streets are not made for skateboarding, but there may be a solution to that, too.

At least three municipalities are considering constructing special parks exclusively devoted to skateboarding. In other areas of the country, such as California and Florida, youth are paying about $5.00 an hour to skate on the smooth concrete waves, banks, and hills. The parks have proven so successful in these states that more than 100 are being constructed and many more are being planned.

Those in favor of such special parks contend that if the parks are supervised properly, they will provide wholesome recreation for the entire family. They further state that if skateboarders are required to wear helmets, gloves, elbow pads, and knee pads, accidents will be kept at a minimum. "We have to accept the fact that children are going to skateboard regardless of what adults say, so let's put some safeguards on it," says one California recreation director. Most proponents say skateboarding is no more dangerous than most contact sports and that injuries occur because it is such a new pastime.

Opponents of the new parks argue that skateboarding is dangerous, particularly for young children. Accidents happen every day. The most common injury is a broken wrist because skateboarders break their fall with their hands. Others contend that it is a fad and the interest will decrease in a couple of years. "For that reason, it doesn't seem logical to set aside precious parkland for this type of activity," states one public official.

As the director of parks and recreation in Bennetville, Nebraska, you are faced with a dilemma. Many citizens in the community are pressuring the park board to construct a skateboard park. This pressure is coming from parents whose children are participating in this activity in the streets and on the sidewalks. To date, one youth has been seriously injured and three have broken their arms in skateboard accidents. One city councillor has asked for the passage of an ordinance prohibiting all skateboarding in the community. This controversy has been going on for the last 6 months. As a result, the mayor and council have requested you develop a report, including a series of recommendations addressing these issues.

Problem

Should special parks be developed for skateboarding? Is skateboarding, in fact, a dangerous sport? What has been the experience of other communities regarding this activity? Should this activity be permanently banned in the community? Should parkland be used for this activity? Under what conditions would you allow skateboarding in public parks? What recommendations would you make to the mayor and council?

Suggested Key Words and Phrases for Internet Search

Skateboard safety

Skateboard park – Pros – Cons

Skateboarding issues

Skateboarding culture

Skateboarding debate

Urban skateboarding

_____ **Case Study 70** _____
Educational Health Sessions in Recreational Summer Camps

Situation

The University of Miami Miller School of Medicine has created a program, Fit to Play, in which medical students take field trips to Miami Dade Parks Summer Camps and educate the campers (aged 6–14) on nutrition, fitness, tobacco use, anxiety/stress management, and sun protection. These are recreational summer camps, all of which provide various recreational activities for the campers. During the Fit to Play program, the campers are separated into small groups based on their age, and for 2 hours they rotate through five interactive and fun sessions in which they learn about the aforementioned five topics. For example, the campers receive an activity and coloring book on the dangers of tobacco, receive sunblock, participate in stress reduction activities, receive a stress ball, make a bracelet out of beads that change color when there is UV light so they know when to put on sunblock, touch and feel synthetic fat and muscle, and choose flash cards on healthy versus unhealthy foods. The medical students provide age-appropriate education using a developmentally appropriate educational approach. All educational sessions are under the close supervision of an experienced pediatrician and educator. For the remainder of the day (before and after the educational sessions), the campers participate in their usual recreational camp activities.

This activity has been performed for 5 years, and the camp staff survey the campers after the sessions. Uniformly, there has been positive feedback from the campers and staff, who stated that they enjoyed the activities and learned a lot. Anecdotally, some campers have successfully pressured their parents to stop smoking and many have begun eating a healthier diet. Some staff have stopped smoking as well. There have been a few instances in which information such as child abuse was uncovered.

The five areas of education were chosen for the following reasons:

1. Nutrition

    The Centers for Disease Control and Prevention (CDC, 2015a) reports the following childhood obesity statistics:

- "Childhood obesity has more than doubled in children and quadrupled in adolescents in the past 30 years" (Childhood Obesity Facts, para. 1).
- "The percentage of children aged 6–11 years in the United States who were obese increased from 7% in 1980 to nearly 18% in 2012. Similarly, the percentage of adolescents aged 12–19 years who were obese increased from 5% to nearly 21% over the same period" (Childhood Obesity Facts, para. 1).
- "In 2012, more than one third of children and adolescents were overweight or obese" (Childhood Obesity Facts, para. 1).
- "Obese youth are more likely to have risk factors for cardiovascular disease, such as high cholesterol or high blood pressure. In a population-based sample of 5- to 17-year-olds, 70% of obese youth had at least one risk factor for cardiovascular disease" (Health Effects of Childhood Obesity, para. 1).
- "Obese adolescents are more likely to have prediabetes, a condition in which blood glucose levels indicate a high risk for development of diabetes" (Health Effects of Childhood Obesity, para. 1).
- "Children and adolescents who are obese are at greater risk for bone and joint problems, sleep apnea, and social and psychological problems such as stigmatization and poor self-esteem" (Health Effects of Childhood Obesity, para. 1).
- Healthy lifestyle habits, including healthy eating and physical activity, can lower the risk of becoming obese and developing related diseases (Prevention, para. 1).

2. Fitness

   The CDC (2015b) reports the following on physical activity in childhood:

   - "The U.S. Department of Health and Human Services recommends that young people aged 6–17 years participate in at least 60 minutes of physical activity daily" (Physical Activity Facts, para. 1).
   - "In 2013, 27.1% of high school students surveyed had participated in at least 60 minutes per day of physical activity on all 7 days before the survey, and only 29% attended physical education class daily" (Physical Activity Facts, para. 1).

   Regular physical activity in childhood and adolescence improves strength and endurance; helps build healthy bones and muscles; helps control weight; reduces anxiety and stress; increases self-esteem; may improve blood pressure and cholesterol levels; helps reduce the risk of developing obesity and chronic diseases, such as diabetes, cardiovascular disease, and colon cancer; reduces feelings of depression and promotes psychological well-being; and may help improve students' academic performance (CDC, 2015b).

3. Tobacco use

    The CDC (2013, 2015c, 2015d) reports the following on tobacco use:

    - "Cigarette smoking causes about one of every five deaths in the United States each year" (CDC, 2015c, Cigarettes and Death, para. 1).
    - "Cigarette smoking is estimated to cause more than 480,000 deaths annually" (CDC, 2015c, Cigarettes and Death, para. 1).
    - "Exposure to secondhand smoke causes nearly 41,000 deaths each year among adults in the United States" (CDC, 2015c, Secondhand Smoke and Death, para. 1).
    - In 2012, 6.7% of middle school and 23.3% of high school students currently used tobacco products, including cigarettes, cigars, hookahs, snus, smokeless tobacco, pipes, bidis, keteks, dissolvable tobacco, and electronic cigarettes (CDC, 2013).
    - "National, state, and local program activities have been shown to reduce and prevent youth tobacco use when implemented together" (CDC, 2015d, Reducing Youth Tobacco, para. 1). They include community programs and school and college policies and interventions coordinated and implemented in conjunction with efforts to create tobacco-free social norms.

4. Anxiety/Stress Management

    The National Institute of Mental Health (NIMH, n.d.) reports the following on childhood anxiety:

    Anxiety is a normal reaction to stress and can actually be beneficial in some situations. For some people, however, anxiety can become excessive, and while the person suffering may realize it is excessive they may also have difficulty controlling it and it may negatively affect their day-to-day living. Anxiety disorders are among the most common mental disorders experienced by Americans. (para. 1)

    - Anxiety disorders affect 1 in 8 children. Research shows that untreated children with anxiety disorders are at higher risk to perform poorly in school, miss out on important social experiences, and engage in substance abuse.

- 25.1% of 13–18-year-olds have anxiety, with 5.9% having been diagnosed with a severe anxiety disorder.
- Anxiety reducing techniques such as meditation, deep breathing exercises, and other activities have been shown to decrease the level of anxiety and improve daily coping skills. (NIMH, n.d.)

5. Sun Protection

   The CDC (2014) reports the following on skin cancer:
   - The incidence of skin cancer has increased in all ages including in children.
   - Early exposure to the sun and sunburns in childhood increases the risk for developing skin cancer.
   - Skin cancer can be prevented by reducing exposure to the sun through avoidance and appropriate protection.

Problem

Is it appropriate for the campers to have their camp time turned into an instructional educational session on their health? Should there be a separation between camp and the doctor? Are the five topics ones that you would choose to be most beneficial? If there is only time for four to five topics, what should the topics be? Should camp staff be in the sessions supervising the children, or should the medical school be responsible for supervising the campers during the sessions that are occurring on camp grounds? Should the camp staff participate in the education? Do the parents need to be informed of this activity if nothing is done other than education? Does the camp need a release form from the parent/guardian? What should the park do with the information that may be uncovered during these sessions (i.e., the camper is stressed out because he or she is being abused)? Is it the responsibility of the camp or the medical school to deal with the information uncovered by the medical student? Should there be an exam or other activity to assess what the children have learned? Should there be a prize for participation or a raffle in which only a few children receive a prize? Should the parks help out with funding of transportation of the medical students, lunch, or handouts/giveaways?

Suggested Key Words and Phrases for Internet Search

Childhood obesity

Childhood nutrition

Exercise and fitness in children

Tobacco use and tobacco prevention
   in children

Skin cancer and prevention

Stress management in children

Anxiety disorders in children

References

Centers for Disease Control and Prevention. (2013). Tobacco product use among middle and high school students — United States, 2011 and 2012. *Morbidity and Mortality Weekly Report, 62,* 893–897. Retrieved from http://www.cdc.gov/mmwr/preview/mmwrhtml/mm6245a2.htm?s_cid=%20mm6245a2.htm_w

Centers for Disease Control and Prevention. (2014). What are the risk factors for skin cancer? Retrieved from http://www.cdc.gov/cancer/skin/basic_info/risk_factors.htm

Centers for Disease Control and Prevention. (2015a). Childhood obesity facts. Retrieved from http://www.cdc.gov/healthyschools/obesity/facts.htm

Centers for Disease Control and Prevention. (2015b). Physical activity facts. Retrieved from http://www.cdc.gov/healthyyouth/physicalactivity/facts.htm

Centers for Disease Control and Prevention. (2015c). Tobacco-related mortality. Retrieved from http://www.cdc.gov/tobacco/data_statistics/fact_sheets/health_effects/tobacco_related_mortality/

Centers for Disease Control and Prevention. (2015d). Youth and tobacco use. Retrieved from http://www.cdc.gov/tobacco/data_statistics/fact_sheets/youth_data/tobacco_use/

National Institute of Mental Health. (n.d.). Any anxiety disorder among children. Retrieved from http://www.nimh.nih.gov/health/statistics/prevalence/any-anxiety-disorder-among-children.shtml

Case study provided by Donna E. Wiener, University of Miami, Miller School of Medicine.

Case Study 71
Controlling Vandalism in Parks

Situation

The topic of vandalism on public buildings and community recreation facilities is large, complex, and diverse. The only true and fully understood fact regarding vandalism is that millions of dollars of public and private funds are wasted each year trying to cope with this unpleasant and growing problem. Although the cost of graffiti in the United States has yet to be effectively documented for many communities, property owners, and public agencies, costs are rising each year. A 2006 survey of 88 cities in Los Angeles County on graffiti found that removal costs were about $28 million. The City of San Jose spent approximately $2 million in 2006 fighting graffiti. The City of Chicago budgets annually about $2.8 million for graffiti removal.

In New Orleans, extensive vandalism is casting doubt on whether its pool in the Delachaise neighborhood will open this summer. The JP Lyons Pool may not open because of $200,000 in damage associated with copper thieves at the complex.

In a city in Minnesota, leaders from the

> VFW and the American Legion invested their time and money to transform a 10,000-square-foot swath of city land into a veteran's memorial park.
>
> The centerpiece of the new park was an engraved granite monument in recognition of U.S. veterans.
>
> But in early June, before the veterans and city officials could hold a public dedication ceremony for the monument, vandals destroyed it. The heavy 3-by-5-foot granite plaque that read "All Gave Some, Some Gave All" was tossed on its side, cracked, and unfixable. (Helms, 2015, p. 8)

Replacing the monument costs over $5,000.

From 2007 to 2011, the San Francisco Recreation and Park Department has spent nearly $1.8 million repairing and replacing equipment; buildings; and even trees, lawns, and flowers damaged or destroyed by vandals. In all, 17,108 incidents of vandalism were reported from January 1, 2007, to December 31, 2011. Work crews spent 22,266 hours of labor fixing the damage. About half way through 2012, more than 1,400 vandalism-related incidents had been attended to, costing the city more than $156,000 (Gordon, 2012).

A Midwestern city had purchased a new playground structure to replace old, outdated equipment. All the new playground pieces sat boxed up and unattended in the park, awaiting installation. It was a tempting sight for arsonists, who torched the entire load.

Public officials often ask questions, such as what is vandalism and why do individuals commit these crimes? Some experts claim that individuals ascribe to anger or envy or to spontaneous behavior possibly for peer acceptance or satisfying the gang culture. Greed motivates vandalism as do political ideologies. Often, these people are bored. When they do not have enough to do, they may gather with other people and search for meaningful entertainment. For some, entertainment comes in the form of damaging or destroying things. They may have little or no relationship with the thing they are damaging. The core problem is that the person or group is struggling to avoid boredom. Therefore, vandalism provides a level of temporary excitement and intrigue.

Council members in Chester, Illinois, are considering options to deter vandalism to restroom, playground equipment, shelter houses, and tennis courts. Suggestions have been made, including use of surveillance cameras, time clocks, closing the parks at dark, and increased police presence. Mayor James Murphy proposed that he appoint a committee of the director of park and recreation, the chief of police, and the director of public works to study the vandalism issue and recommend how the city can cope with this serious problem. Councillor Betty Stangle suggested that one council person and three citizens from Chester also serve on this committee. Councillor Jack Dorvee made a motion to accept the mayor's suggestion. The motion unanimously passed.

Problem

Outline the goals and objectives of the committee. What other agencies should be allowed to provide input to the solutions to the vandalism problem? Should a consultant be employed to assist the committee? If yes, what would be the consultant's role? What techniques can be used to involve the entire community? Should the board of education be involved? Would a vandalism program in the schools be an effective approach? Should more police be employed for assignment in the park? Would the visible presence of uniformed police staff in the parks decrease vandalism activity? How can the media be used in helping with the vandalism issue? Is the general public aware of how serious vandalism is in the community? Is the community aware of the cost of vandalism to the community? What role can the criminal justice system play in vandalism activity? What role can volunteers play in reducing vandalism? What procedure could be established to measure the effectiveness of reducing vandalism in the community? What materials should be considered to ensure durability to prevent vandalism and graffiti? How can equipment and recreation space be designed to reduce the amount of destruction? Would cameras in indoor facilities and parks be effective in reducing graffiti and destruction of equipment?

Suggested Key Words and Phrases for Internet Search

Vandalism – Park and recreation facilities
Vandalism – Definition
Park vandalism

Who commits vandalism?
Vandalism – Police control
Combating vandalism
Vandalism problems

References

Helm, M. (2015, March–April). Combating vandalism in city parks. *Minnesota Cities,* 8–10. Retrieved from http://lmc.org/media/document/1/mncitiesmarapr2015.pdf?inline=true

Gordon, R. (2012, June 4). Vandals deface city's renovated parks, playgrounds. Retrieved from http://www.sfgate.com/crime/article/Vandals-deface-city-s-renovated-parks-playgrounds-3606472.php

Material in this case study from Helms (2015) used with permission from Claudia Hoffacker, publication manager, Minnesota Cities.

Case Study 72

Stop Appealing to Billionaires' Egos With Naming Rights

Situation

The village of Riverville, South Dakota, population 7,300, is approached by a local businessman who wishes to donate money to support development of athletic facilities at one of the village's key parks. In return, the businessman proposes naming a field after his business. The specific project would support the addition of field lights at the soccer–football complex.

The parks and recreation department is governed by elected officials on the village board of trustees. It is funded primarily by real-estate and utility taxes from village residents as well as by recreation user fees. A small but significant portion of revenue is also fund-raised from community businesses via team sponsorships. The population served by the department programs includes village residents as well as nonresidents. In recent years, 30% to 40% of the program participants resided outside the village, primarily in Riverville Township. The village of Riverville boundaries continue to grow and expand into Riverville Township. Essentially, the parks and recreation department serves a population of approximately 14,000, which includes the village of Riverville.

Participation for recreation programs continues to rise, and demand for enhanced and expanded facilities is high. A naming rights program could reveal new revenue streams and could help to address some of the ongoing facility development needs. As federal and state grant funding sources decrease, staff are tasked with providing excellence with less funding. As a result, alternative revenue sources are required to meet the expectations of the community.

Staff conduct research for several months using comparable model agencies in forming a naming rights policy. The board of trustees is open to any additional revenue. You must present all sides to this important decision that will shape the community going forward. The naming of parks and recreation facilities is complex and sometimes emotionally evocative.

The following input from the community was gathered:

- "I understand the need for additional revenue, and I don't mind supporting it, but the last thing I want to see is business signs all over the ball diamonds. I can't stand the clutter!"
- "Public property is not just bricks and mortar. Names are, for the most part, permanent, and say something about how our community presents itself and its heritage."
- "I'm all for it, our taxes are too high already. I'll name anything, even toilets if it saves taxpayer dollars!"

- "If we can fund improvements without raising taxes and fees, then it sounds good to me. This town needs more money for parks and recreation."
- "They do it on universities to fund facilities, so why can't we? Seems like a pretty reasonable approach to me."
- "When I go to the parks, I go to escape the constant barrage of advertising and signage, does this mean I'm going to have that at the park now? Advertising on signs and facilities on every corner?"
- "As a board member, I feel it's important to weigh the long-term impact of any decision I make. I would like to know the long-term implications for naming our community assets."

You, as the director of the parks and recreation department, have been asked by Mayor Sullivan to establish a naming rights policy for Riverville.

Problem

Is naming facilities consistent with the mission of your agency? What is the purpose of the naming rights policy? What are the criteria for naming parks and facilities? How much revenue could be generated by naming the parks and facilities? What strings could be attached to the additional revenue from naming parks and facilities? What specifically can be named in the park system? Who determines what can be named, and what is the process for approval? What happens if a person or organization for whom a park was named faces criminal charges, bankruptcy, or another negative situation? Should "renaming" existing parks be considered? What could be the repercussions to renaming parks and facilities? Who will pay for new signage that comes with a newly named or renamed park or facility? What are the restrictions on signage/branding? What are the long-term implications for your agency?

Suggested Key Words and Phrases for Internet Search

Naming rights procedures
Recreation facility sponsors
Naming rights benefits

Naming rights – Revenue source
Purchases – Naming rights
Naming rights – Downside

Case study provided by Dan Waldinger, director, park and recreation, Mahomet, Illinois.

_____ **Case Study 73** _____
Hiring an Interim Executive Director

Jane Nelson, deputy director of Hudson Falls Park District, became the sixth staff member to officially resign in 5 weeks after a heated debate at this week's district board meeting that put citizens at odds over their role in planning recreation programs. Nelson said her decision was for personal and professional reasons. Several citizens and board members claim hostile politics and personal attacks played a role. Nelson's departure followed that of the recreation director, superintendent of parks, business manager, and purchasing agent, all of whom resigned amid heavy scrutiny in wake of a $215,000 unauthorized expenditure for a swimming pool filter at a neighborhood pool.

Early this month, the park district board asked Nelson to serve as interim director until a permanent director could be hired. Nelson said she was interested in serving only for 3 weeks to 1 month, until the district was able to fill a long-term interim position. The board chair, George Lemery, indicated Nelson said that serving as interim director was not worth the criticism and demands from citizens who are heavily involved with the districts everyday operations.

The most active of these critics is John Nichels, the owner of a local Hudson Falls Accounting firm. He recently sent Nelson an e-mail voicing his disapproval of her decision to not stay on as interim director. Marie Moore, an active participant in many district recreation programs, said, "Nelson has the responsibility to step up and fill the interim position until a permanent director is employed." Mary McArthur said, "If we are not careful, we'll end up spending $100,00 to hire, train, interview, then dismiss the interim director. It will take the new director time to 'learn the ropes' and become comfortable with the district operation." McArthur also pointed out, "I would hope Nelson would make a decision before dissatisfaction mounts with the irritability of her reluctance on the importance of the issue. We should show respect and support, and maybe she will continue on a permanent basis."

The most active of the critics is the audit and budget director for the park district, David Donavan. He sent Nelson an e-mail voicing his disapproval of her decision to not stay on as director. The e-mail of public record was republished in the *Hudson Falls Gazette*. Donavan also added that he hoped Nelson would reconsider her decision. The outgoing recreation director pointed out that despite her efforts to avoid the spotlight, she was unable to escape being the target for the critics. She did not want to be in a negative environment where critics continue to express their feelings about the park districts. She also commented, "Nelson was honest and straightforward and yet she still received verbal attacks."

Problem

Should Jane Nelson stay on as deputy director until a new deputy director is employed? If she agrees to stay on, what conditions should the park district board set? If she does not continue until a new deputy director is employed, would this be considered unethical? From the information you now have, describe the problems for the Hudson Falls Park District. Describe what you think should be done. Under the circumstances, do you believe that Nelson would successfully serve as an interim director? Explain your answer. At this time, what should be done about the $215,000 unauthorized expenditure? Should a private consultant be employed to study the issue and recommend solutions to this situation? How would citizens of the district become involved? Would it be wise to appoint a citizen's advisory committee? If yes, what would be their role? Write a statement concerning their duties and responsibilities.

Suggested Key Words and Phrases for Internet Search

Interim leadership

Interim director responsibility

Hiring an interim deputy director

Interim deputy director

Interim deputy director contract

Interim deputy director –
  Professional ethics

_____ Case Study 74 _____
The Center Is Closed

Situation

The Dyland City Recreation and Park Department recently eliminated a teen-center program. According to city officials, it was closed because of the "frequent" and severe vandalism that has occurred during the past year. Vandalism included writing on walls, breaking and entering the premises, destroying property, starting fires in the building, setting off fire extinguishers, and breaking windows. The youth were frequently violating the rules and regulations set by department personnel. This included smoking, spitting on floors, and using improper language.

You are a recreation consultant with the state recreation commission, and the League of Women Voters has asked you to attend a public meeting and discuss the youth program. The only information you are given is a recent news release by the recreation and park department. It reads as follows:

> The teen-center program operated by the recreation and park department for the past several years has been guided by the teens and has until recently enjoyed popularity and success among them. This success was facilitated by the efforts and cooperation of the professional staff. The professional staff included a male and a female supervisor who are college trained in the field of community recreation. Both supervisors have had over 5 years of experience in dealing with

youth. Along with the teen-program responsibility, the supervisors conducted programs for grade school children, junior high school students, and young adults, in arts and crafts, sports, physical fitness, and special events. It has been obvious that teens in the program have not respected staff. Recently, the supervisors' job has become more that of police officers than of recreation leaders. The teens have flaunted their authority and therefore hurt the program. The staff of the recreation and park department have decided not to continue the program under present conditions. Center staff are not employed to play the role of police nor to hold keys . . . open doors . . . and to be spectators at scenes of chaos and destruction that are unfitting, immature, and self-destructing for the teens. The recreation staff are employed to coordinate teen programs as much as possible so they form a successful and rewarding experience for all who participate.

It is with great reluctance that the recreation and park department finds it necessary to close the center. The center will remain closed until some indication is given that changes will be made in existing conditions. If there is no evidence of this, the program will remain closed and other groups will be given use of the facilities.

In discussing this by telephone with the president of the League of Women Voters, you are informed that three councillors have commended the recreation and park department for taking such a stand. "It's about time public officials took a stand on this teenage nonsense." The School Principals' Association has indicated that the department was wrong in closing the center. The two newspapers have not taken a position, but have publicized the closing of the center a great deal. A league member who has found out that you have been asked to attend the meeting indicates, "This is a local problem, and the state recreation commission should stay out of it." She informs the president that she will attend the meeting and indicate her feelings. The community is concerned and a large turnout at the meeting is expected.

Problem

Should the center have been closed? Why? Do you think the press release explains the problem? Why? As a consultant, should you get involved in this local issue? What is your role in this situation? If you become involved, what would you say? Write a press release to publish in the newspaper concerning the role of the state recreation commission in this situation. Prior to going to this meeting, what should you do to become more familiar with the situation? What other information would be helpful?

Suggested Key Words and Phrases for Internet Search

Damage and vandalism in recreation
Park and recreation vandalism
Safety and vandalism

Vandalism - Police department
Managing vandalism

_____ **Case Study 75** _____

Planning Recreation Facilities

Situation

A city with a population of 100,000 is divided into three large neighbor-hoods or small districts, each with its own distinctive characteristics and needs. They are known as North Side, West Side, and South Side areas, respectively. The situation in these areas is as follows:

North Side:
1. Has 36% of the existing public recreation areas.
2. Has 25% of the citywide attendance and registration at public recreation centers.
3. Has the smallest number of voluntary agency programs (Boy Scouts, Girl Scouts, YMCA, and the like) in the city.
4. Has a fair amount of commercial recreation facilities (bowling alleys, movie theaters, and the like).
5. Population
   a. Has 31% of the population.
   b. Has the highest percentage of teenagers in proportion to its population.
   c. Has the lowest number of minority groups.
6. Has a high rate of juvenile delinquency.
7. Has a high economic and employment level.
8. Has a relatively low illness and mortality rate.

West Side:
1. Has 34% of the existing public recreation areas.
2. Has 35% of the citywide attendance and registration at public recreation centers.
3. Has an average number of voluntary agency programs (Boy Scouts, Campfire Girls, YMCA, and the like) in the city.
4. Has an overabundance of commercial recreation facilities (bowling alleys, movie theaters, and the like).

5. Population
   a. Has 33% of the population.
   b. Has average number of teenagers.
   c. Has an average but increasing number of minority group families.
6. Has an average rate of juvenile delinquency.
7. Has a low economic and employment level.
8. Has a relatively high illness and mortality rate.

South Side:
1. Has 30% of the existing public recreation areas.
2. Has 40% of the citywide attendance and registration at public recreation centers.
3. Has the most voluntary agency programs in the city.
4. Has few commercial recreation areas.
5. Population
   a. Has 36% of the population.
   b. Has lowest number of teenagers.
   c. Has the largest proportion of minority groups.
6. Has a very low rate of juvenile delinquency.
7. Has an average economic and employment level.
8. Has a low illness and mortality rate.

Problem

The city has voted a limited amount of money, sufficient to provide additional public recreation facilities in only one of the three areas. In which area should the new facilities be placed? What other factors not mentioned need to be considered? What recommendations should be made in establishing a long-range recreation facilities plan for this community? What important elements should be kept in mind? Should the population of the entire city be involved in the decision-making process? Would you conduct a community survey?

Suggested Key Words and Phrases for Internet Search

Commercial recreation
Construction
Facility management
Master plan
Short-range planning
Voluntary agency program

Comprehensive planning
Equity
Long-range planning
Nonprofit organization
Urban planning

_____ **Case Study 76** _____
Mayor: Bring Bikers Back—Negative Activities Concern Officials

Local officials are looking for ways to make motorcyclists feel comfortable returning to the area for a convention after a weekend marred by vandalism and unruly behavior. The trouble was attributed not to participants in the annual rally, but to outside individuals drawn to the area during the week by the event.

The village mayor, George Lemery, called a meeting Tuesday afternoon with police, government, and business officials at the county municipal center to discuss negative activity that occurred during the week. He said massive amounts of vandalism, large crowds, and street brawls, such as one in front of Skippers Nightclub on Cherry Street on June 7, which injured a few county sheriff's officers, caused many cyclists to either leave the convention early or make this event their last. "I've gotten more and more e-mails from the cyclists saying they don't want to come back," Lemery said. "The people causing these problems, which mostly occurred Friday and Saturday night, are not necessarily the bikers, young kids, or teenagers. They are people coming to the area for the thrill of being part of a large scene. The problems are caused by folks that really don't have any redeeming value of the activity."

Tom Sawyer, supervisor of the sheriff's deputies, said that from June 2 to June 7 peace officers made nine unlawful possession of marijuana arrests and cited seven people with disorderly conduct, one with harassment, and two with alcohol beverage control or open container violations. The peace officers, Deputy Sawyer said, also assisted police in three large fights, one at Sweey Bar and another in front of Skippers Nightclub. The trouble hot spots this year, said the county sheriff, were in from of Capri Pizza and Lake Grove Casino. But Chief Deputy Shane Haven pointed out that the establishments were not at fault for the violence and vandalism. They were just the locations where crowds congregated. "It has nothing to do with these establishments. We just use them as landmarks," he said.

Although discontinuing the event would solve the problems, the county sheriff said taking that drastic of a step would be "crazy." "I don't know how you stop people from coming to see the event. The problems aren't caused by the people who come for the cycling event. It's the tagalongs," he said. The sheriff suggested upping the police presence in the village throughout the week with not only uniformed officers, but also undercover officers patrolling the streets. He said it would only take one or two arrests by an undercover to make a difference. "If 50 to 60 people see that, it will spread like wildfire. People might say, 'Maybe next year I won't go there because you don't know where those guys are.' From a police perspective, that's all I can do," he said.

Sheriff's officers discussed other facets of enforcement, such as roadblocks and checkpoints. But an overall solution to problems occurring during the cycling event was not reached at Tuesday's meeting. Mayor Lemery said he wants to continue the cyclist event because it serves as a tremendous engine for the economy.

Problem

What other organizations besides the ones mentioned should be invited to the meeting? Should the cyclists group be represented? Should the business community become involved? What responsibility do the owners of Skippers Nightclub, Capri Pizza, and Lake Grove Casino have in this situation? Should the event be discontinued? Will police presence in large numbers eliminate the problem? How can the news media assist with eliminating the vandalism problem? Would roadblocks or checkpoints be effective? Is Homeland Security a possible source of assistance and information? Should the National Guard be informed of the event? Should the mayor appoint a special committee for this event?

Suggested Key Words and Phrases for Internet Search

Communitywide special events
Special event security resources
Special event management

Special event planning
Special event checklist
Major event security

_____ **Case Study 77** _____
Alcoholics and the Disciplinary Board's Dilemma

Drug and alcohol use has become a major problem in the workplace according to the Substance Abuse and Mental Health Services Administration (SAMHSA, 2014). Of 21.6 million adults with substance dependency, 11.3 million (55.7%) were employed full time. According to the National Council on Alcoholism and Drug Dependence, alcohol and drug users are far less productive, use 3 times as many sick days, are more likely to injure themselves or others, and are 5 times more likely to file workers' compensation claims.

Situation

Peter Morrsey has for the last 7 of his 8 years worked with the Lake George Park and Recreation Department as a foreman in the park maintenance division. In his early years with the department, he was active in the union and help positions on the negotiating committee and as a steward, but for the last few years, his interest in the union has lagged and he no longer actively participates in its administration.

Morrsey is not well liked by his fellow employees. He takes no active interest in off-the-job activities of his staff. Because he has been with the department for many years, he is on close terms with the supervisor of parks and several city council members. Although Morrsey is sometimes hard to get along with, his bosses consider him a loyal employee and a capable worker. His troublesome fault is his love for beer.

On the morning of October 1, Morrsey reported to work at 7:30 a.m., his regular check-in time. At 8:30 a.m., he asked for and received permission to return to his home. His excuse was that a furnace repairman was coming to look at the heating system. At about 1:30 p.m., Morrsey reported back to work and immediately went directly to his job. Shortly after his return, the supervisor of parks discovered that Morrsey was drunk and unable to do his work properly. It only took a short time for the supervisor to see that Morrsey had been drinking. He was staggering and had the odor of alcohol on his breath.

The supervisor immediately took Morrsey from his job and to the office of the superintendent of parks. At this time, Morrsey confessed that he had been drinking beer earlier in the day, but he said he only had four glasses, and these were before his lunch. The supervisor and the superintendent then took him to the director of parks and recreation, who immediately discharged him.

Morrsey, not wanting to lose his job and not wanting to take this as the final word, appealed his case through the personnel department to the city disciplinary board. The board comprised the supervisor of parks, the director of public works, a foreman in the water department, and the assistant city manager. A member of the union was also present at the hearing as an observer. At the hearing, Morrsey pleaded his own case: "I have given the best years of my life to the parks and recreation department—my most productive ones. Now that I am 55 and have reached the end of my usefulness, you are going to fire me and force me to start anew with another job. I'm too old to do that. Here I have seniority and security. I want to stay here. If I am allowed to return, I promise that this will never happen again."

The records disclose that Morrsey had been suspended twice for short periods for being drunk on the job. He was told on the last occasion, about 12 months ago, that the next time he came to work under the influence of alcohol he would be dismissed at once with no possibility of returning.

About 6 weeks after the hearing, the board reached its decision. Morrsey would be allowed to return to work after a 60-day suspension, but if it happened again, he would be dismissed. The notes and minutes of the meeting, along with the judgment, were filed in Morrsey's personnel folder. Morrsey commented to his fellow employees that he thought the union observer, who had no vote, was instrumental in persuading the board to give him another chance.

Problem

Should Peter Morrsey be allowed to return to work? For this problem, what information should be used to make a decision? For example, is it important to know if Morrsey was home with the furnace repairman? How would you determine this? Were the purposes of disciplinary action accomplished in this case? Should Morrsey have been allowed to go to the disciplinary board? Why? Why do you think the union observer was invited to sit in on the hearing? What should organizations do to help employees with alcohol problems? If you were a member of the disciplinary board, how would you have voted on the Morrsey case? If you were the director of parks and recreation, how would you react to the decision of the disciplinary board?

Suggested Key Words and Phrases for Internet Search

Managing employees - Disciplinary issues

Disciplinary board decisions

Supervisor - Disciplinary decisions

References

Substance Abuse and Mental Health Services Administration. (2014). *Results from the 2013 National Survey on Drug Use and Health: Summary of national findings* (NSDUH Series H-48, HHS Publication No. SMA 14-4863). Rockville, MD: Author.

Case Study 78
Building the Ideal Boys and Girls Club

Over the past decade, the directors, board members, and friends of the Boys and Girls Club have spent considerable time, money, and energy toward building the "ideal boys and girls club." This extraordinary effort has been justified not only in terms of the obvious needs in the community, but also in the belief that the club's success could and would serve as an inspirational model for other Boys and Girls Clubs to follow. To a great extent, the club has been successful in reaching it goal of providing the "ideal club" when applying the criteria of success used within the club system. On the other hand, it is clear that the club has not provided a "model" widely embraced by other clubs in the metropolitan area.

The club is surrounded by one of the most complex diversified neighborhoods in the city. It is frequently referred to as a major melting pot of social, cultural, economic, ethnic, and racial conglomerations. It is similar to, but unlike, other neighborhoods of its size in the city.

The club is a well-equipped modern facility, which has the outward appearance of a bank or medical building. It is a well-financed organization with the largest budget of any club in the city. Although most of the board members of the organization live outside of the neighborhood, many have their places of business in the area. For the most part, these individuals are influential leaders; they not only contribute large sums of money toward the financial support of the club, but they also take a serious interest in the problems of the community.

The present director and the former director of the club are also considered as key elements in the organization. Although both individuals are highly skilled club workers, their greatest strength is in the charismatic quality of their personalities. They have been successful in getting many people to follow them even when there has been frequent disagreement with their methods. Also, both have been generally successful in maintaining continuity in staff over the years, and this has contributed greatly to the steady growth of the organization.

Another strength of this club is the ability of the professional staff to maintain personal interest and concern for individuals while conducting mass recreation programs. Sometimes, however, the workers begin seeing themselves as counselors or therapists. Although they do reasonably well in performing the role of counselor, the time demands required to perform their roles well have a deleterious effect on their other roles. Consequently, they do not have sufficient time to devote to supervising part-time employees and junior staff. This has contributed to a general deterioration in quality of recreation programs and to a low staff morale.

Some of the strengths of the club may also be considered weaknesses. For example, the increased emphasis on developing the ideal club has displaced some goals considered primary in terms of Boys and Girls Club philosophy. This has resulted in the downgrading of importance of the recreation programs in the club and has tended to subvert the democratic social-group-work principles upon which club leadership is usually based.

As the club has become more like a comprehensive caretaking service agency, the staff have moved toward professionalism and the structure of the organization has become more rigid and formal. Regimentation has resulted in increased emphasis on conformity. Children have had decreasing involvement in the decision-making process, which has affected their degree of investment in the life of the club. The club director has become more aware of the problems the club is facing and has become more autocratic in leadership style.

The more autocratic the director becomes, the less subordinates are able to make decisions to improve the situation at the program level. Their frustrations have led to job dissatisfaction and some staff departures.

Even though the club has outward appearances of success, early signs of organizational deterioration are apparent. Recreation programs are no longer as fun as they once were. Staff roles are conflicted between recreation and counseling. Three of the five professional staff members have resigned to take other jobs in the Boys and Girls Club system. Community support has decreased.

The board of directors fires the club director and hires you as the new administrator to come into this situation and bring it back to its former position.

Problem

Why is the Boys and Girls Club going through organizational decline? What responsibilities does the board have in correcting the situation? What goals and objectives should be revised? Has too much emphasis been placed on building the "ideal" Boys and Girls Club? Has the board failed in its responsibilities of overseeing the direction of the club organization? To what extent has community involvement been used? Why has there been so much staff turnover? Should the staff be spending time in serving in counseling situations? Write job descriptions for the Boys and Girls Club director and program director. What information is needed for you to assess the situation?

Suggested Key Words and Phrases for Internet Search

Team development training
Leadership management principles
Motivating staff
Boys Club of America history

Boys and Girls Club – Facing future
Program and services – Boys and Girls Club

_____ **Case Study 79** _____
The Tennis Association Monopoly

Situation

For the past 8 years, the Owensville Tennis Association, a group of tennis enthusiasts, has leased from the city for $1.00 a year a tennis-club complex that includes 16 tennis courts and a clubhouse with showers, snack bar, and lounge area. Upkeep and maintenance is the responsibility of the city recreation and park department. To use these facilities, residents in the community pay a membership fee to the tennis association. The association retains this fee to employ personnel to supervise the area. The personnel employed are directly responsible to the board of directors of the association. The recreation and park department has no jurisdiction over the operation of the tennis association or its program. The president of the association also serves as a chairperson of the recreation and park advisory board, and because of his position, he has been able to influence other members of the recreation and park board not to disturb the administration of the tennis association.

Because you have been on the job as director of recreation and parks for only a few months, you have not had the opportunity to review all existing lease agreements. However, while you are attending the North End Civic Association meeting, a citizen informs you that he attempted to use the tennis-club facilities, but he was turned away because he would not purchase a membership. He indicated that this was unfair, because these are publicly owned facilities. The attendant on duty told him that he was required to fill out a membership application that then would need approval by the board of directors of the tennis association before he would be permitted to play. You reply that you are not familiar with the details of the tennis association operation, but that you will look into the matter.

You immediately contact the chair of the recreation and park advisory committee and request an opportunity to discuss this situation. Upon hearing your concern, he becomes defensive and tells you that the association has operated this way for years and that he can see no reason to change it. He further informs you that he wants the matter dropped and does not want you to discuss it with other board members. You tell him that the present operation of the tennis association is not in the best interest of all the citizens in the community and that you feel obligated to make your views known to the board at the next meeting. He informs you that if you are wise, you will not bring this to the attention of the board, and if you do, there will be repercussions.

Problem

What should be the policy regarding the leasing of public facilities to private groups? Will you bring it up to the board? Under what conditions is it acceptable to charge a membership fee for the use of facilities? If you decide to bring this situation to the attention of the board, what strategy will you use? Will you discuss the situation with the mayor and the council before you bring it to the attention of the board? How would you gain public support for your position?

Suggested Key Words and Phrases for Internet Search

Public property – Private use
Leasing public facilities for private use
Leasing city-owned recreation facilities

Public sector leasing
Leasing public facilities to private concerns
Legal considerations when leasing public facilities

Case Study 80
Teenagers Create Problems in Local Park

Many cities and recreation agencies are declaring war on gangs. The crackdown includes beefed-up patrols and a court order that draws the line in the sand. The message is being sent loud and clear to gangs that there will be zero tolerance for their illegal activity. Police agencies will be proactively making patrol visits at recreation centers, parks, beaches, and other recreation facilities.

Situation

As superintendent of recreation in Mechanicsville, Ohio, you have recently been made aware by your staff and neighborhood residents of the problems at Leal Park. For the past 6 months, a large group of teenagers has been gathering and loitering at the park. During this period, reports of vandalism, beer drinking, smoking marijuana, and cars speeding up and down the parking lot have been reported to your department. It has also been reported that trees have been damaged and burned and picnic tables and signs have been destroyed. Bullying has also become a problem. The police have also received these complaints and have made a few arrests for drinking alcohol in the park, but will not arrest anyone for loitering, because the conviction process is difficult and there is not enough time or personnel to watch the park more closely. Your staff have mixed feelings on how the problem should be handled. Some feel the recreation department should plan activities and programs for the youth. It is also suggested that the park remain open until 3:00 a.m. and that the department provide supervision until the park closes.

Other members of the department feel that park supervisors should be deputized and allowed to arrest individuals who are breaking the law. The recreation and park advisory council feels that the city should institute a curfew requiring all youth under age 18 be off the streets by 12:00 midnight. The chief of police has rejected this idea because of the lack of personnel to enforce it.

In a recent editorial in the newspaper, the police called for immediate reaction by the city fathers and the recreation department. Because this problem is part of your responsibility, you have been asked to draft a plan of action to alleviate the problem. You have decided to call a staff meeting and discuss solutions with your recreation supervisors.

Problem

What program would you recommend to alleviate the problem? From what other groups would you solicit help in solving the problem? How would a curfew be helpful? How would you respond to the newspaper editorial? Do you feel it would be helpful to deputize the recreation supervisors to allow them to make arrests? Should your staff report to the police individuals drinking alcohol and smoking marijuana? Is it advisable to leave the park open until

3:00 a.m.? How can volunteers assist with this problem? What role should the police department play in eliminating this problem? What relationship should exist between the police department and the park and recreation department?

Suggested Key Words and Phrases for Internet Search

Teenage curfew

Troubled teens in the recreation program

Public parks – Teen hangout

Teenager – Peer hangout

Where do teens hang out?

Best teen hangouts

Case Study 81
Festival Seeks to Extend Reach

Situation

Corinth has the biggest festival in the county. Despite 3 years of huge crowds—7,500 to 10,000 people—for the annual Summer Night festival, the news has not reached the suburbs.

Organizers want the festival to be a countywide affair, drawing residents from as far away as Glens Falls and Ft. Ann. They marketed it extensively in the suburbs this year in hopes of increasing suburban attendance. But with less than 2 days to go, many of the towns' key communicators are completely unaware of it. Town clerks, politicians, and residents in Glens Falls and Ft. Ann do not recognize the name of the event on Wednesday, and in Boltan Landing, the normally active senior center is not abuzz with plans to attend, Director John DeGeorgio said.

Barbara Dening, Ft. Ann town clerk, confessed that she is not aware of any festivals located in Corinth. "I've never really attended anything over there," she said.

Glens Falls Park Director James MacFarland—who knows about Summer Night, though he has not attended—said town residents are simply too busy to go. "There's just lots to do in the summer," he said. "Summer sports leagues, baseball—people are living very busy lives." But he also noted that the town's Freedom Park music concerts are "blooming" and that Collins Park was filled with people for the early Fourth of July celebration. So why do they not cross the river to Summer Night?

"To my knowledge, I think the publicity's been good," he said. "The events are good. People like what's going on in Corinth. I hear people talk about Rocko's [restaurant]. But you know, you just can't be in two places at once."

In Cleverdale, the only suburb that still runs a massive town festival, the level of enthusiasm is higher, Deputy Town Clerk Val Sommo said. She has been extolling the virtues of the festival and cannot wait for it to begin Friday.

"I remember one year, they had a sand castle going," she said. "It was Hogwarts, I think." (The sand sculpture will return this year, though probably not with a Harry Potter theme.)

Corinth officials theorized that many suburban residents do not attend because the festival is too young to have become a tradition.

"People know when Niska Day is. They look forward to it all year," Niskayuna Parks and Facilities Coordinator Kathleen Gansfuss said. "It will happen in Corinth, too. It's just a matter of getting it into people's minds." County events organizer Wendy Voelker is counting on that.

"We want this to be a premier regional event," she said. "It is a great way to bring the community together. Downtown Corinth has been the focus of economic development, so we want to bring people there and showcase it."

She modeled it on the First Night festivals celebrating New Year's Eve, deciding that the events would be perfect if they were not held in December. "I got a lot of ideas from First Night, but doing it in summer, you don't have to worry about the freezing temperatures. You don't have to worry about the snow," she said.

As in previous years, the Corinth free event will include music, children's activities from 4:30 to 8:30 p.m., a sand sculpture, and a puppet show at 6 p.m. A hypnotist will also run three shows during the evening, which ends with fireworks at 10 p.m. New events include the Price Chopper bouncy bounce and Native American entertainer Kevin Locke. Locke is a hoop dancer and traditional storyteller, who will play the indigenous Northern Plains flute.

Summer Night will run in conjunction with Art Night and the first Culturefest Concert, which will be held at Jerry Smith Park at 6 p.m. The concert will include the Argle Church Mass Choir, a gospel hip-hop artist, an inspirational poetry jam, and a dance performed by the Heart and Soul group. Musicians downtown will be the Foy Brothers Band, the Frank Capri Trio, Yuko Kishimoto, the Corinth Symphony Orchestra, Sensemaya, and Ernie Williams.

Problem

Why do you believe the Corinth Summer Night festival is not drawing citizens from the suburbs? What is the best way to determine the answer to this question? Design a survey to collect information. Find out why suburban citizens do not attend Corinth's Summer Night festival. What advertising techniques can be used to attract people from the suburb communities? What role can the city council play in promoting the event? Should the event be held in the spring or fall instead of the summer? What community organization in Corinth could assist with the event? How can the downtown businesses contribute? How can the local newspaper, *The Post*, become involved? Develop a plan for advertising and promoting the event.

Suggested Key Words and Phrases for Internet Search

Media – Promoting festival
Marketing events
Sponsorship of summer events

Festival marketing
Summer activity marketing
Survey festival attendees

Case Study 82
Mayor Plays Politics With Recreation Jobs

Situation

A community in which you are director of recreation and parks has a five-member board appointed by the mayor. After the last election, the new mayor appointed two new members to the board, George Anderson and John Cabbott. A number of influential people in the community have indicated that these appointments were made so the mayor would have more control of the recreation and parks board and that certain individuals would be permitted to obtain a job in the recreation and parks system. The chair of the board is a close friend of the mayor; however, by his past performances, he has shown he is sincerely interested in the success of board activities. The other two board members act independently and do not "owe" their appointments to the new mayor, but each has only 1 year left to serve.

Prior to the first meeting attended by the two new board members, Cabbott takes you to lunch to discuss changes he would like to see in the operation of the board. He indicates the mayor should have more control over the appointments of staff members and that he should have the opportunity to approve or disapprove of them. He states further that George Anderson agrees with him and that Mike Slade, the board chair, will also agree to the mayor's wishes. Cabbott informs you that at the next regular meeting he will be proposing several new appointments. These appointments will fill professional and nonprofessional positions. He encourages you to support these appointments.

Problem

What action would you take? Would you discuss this with Mike Slade, the board chair? Would you go directly to the mayor? Would you inform your staff of this meeting with Cabbott? Would you approach Anderson? Would you discuss it with the other two board members? Should you not do anything until the subject comes up at the meeting? Should you agree to the appointments in the nonprofessional staff, but not in the professional staff? Should you go to the newspapers with your problem? Why? What is your position as to the acceptability of the patronage system?

Suggested Key Words and Phrases for Internet Search

Getting a city job
City council – Job appointments
Favoritism – Cronyism – Nepotism

Mayor influences city jobs
Ethics – City job appointments
Political guide lives in hiring state

_____ **Case Study 83** _____
Are Teen Programs Outdated?

Situation

Teenagers today live in a society of entitlement that promotes self-centeredness, ungratefulness, and laziness. Some people refer to this as teenage retirement—provided with everything, earning nothing. Teenage retirement produces adolescents who are bored with life, disrespectful, wasteful, and unhappy. Of course, all teens are not of this type. Many recreation program planners are finding that offering activities for teenagers is the most difficult task in all age groups.

After years of operating successful recreation programs, teen-center agencies have abandoned formal programming. Teen programming is now limited to classes and athletic teams designed to interest youth from junior high school to adulthood. Some of the most successful programs are girls softball leagues and boys basketball programs, in which boys try to become like Michael Jordan or LeBron James.

Do the participants indicate that the teen program is successful? "It is difficult to tell," says City Teen Director Joe Benson. Part of the problem is that the agencies are making slow progress in finding out the needs of teenagers in Melville. "Everything we are doing now is experimental," says Benson. "Things are always changing with teenagers. Other age groups are more predictable; we usually know what they want."

"What the teens do not want is a teen center," Benson says. "For some reason, a program that years ago used to draw up to 600 teenagers to Lion's Den, the city's teen center, no longer is popular or of interest."

Jack McDougal, youth activities director for the City of Dryden, 17 miles south of Melville, says, "When teen centers first started opening they were successful, but once the work was done and the centers became a pattern across the country, the teenagers seemed to stop coming."

Oscar Brown, a park and recreation commissioner and the former director of the Lion's Den in Melville, feels differently. He states that there is definitely a need for a teen center in the City of Melville. He questions how much of a test "the old way was given." "The Lion's Den used to draw 500 to 600 teenagers after high school athletic contests. Since it was torn down, there hasn't really been a good spot with the right kind of facilities," says Brown. Brown is now a history teacher at the high school and says that from talking with students, he thinks they would like to have a center again. They have no place to go now. They do not want to go back to school for most events. Brown believes, "The programming we have now is great, but we still need a center facility. It would serve a larger number of teens. Teens need a place to visit, sit, and talk. We don't need a lot of duplication in programming; however, I'm sure that is the kind of thing the schools will not do. I support a teen center in the future," says Brown.

Robert Towers, director of recreation and parks in Melville, indicates that many recreation professionals have raised the question of whether they should program for teenagers at all. "I feel we should," says Towers. "But I don't think we can justify the expenditure on a center that no one uses. We have tried to give the 'drop-in' approach a chance, and it didn't work. We constantly must ask, can we do better?" Towers says the department will keep a close watch on the success of the current teen program. More changes may be made in the future.

Problem

Should recreation and park agencies be concerned with the programs for teenagers? Are teen centers out of date? Should Melville reestablish its teen center? To what extent does location of such a facility affect its success? What are the best methods of determining the program need of teenagers? Describe in detail the methods you would use to determine program need. If a teen center is to be built in Melville, what type of facility should be constructed? Sketch a drawing of or describe your proposed facility.

Suggested Key Words and Phrases for Internet Search

Youth activities
Recreation for teens
Wilderness programs for teens
Recreation services – Peter Witt

Retention of teen recreation
   programs
Trends for teen recreation

Case Study 84

Responding to the Demands of the Dunkin Recreation Center

Situation

You have assumed the position of superintendent of recreation for Long View, Virginia, a community of approximately 100,000. On the second day on the job, you receive a telephone call from the athletic supervisor in one of the department's four regions. He requests you meet with him on Friday at the

Dunkin Recreation Center to discuss the softball league program for that center. You agree to do this.

The Dunkin Center is in a poor neighborhood of the community and has had many problems in the past, one of which was gang control. However, this problem has subsided during the past 2 years. The center programs are heavily subsidized by tax funds.

When you arrive at the center, you discover that what you thought was going to be a meeting with the athletic supervisor turns out to be a meeting between you and 15 softball program participants. The athletic supervisor is also present. The meeting opens with the athletic supervisor listing the problems that he and the participants see in the program. Their demands include the following:

1. Their field be maintained as well as others in the community.
2. Trophies equal in value to those presented in other city leagues.
3. The umpires be paid at the same rate as others throughout the city.

A spokesperson for the participants emphasizes their support for the athletic supervisor's proposals. Their plea is demanding and somewhat threatening. They insist that you meet with them next week and discuss your proposed solution to these problems.

Upon returning to the main office, you begin to examine their claims immediately. You find that their field is in poor shape, mainly because of vandalism, which appears to have been caused by neighborhood residents. The trophies are not the same as those of the other leagues in the city because entry fees for the Dunkin Recreation Center League are less than a quarter of those for the other leagues throughout the city. The fees charged to other leagues in the city also pay for umpires, scorers, balls, bases, and a league supervisor. The umpire fees for the Dunkin Recreation Center League are lower because of the low entry fee and because most of the umpires in the league are not certified. It is also a problem to get certified umpires to work at the Dunkin Recreation Center. This is due to past problems: gang fights, assaults, and shakedowns.

Problem

Would you meet with this group in 1 week? How would you respond to the group's request? Do you feel you have been set up by the athletic supervisor? Do you have a discussion with your supervisor? What reaction do you have to the athletic supervisor's behavior? Should he be reprimanded? Are the complaints from the group legitimate? Would you suggest increased entry fees so better services can be provided? Should the city further subsidize the program so more and better services can be provided? What can you do to involve the neighborhood residents in reducing vandalism at the park? What responsibility does the athletic supervisor have for this problem?

Suggested Key Words and Phrases for Internet Search

Citizens make demands
Citizens want their voices heard
Voter opinions important
Town hall meetings

Citizen opinion in decision process
Understanding citizen perspective
People – Participation – Involve

_____ Case Study 85 _____

Disgruntled Citizens Will Prevent Demolition

You are a member of the park board in Fairing, Indiana, a town of approximately 60,000. In 2009, the citizens of Fairing passed a bond issue that allocated $1,500,000 to build a recreation facility in the northeast end of the community. Three years have passed, and the facility has not been built. However, after a great deal of work, you are now opening bids for construction of the facility. Because of inflation, prices have skyrocketed, and costs are now about $600,000 above the original estimates. Because of the increased costs, the new center will now consist of a gymnasium, showers, stage, and a small activities area. Initially, the plan also included a library and small theater. The new recreation facility would replace the present Washington Center, which has served the residents of the northeast end for approximately 30 years.

Community members are disgruntled with the park board about the change in plans. They have expressed a need for a comprehensive recreation facility because this center is the only park district facility in the community. The disgruntled citizens have organized a steering committee, which has submitted a position paper to the park board that includes the following: (a) the only acceptable facility is a complete facility; (b) the present facility is understaffed and lacking in program space, and this problem must be eliminated; (c) the citizens of the north end will not allow demolition of the present facility unless a complete facility is constructed; and (d) 50% of the construction workers on the new facility must be minorities.

Not only is the community upset, but one park board member is also. This board member and other citizens of the community have vowed that they would go to jail before letting the present building be razed if their demands are not met. Members of the community are currently picketing the offices of the demolition firm, and the contractor has refused to demolish the building for fear of his employees' safety.

The park board insists that it does not have the financial resources to meet the demands of the community.

Problem

What choices does the park board have? Should the park board meet with the citizens? What other sources of funding are available to the park board? Do you think the board is being unreasonable? How would you react to the one board member? Are any of the demands of the board negotiable? What action would you recommend to the owner of the demolition company? Would you authorize demolition of the existing center? What are the legal ramifications of this problem?

Suggested Key Words and Phrases for Internet Search

Recreation centers – Community togetherness

Recreation centers – Benefits

Why community recreation centers

Recreation center facilities

Community recreation

Community center programs

_____ Case Study 86 _____
The Tornado Watch Policy

Situation

You are supervisor of recreation centers and playgrounds for the community of Stillwell. It has a population of about 25,000. During the summer months, you direct and supervise the operation for 13 playgrounds throughout the city. During last year's program, you witnessed a devastating tornado that claimed the live of 32 people. Three of the victims were participants on the playgrounds. Immediately following this tragedy, your department was criticized because it did not have written policies concerning evacuation of the playground area during a tornado alert. The director of recreation and parks has instructed you to develop guidelines from which the department may establish policies for tornadoes. These guidelines are to include information concerning the following:

1. Communication between city hall and playground locations.
2. Warning systems.
3. Procedures for the evacuation of the playgrounds.
4. Desirable location for shelters.
5. Relationship between the recreation department and the civil defense department during the tornado watch.
6. Staff responsibilities during tornado watch.
7. Provisions for participants with disabilities during the tornado watch.
8. Conduct of individuals while in shelter areas.
9. Procedure of releasing playground participants after the all-clear signal has been sounded.
10. Management of shelter area during tornado alert.
11. Drill procedures for the tornado alert.

Problem

Establish guidelines for the items suggested in the aforementioned situation. How would you disseminate this information to the program participants and to the general public? How would you train the playground staff in the use of the tornado policy? What knowledge and skills should playground staff possess that would be helpful during a tornado alert?

Suggested Key Words and Phrases for Internet Search

Tornado safety tips

Preparing for tornadoes

Tornado facts

Tornado disaster information

Surveying natural disasters

Tornado recovery

Case Study 87
Promotion Will Determine Success of the Racquet Club

Situation

You have been employed as a consultant to the Saratoga Racquet Club, a private commercial recreation facility. Your principal responsibility is to design a public relations and information campaign that will attract new members 6 months from now, when the facility opens.

Saratoga is a community of approximately 50,000, with a median family income of $35,000. At present, there are no other indoor racquetball facilities in the community. Tennis is popular because of the instructional program and tournaments offered by the city recreation department. The only exposure the community has had to racquetball is through the use of three courts at the local YMCA. There are four radio stations in the community, one of which devotes its programming to teenagers; a morning and an evening newspaper; and three television stations, one of which is a public education station affiliated with the local university.

Upon accepting this assignment, you are informed by the owner and the builder that the following facilities will be included in the new recreation development: six indoor tennis courts; 12 air-conditioned racquetball/handball courts; a supervised nursery; a well-equipped exercise room; carpeted locker rooms; a furnished lounge area; a pro shop with the latest tennis, handball, and racquetball equipment; and a steam room, whirlpool, and sauna. A large room with a kitchenette for social activities will also being included. Annual membership fees have been established at $50 for an individual and $75 for a family. People wishing to use the tennis courts or the racquetball courts must pay an hourly rental fee of $10. The club will be open daily from 6:00 a.m. to 11:00 p.m.

You have been told that the maximum amount of money that can be spent during the next 6 months on the campaign is $25,000. Advertising on radio, on TV, and in the newspapers and any promotional brochures must come from this amount.

Problem

Plan a detailed promotional campaign for the opening of the racquet club, not to exceed $25,000. What would be the most effective way to spend the allotted money? Which of the media mentioned would be the most effective in publicizing the program? Develop a promotional brochure describing the club facilities and why individuals should join. What promotional techniques would encourage individuals to join *before* the club opens? Which public relations and information programs would require little or no expenditures of funds? What assistance would you need to carry out your proposed programs? Outline your entire campaign.

Suggested Key Words and Phrases for Internet Search

Marketing	Buying motives
Media promotion	Buyer motivation
Budgeting	Consumer benefit

_____ Case Study 88 _____
Is the Community Ready for Tourism Planning?

Situation

Webster County is the fourth largest county in Idaho. It has a population of over 120,000 people and is located in the northernmost part of the state. It has a 200-year-old heritage that celebrates its rich history and attractions that highlight its outdoor park and recreation facilities. It also provides several national parks, picturesque mountain ranges, and numerous lakes.

Tourism affects the viability of an area. It affects the number of available jobs, affects local economic stability, and increases spending, to name a few. An active tourism program helps to showcase local products, encourages visitors from other areas, brings success to local events, and provides opportunities for local businesses. An effective tourism program provides a positive sense of community pride and encourages citizens to maintain traditions and identity. Ecotourism places greater focus on natural resources by providing recognition of the importance of the visitor experience.

Webster County supervisors have decided to leave the county tourism department without a director indefinitely, hoping a study of tourism promotion efforts will give them an idea of how to fund programs in the future.

Barb Ellesworth, chair of the county board of supervisors tourism committee, said that tourism leaders have been meeting with business owners, including members of the Webster County Lodging Association, to discuss tourism promotion. Supervisors are trying to figure out how to proceed with promotion after the director retires in late June. Tourism promotion is funded by a 4% bed tax on hotel, motel, and bed and breakfast rooms.

A number of business owners have expressed concerns on tourism issues with the county board during an hour-long discussion during last month's meeting. A study in 2012 that questioned some aspects of the tourism department was discussed as were concerns that the department does not do enough to stay current with technological promotional venues. Lincolnshire Supervisor Bernard McGuire said he has concerns about whether input from the business community in the entire county is being solicited: "The only thing I'm hearing is the voices from people from Lake Decatur." McGuire also questioned proposals by some lodgers to scale back or cut back the print visitor guides, because rural areas of the county have spotty cell phone and Internet service that makes accessing electronic versions difficult. He is also concerned that there is no plan to hire a new director or consultant to review the tourism department. Ann Carpenter, the creative director of the department, stated that department efforts are so ingrained that change is going to be difficult to introduce.

Problem

What information do you need to develop a long-range plan for Webster County tourism department? Should the county board hire a director for the tourism department as soon as possible? If yes, develop a job description for the position. What should the relationship be between the department of tourism and the business community? Should the former director play a role in the future of the department? If yes, what should it be? If no, why not? How can social media be used to improve the promotion? What role can Ann Carpenter, the creative director, play in implementing changes? What strategies should be employed in implementing changes? Should the board consider a tax increase to support the tourism department?

Suggested Key Words and Phrases for Internet Search

Travel forecasting

Tourism economic impact

Tourism industry

Creative tourism

Trends – Use tourism

Tourism research

Case Study 89
Nativity Scenes Barred From Public Park

Every year during the Christmas/holiday season, nativity scenes are displayed in communities throughout America. Many of these displays occur on private property and are sponsored and maintained by private citizens. But many of these displays occur on public property and are sponsored and operated by public officials. Some are privately sponsored, but operated on public property.

The display of nativity scenes on public property has perplexed the courts, the public, and public officials for many years. In fact, the United States Supreme Court said that the review of such cases "is a delicate task" (*Allegheny v. ACLU*, 1989).

When ruling on the topic, the Supreme Court made clear that determining the constitutionality of religious displays requires the court to undergo an intense review of the "unique facts" of the particular case to "determine whether the nativity scene constitutes an endorsement or disapproval of religion" (*Lynch v. Donnelly*, 1984). See also "Nativity Scenes and Christmas Carols in Public Places" (Staver, 1999) and "Religious Holiday Displays on Public Property" (Markert, 2008).

In her concurring opinion in the *Lynch* case, Justice O'Connor explained that not all government actions acknowledging religion or a religious belief are unlawful. She used as examples that the government closes its offices and declares Thanksgiving and Christmas to be national holidays and that "In God We Trust" is printed on money, despite the obvious references to religion in these instances. These acknowledgments by the government, she wrote, reflect American culture and serve the purpose of "solemnizing public occasions, expressing confidence in the future, and encouraging the recognition of what is worthy of appreciation in society."

Only when the government action goes further and serves as an "endorsement or disapproval of religion" is the government action unlawful. For instance, the Supreme Court struck down a "moment of silence" law and a "creationism" law in the public schools on the ground that both specifically endorse a government policy in support of religion (*Edwards v. Aguillard*, 1987; *Wallace v. Jaffree*, 1985).

In the case below, determine if the "unique facts" of the nativity scene merely acknowledge religion as part of American culture or go further and send the message that public officials "endorse" religion.

Situation

You are the public parks and recreation director of a large metropolitan area. For 3 weeks before Christmas each year, your staff set up a sparkling Christmas tree in the park downtown. In addition, you also fence off a quarter of the park and allow reindeer to graze in that portion of it. The scene is breathtaking, and thousands of people come to view it each year. The local chamber of commerce, recognizing the numerous people your department attracts into town with the exhibit, underwrites most of the costs.

Because you are a public agency, you have attempted to avoid references to the religious connotations of the holiday season in the park. To make sure that groups that might promote controversial religious ideas do not have access to the park during December, your agency has adopted a policy that no group is allowed to use the park during the holiday season. The parks department treats all groups equally by the policy of not allowing any group access.

Jessee Fredericks, president of the Prince of Peace Foundation, wants to install a nativity scene in the park. He claims that the three fourths of the park that is not being used for the town display is public land and that he has a right to use it. He contends that to forbid the group from using the land denies a First Amendment right to free speech on public ground.

Problem

Does Fredericks have a right to use the park to set up a nativity scene? Would he have the right to use the park if he wanted to set up a scene that had no religious undertones? Is the park policy of denying all groups access acceptable? Is not being able to use the park as a group a form of censorship? Can the parks department legally tie up public land for an extended time with a display? Can private citizens tie up parkland for an extended time with a display? Do your personal religious values play any part in this situation? If so, how? How can you vouch that you are being fair, realizing that your own religious views color your interpretation of the situation?

Suggested Key Words and Phrases for Internet Search

Religious symbols on public property

Nativity scene – Public parks

Public – Sponsorship – Nativity scenes

Private sponsorship – Nativity scenes

Publicly sponsored nativity scenes – Constitutional rights

Faith and freedom

References

Allegheny v. ACLU, 492 U.S. 573, 623 (1989).

Edwards v. Aguillard, 482 U.S. 578 (1987).

Lynch v. Donnelly, 465 U.S. 668, 694 (1984).

Markert, R. S. (2008). Religious holiday displays on public property. Retrieved from http://ffrf.org/faq/state-church/item/14019-religious-holiday-displays-on-public-property

Staver, M. D. (1999). Nativity scenes and christmas carols in public places. Retrieved from http://www.jesus-is-savior.com/Believer's%20Corner/nativity_scenes.htm

Wallace v. Jaffree, 472 U.S. 38, 60 (1985).

Case Study 90
Select, Hire the Best Job Candidate

Hiring employees is important. Effective employees operate and bring success to organizations. Many managers and senior executives fail to recognize the importance of this task. A major challenge for an organization is establishing its reputation, that is, ensuring the organization's name is synonymous with good work, quality service, and professionalism. It is vital that the right people are hired for every job. The cost of hiring the wrong people can affect financial structure, the effectiveness of the organization, and ultimately its failure.

Situation

As general manager for a large park and recreation department, you must decide who will become director for the administrative section of the organization. You have narrowed your selection down to three candidates. All are staff members in the department. You also establish guidelines for the selection process. These include the following:

1. The potential of becoming general manager of the county recreation and park department.
2. Completed a minimum of 5 years of employment with the department.
3. An excellent health record and willingness to take a complete physical examination.
4. Earned at least a master's degree.
5. Demonstrated through his or her performance that he or she can cooperate with people.
6. A proven ability to speak before public groups and convey the concept and function of the department.

From the information in the table on the next page, which candidate you would select?

Problem

Which one of the three candidates would you recommend? Why? How much importance should be placed on education and experience? Which do you feel is more important? Why? To what extent should the age factor be considered? Would you have an employee who is too aggressive rather than one who is too complacent? Why? How important is it that the new director of administration be accepted by the staff? Discuss in detail your reason for recommending one of the three candidates. Should an in-house committee be appointed to assist in the selection? Should the general public be involved in the process? Write a job description for the position. What additional information on the candidate would be helpful in making the decision? Develop a series of questions you will ask each candidate.

Name	Present position	Performance evaluation rating	Length of employment	Health	Age	Education	General comments	Ultimate goal
John Buck	Assistant director of recreation	Has received excellent rating on three occasions	3 years with the department	Excellent	28	Completing PhD in administration	Very aggressive; sometimes too pushy but gets the job done; liked by some staff, other feel he is an opportunist	To be head of large department
Don Craven	Assistant director of parks	First three ratings were good—the last four have all been excellent	7 years with the department	Was treated for heart murmur as a child; doctor has indicated this is no problem	40	BS degree in horticulture; has taken extension courses at university	A slow starter; quite well organized; low-pressure type, gets the job done; liked by staff	Has not specified ultimate goal
Nora Sullivan	Assistant director of administration	All ratings have been good except the last one; problem: getting complacent in the job; needs more drive	12 years with the department	Had polio as a child and walks with a slight limp, which does slow down maneuverability; other than that health is excellent	49	BS in physical education and MS in recreation administration	Has lived the community all her life and probably will not leave; somewhat fixed with her ideas, sometimes not too flexible; well liked by all staff; probably would be staff choice	Has not indicated but probably will be interested in opening

Suggested Key Words and Phrases for Internet Search

Employee selection process
Human resource recruitment
Employment – Tests – Selection
Employee – Selection – Hiring

Employee – Assessment
Structured interviews – Employee
  selection

_____ **Case Study 91** _____
Dropping Gymnastics Huge Disappointment

Situation

When the Stangle County YMCA relocates to the southwestern part of the county in March, it will terminate its competitive gymnastics program. This is unfortunate. The YMCA gymnastics program has been building strong bodies and minds for many years. Many dedicated young men and women—gymnasts and coaches—are extremely sad to see the YMCA decide not to support competitive gymnastics.

The decision to terminate gymnastics was made in late 2010, yet YMCA CEO Pat Benway only notified parents at a meeting on January 26. In a meeting that was nothing less than stunning, a confused Benway said that information about the gymnastics program had been deliberately suppressed, yet he was unable to articulate any reason for withholding this information from YMCA members and gymnastics families.

He made it clear that this decision was not his to make, but that it was instead driven by consultants. Finally, Benway said that the competitive gymnastics program was terminated because the parents of the gymnasts did not contribute a single penny to the new building. Carrie Paule, mother of an active gymnast, stated, "The fact that I hold a letter from Benway thanking me for my donation makes this claim false. As parents, we were not notified that the new facility was being constructed under a pay-to-play paradigm." She continued, "For more than a year, our kids have been excited that the new YMCA would soon be their gymnastics home."

Parents now have to tell them that they will not have gymnastics at all. Paule said, "But beyond sadness of losing competitive gymnastics, we are absolutely shocked at how our children have been treated by the management of the Stangle County YMCA. We thought that the YMCA stood for respect, responsibility, and honesty."

Problem

How should Pat Benway respond to the disgruntled gymnastics parents and participants? Does his statement about donations coincide with the goals and objectives of the YMCA? Should Benway have included the gymnastics group in the decision-making process? Is the pay-to-play policy an acceptable procedure? Explain. Is this situation relatable to the satisfaction of the YMCA and gymnastics group? Should Benway be held responsible for not informing the board? Should he be scorned for his actions in dealing with the situation? Is there a compromise that would be acceptable to the YMCA and the gymnastics group?

Suggested Key Words and Phrases for Internet Search

Goals and objectives – YMCA
Public relations – YMCA
YMCA – Public policy

YMCA – Sales – Marketing
YMCA – Community involvement

_____ **Case Study 92** _____
The Pros and Cons of Awards

Do park and recreation departments keep trophy enterprises in business? Have we gone overboard in giving trophies to participants for just showing up? Trophies were once rare. In the 1960s, they began to be mass produced and were promoted to teachers and coaches and sold in sporting goods stores and jewelry stores. Experts now say participation trophies and prizes are given to assure children constantly that they are winners. In Southern California, a regional branch of the youth soccer organization (AYSO) hands out roughly 3,500 awards each season. It is estimated that local branches spend as much as 12% of their yearly budget on trophies. It is estimated that it is now a $3 billion a year industry in the United States and Canada. The need for youth awards is now a major discussion among recreation professionals. Recently, the Keller Youth Association's football league in northern Texas decided it will no longer give trophies to kids just for showing up.

Situation

In Clawsonville, the park and recreation board operates four recreation centers. During the weekly meeting of the center directors, the question of awards was discussed. One thing was sure: There were different opinions among the directors as to the value of awards. Some questioned whether awards should be continued.

In the centers, one set of awards was given for passing certain designated tests in nature lore, athletics, aquatics, and other activities. Another set of awards was given to those who showed themselves outstanding leaders, that is, cooperative, enthusiastic, friendly, helpful to others, and unselfish.

It was generally agreed that awards depending on the passing of specific tests should be discontinued. The tests were relatively easy, and almost any youth could pass them with little effort. The question of the outstanding-leader award was more difficult to settle. The staff were divided as to the desirability of this award. The older participants tended to support the outstanding-leader award more than the younger participants.

After a number of meetings of the directors, several who were in favor of the outstanding-leader award had changed their minds and were now in favor of abolishing it. As time progressed, other directors and many of the participants showed less enthusiasm for this award. Finally, by vote of the staff and participants, the outstanding-leader award was abolished.

Problem

List the pros and cons of an award system. To what extent do participants work directly for awards rather than for achievements? Do you agree with the decision to abolish the award for passing specific tests and the outstanding-leader award? Why? Why do many recreation programs have award systems like the one described? Do you agree with the way the award system was administered in the centers? What does winning an award do for a child? How does a child's failure to win an award affect him or her? Are youth given too many awards? Why does the possibility of earning a trophy motivate youth? Have you ever received a trophy you felt you did not deserve?

Suggested Key Words and Phrases for Internet Search

Athletic awards
Trophies – Youth sports
Youth sports award
Awards – Youth value

Trophies – Pros and cons of youth
  programs
Youth trophy sales

_____ **Case Study 93** _____
Grand Jury to Investigate the Park Board

Situation

The president of the park board, Seely Thompson, opened the morning newspaper and read the headlines: "Grand Jury to Investigate Park Board." Naturally, he was surprised because he was unaware of any problem with the operations of the park board. He immediately called an emergency meeting of the five-person board to discuss the situation.

Thompson appealed to Howard Cascade, a new board member, for cooperation instead of criticism while the board was trying to get going on a greatly expanded park program. Thompson's remarks came after Cascade reported that he requested the state's attorney general look into the activities on the board.

In a letter, Cascade told the attorney general that a board member was receiving compensation for conflict of interest. He was referring to payment of $281.20 to Burt Sloan, an attorney and member of the board, for legal services in negotiations for an option on an 80-acre tract of land west of the city. Sloan performed this service for the board while the regular board attorney was out of town on vacation. Thompson stated, "Sloan helped us out in a tight spot, and he certainly did not overcharge us for the service. I don't know why there is any fuss; nobody made any big money on this transaction."

Cascade further said that he asked the attorney general to investigate nine items relative to park board activities including the following:

1. Minutes of the board proceedings are seldom kept.
2. Board equipment and employees have been used for board members' personal gain.
3. Checks are being written before the board meets to approve or disapprove the bills.
4. Board members are receiving compensation for conflict of interest.
5. A board employee was arrested in another city at 3 a.m. driving a park-district truck.
6. The board does not keep a regular book or record of all ordinances.
7. Board funds are in the First National Bank and in the savings bank, and two park-board members are presently serving on the boards of directors at these banks.
8. The board does not use formal bidding procedures.
9. Debts are being created without first issuing purchase orders.

Other board members are upset that Cascade did not discuss his accusations with the board prior to his writing a letter to the attorney general. However, all of them indicate they will welcome the investigation and will cooperate fully.

Problem

Should Cascade have discussed his letter with the board prior to sending it to the attorney general? Why do you think Cascade is requesting an investigation? Do you feel that Burt Sloan has a conflict of interest? Should a board member be permitted to provide a service to the board for which he will receive compensation? What is the law in your state regarding this? What records should be kept by the park board? Should employees be permitted to use board equipment for personal use? What procedure should be established to permit the payment of bills? What policy would you suggest for the deposit of park-board funds in the local banks? What bidding procedures would you recommend to the park board? What state laws in your state affect bidding procedures? Recommend a purchase order and voucher system that would adequately facilitate park-board business.

Suggested Key Words and Phrases for Internet Search

Park board subpoena

Response to grand jury

Grand jury system

Board members – Ethics

Bidding procedures

Testifying before grand jury

_____ Case Study 94 _____
Will Halloween Trouble Hasten Passage of Nuisance Party Law?

Assume you are director of parks and recreation in Athens, Ohio. Your department is in charge of the city's annual Halloween event. The mayor has asked for your input and suggestions concerning the working draft of the nuisance party ordinance being proposed by the city council. His primary concern is how it would affect the department of parks and recreation.

Situation

In mid-October, Athens City Council let it be known that it was working on a draft of a "nuisance party" ordinance, which if passed would give police more power to shut down wild house parties that generate multiple misdemeanor citations.

Opinions were predictably mixed on the merits of such a law. But then came Athen's annual Halloween street party on Nov. 1–2. Around 5 a.m. Sunday, a small scale "riot" took place in the Mill Street area student neighborhood, in which partiers set fire to furniture in the street, overturned a car, and pelted police and firefighters with bottles and other projectiles.

Has the incident made passage of a nuisance party law more likely? And would having one on the books have helped?

Athen's Police Chief Rick Mayer is spearheading the push for the new law, modeled on one adopted by Oxford, Ohio. He said shortly after Halloween that having a nuisance party law might have helped head off the Mill Street area disturbance if it had been used earlier in the evening.

"It may have helped on some of the houses," Mayer said, suggesting that if some of the rowdier house parties had been broken up hours before the disturbance, their participants might not have taken part in the later problems.

At-large council member Jim Sands said he believes the events of Halloween probably will increase public pressure on council to adopt the nuisance party ordinance, despite concerns among Ohio University students that it could infringe their rights.

"I think it will probably give it a boost," he said. However, Sands added, the aim of the proposed law was to deal with the day to day problems with house parties in off-campus neighborhoods, not to serve as an extra tool for handling Halloween.

"When I talked to the chief of police this week, he made it clear," Sands said. "That what he is asking for is not something to deal with Halloween. But parties on the weekends, or during spring quarter, that are getting out of hand."

He acknowledged, however, that in the minds of many town residents, that distinction may be somewhat blurred in the wake of the Halloween disturbance and other problems that weekend, including a double stabbing and a reported sexual assault in an OU dorm.

Joanne Prisley, co-chair of the Athens Near Northside Neighborhood Association, said she doubts the Halloween problems will add appreciably to the support for a nuisance law.

"I don't think it will increase it much, because there's already a lot of people in the neighborhoods who are for it," she said. "You have Halloween, and it goes off, and you forget about it. But (these parties) go on day after day."

Sands, who was out with volunteer "safety teams" during the Halloween street party, said the outbreak of destruction and violence during the wee hours of Sunday morning was especially unfortunate, given that the Court Street party itself was fairly mellow and well-behaved.

"The neighborhood we were in . . . they were having parties, there were lots of people, but it was an upbeat mood," he reported. When safety team members had to warn partiers to dump an open beer, or not block the street, he said, "it was all handled with a positive outlook, and so it's just especially disturbing to think that everything was going good and then just fell apart."

Regarding the nuisance party ordinance, Mayor Ric Abel said Wednesday that council members have met Chief Mayer "to ask, how does this really work?" He, like Sands, predicted the violence on Halloween could add to public support for the ordinance, but also like Sands, noted that the Halloween events were hardly the kind of garden-variety party the law is mainly aimed at controlling.

"This isn't something that happened at midnight," Abel said, pointing out that some partiers apparently began drinking early in the day Saturday "and it just kept going on" until early the next morning.

Council member Nancy Bain reportedly called an informal meeting last night, to include members of OU Student Senate and representatives of Athens neighborhood groups, to discuss the proposed nuisance party law. And whether or not such a law is added to the books, Sands predicted, there will be some type of official backlash to this year's party.

"I would feel certain that Halloween 2004 will be dealt with in some ways differently from the last couple years," he said. "But at this point I have no idea where it's going to go."

In an interview over the weekend, OU President Robert Glidden said the university is very concerned about the events of Halloween, and intends to address the problem cooperatively with the city. He suggested that "a police state approach"—including enforced curfews—may be called for to prevent the sort of disturbance that rocked the Mill Street area early on Nov. 2.

Problem

Should the City of Athens work closely with the university to solve the Halloween event problem? What should the relationship be? Should the council vote to pass the nuisance party law? Why? Sands predicted there will be backlash. What might happen? The president of the university wants to do this cooperatively. How might this be done? Should the city establish curfews? Is establishing a nuisance party law an encroachment on individual rights? Students at Ohio University feel the passage of the nuisance party law could be an infringement on their rights. Do you agree with this? Why or why not? Are the parties on campus similar to the city Halloween events? Should this be considered? What relationship should exist between campus police and city police? How would the passage of the nuisance party law affect the city parks and recreation department?

Suggested Key Words and Phrases for Internet Search

Halloween trouble
City and university relation
Student housing – Acceptable
   behavior

Student party complaints
Neighborhood night behavior
Noise complaints

Article by Janet Nester and Jan Strawn, staff writers for The Post. *Published with permission.*

_____ **Case Study 95** _____
Cultural Arts Development in Cities and Neighborhoods

There is an awakening in the United States today to bring a closer relationship to leisure services delivery and the cultural arts. Many park and recreation professionals are recognizing this. With an increase in time away from their jobs, many Americans are searching for leisure, including theater, choral, and instrumental fine arts experiences. The move toward the arts as a choice for leisure has been observed on college campuses, in senior citizens programs, in family programming, in churches, and in the numbers of people attending concerts and visiting museums not only in large cities, but also in smaller neighborhoods. A major obstacle in the arts affiliated with recreation programs is the lack of joint efforts between the trained artist and the recreation administrator. The recreation director is often unaware of the potential power of the arts, not only as a means of enjoyment, but also as a catalyst for emotional involvement, community identification, and personal enrichment.

Situation

Assume you are the director of parks and recreation in Scovoalville, Louisiana, population 200,000. At its last monthly meeting, the parks and recreation board was confronted by a group of 25 people, who requested the department hire a supervisor for the performing arts, to begin a citywide program in the cultural arts. They also suggested that a center be constructed to house the new program. The group hopes the program can be operational in 1 year and the supervisor employed within three months. George Hickey, a board member, said he likes the idea, but indicated there are no funds available to support the program. "We need to discuss your ideas and suggestions with the mayor and the council," said Hickey. Hetle Trombly, a local theater enthusiast, indicated, "There is a lot of interest in the proposed cultural arts program." Tom Stickney, chair of the taxpayer association, stated, "I'm tired of all these programs that will raise local taxes. It's time we start fixing the potholes in our roads, doing a better job of snow removal, and bringing more industry to our community to help pay bills."

John Short, chair of the park board, stated, "It's refreshing that our citizens have attended tonight's meeting and expressed their suggestions for programs the department should be providing. As many of you know, the parks and recreation commission is presently in the process of working on a long-range plan for the department. Your thoughts and ideas are important as we go through this process. Others have mentioned that cultural arts would be an exciting addition to the commission's program. With the commission's approval, I will appoint an individual who can represent the views of cultural arts interest. I should caution all of us. I share the concern of Tom Stickney. With the present fiscal problems facing our city, it is almost impossible to meet all the demands."

Problem

Would it be appropriate to appoint the mayor to the long-range study committee? Is it appropriate for the parks and recreation board to appoint the supervisor for cultural arts? Write a job description for the supervisor of cultural arts. Should the city council approve a tax increase for the cultural arts program? How would you deal with individuals who agree with Stickney? What other groups in the community should be contacted for their support? Should a citywide advisory committee for cultural arts be appointed? If yes, what would be its function? What methods would you use to determine the need for a cultural arts program? What method would you use to evaluate the effectiveness of the proposed program? What roles could volunteers play in establishing the cultural arts program? Explain why it is appropriate for the parks and recreation department to provide the leadership for the cultural arts program.

Suggested Key Words and Phrases for Internet Search

Arts and leisure

Cultural affairs – Leisure

Parks and leisure services

Arts – Culture – Quality of life

Arts and economic prosperity

Finance and operation of performing arts

_____ **Case Study 96** _____
You've Gotta Have Heart

Situation

You are the executive director of a special recreation cooperative that covers nine park districts. The districts realize that they are not meeting the leisure needs of their special populations, because of a small number of identified special populations. They decide to consolidate their resources and populations and to hire a core staff of professionals trained in therapeutic recreation. By pooling resources and special populations, the park districts hope to offer a program of recreational activities equal in diversity, frequency, and quality to those available to residents without disabilities. In addition, all activities will be geared to meet the individual needs of each participant. The cooperative is committed to providing comprehensive leisure services for children and adults with disabilities stated in it guidelines. Programming and budgeting provisions have been made for only people with mental and physical disabilities, behavior disorders, and visual impairments.

The representative districts of each community allocate a portion of funds derived from tax assessments to the special recreation cooperative. The governing board consists of representative directors of parks and recreation and a combination of staff. This board is a policy-making body that may act as a steering force through its committee work and community involvement.

In July, you receive a letter from Jerry Adams, requesting on behalf of several individuals the initiation of a special recreation program designed specifically for people with heart conditions. Adams states that individuals with heart disease cannot participate in the regular park district programs, because they are too strenuous, but that activity is necessary for rehabilitation and prevention of further heart deterioration. Individuals in the community feel that it is the responsibility of the special recreation cooperative to provide for them. After all, is not leisure essential to everyone?

A new program would, of course, mean additional funding. As executive director you feel that this program, although costly, is necessary. Board members are skeptical about this program, however, because they feel that people with diabetes, epilepsy, and other health conditions may demand similar programs.

Problem

What should be the policy regarding heart patients? Why should they be regarded as special? Should the special recreation cooperative be responsible for programming for this group? How would you begin this program? Write a general policy for providing programs for those with health conditions. Outline a program that would accommodate this group. Should funds be cut from other programs to provide for the individuals with heart disease? Should city taxes be levied to support this group? What other sources of revenue are available to support this new program? Would it be possible to increase fees to support this program? What other ideas can be suggested to support this program?

Suggested Key Words and Phrases for Internet Search

Equal rights for people with disabilities

Guide for rights – People with disabilities

Americans With Disabilities Act

Olmstead Supreme Court decision

Equal rights center – Disabilities

Understanding Equal Rights Act

_____ Case Study 97 _____
Living Together: Single Membership

Situation

As director of recreation and parks in Redwood, California, one of your responsibilities is to oversee the direction and management of six municipal swimming pools and four municipal ice rinks. Because these facilities were built and constructed with municipal revenue bonds, the park board has established membership fees to pay for the bonds and for operational costs. The membership fees that were established are as follows:

Family Membership $150.00
   Includes husband, wife, and children under 18 years of age–Single male and/or female with children under 18 years of age.
Single Membership $100.00
   Includes single male and/or female over 18 years of age.
Youth Membership $50.00
   Includes male and/or female under 18 years of age (before Nov. 15).

Recently, Robert Goff entered the recreation office to purchase a membership for the ice-rink facility. The receptionist gave him an application to fill out. Moments later Goff returned the application to the receptionist with a check for $150. Upon checking the form, the receptionist noted that Goff had applied for a family membership and listed his name and that of a George Lemery, Nancy Moyneham, and Marie Paul. The receptionist immediately informed Goff that he was not eligible for a family membership and that each person must purchase a single membership at $100 each. Goff informed the receptionist that the four people had recently bought a house together and were now "living under the same roof," and therefore, they should be eligible for a family membership. The receptionist told Goff that this would be referred to the director of recreation and parks, to make a decision as soon as possible. Because Goff had to go back to work, he requested that the director communicate his decision by mail. After reviewing the situation, the director sent the following letter to Goff:

May 25, 1977

Mr. Robert Goff
21 Valley Road
Redwood, CA

Dear Mr. Goff:

In answer to your recent request regarding the family membership for you and the other three to the Redwood Ice Rink, I wish to inform you that I have discussed the matter with members of the recreation and parks board. Membership categories were established by the recreation and parks board with the approval of the mayor and council. The categories for membership include family membership, single membership, and youth membership.

As outlined in the membership rules, single membership includes any person who does not qualify under the family or youth category. Therefore, Mr. Goff, you and your roommates must take out "single" memberships in order to participate in the Redwood Ice Rink program. The fact that you all have bought a home and are living together is irrelevant to buying membership at the Redwood Ice Rink.

I am available from 9:00 a.m. to 5:00 p.m. each day if you wish to discuss this situation any further.

Mr. Thomas Carroll
Director of Recreation and Parks
City Hall
Redwood, CA

After receiving this letter, Mr. Goff became upset with your response and as a result sent the following letter to you and the commission:

Mr. Thomas Carroll
Director of Recreation and Parks
City Hall
Redwood, CA

Dear Mr. Carroll:

Please forgive me for not having answered your kind letter sooner. I do wish to thank you for the detailed account of the membership regulations to the Redwood Ice Rink. However, I cannot, in good conscience, go along with this philosophy or logic. As a committed campaigner for human and civil rights, I find your regulations to be highly discriminatory against certain individuals. In an age when discrimination is under daily attack in every media, both nationally and locally, it seems incredible that your commission continues to base its distinctions on outdated notions of family. Obviously, I find such "membership categories" to be antiquated and, what is more serious, ethically offensive. Moreover, I would suppose that they are also illegal.

Of course, my complaints cannot be interpreted as an attempt to save money. I think I can afford this extra amount. However, I believe your decision might cause the park board quite a lot of bad publicity and embarrassment. The fact that our group pays our fair share of taxes in this community, yet takes advantage of the family membership plan for the ice rink seems incredible. I am sure you are aware that situations such as this are being dealt with on national and statewide basis. The point is that in this instance the board could use what in law is referred to as "the rule of reason" and make an exception in this case. Instead, the board insists on being legalistic and mercenary, basing their argument on the mythical "what would happen if..." Yes, what would happen if an unmarried couple moved into your community and bought a house? Would you discriminate against them also?

I would suggest that you amend your regulations to deal with these exceptions. In so doing, you would avoid typing individuals according to membership categories.

In light of these comments, I insist that you reconsider your decision in this matter. If you fail to do so and do not respond within a week to 10 days, I shall be forced to forward my complaint to the Civil Liberties Union as a formal complaint against the recreation and parks board and proceed to file suit in this matter.

Yours very truly,

Robert Goff
21 Valley Road
Redwood, CA

Problem

Would you allow the group to buy a family membership? Are there legal implications in this matter? How would you answer Goff's most recent letter? Write a letter of response. What are the implications of this problem? Are there any legal definitions of a "family"? Would you permit a male and female who are living together to join with a family membership? How would you react to the legal suit? What type of defense would you prepare? Are the descriptions of the membership categories clear and explicit?

Suggested Key Words and Phrases for Internet Search

Private club membership
State statute
Fees and charges
Civil rights

Family (legal definition)
Citizen rights
Rights of property owners

Case Study 98
Mr. Eckert Presents the Jaycees' Complaint Situation

Situation

You are the general manager for the Sioux Falls Park and Recreation District. The Sioux Falls Park and Recreation District has always tried to maintain good relation with organizations in the community. Many of these organizations have donated parkland and equipment and, in general, provided the district with a great deal of volunteer leadership. Mr. Jim Frazer, chairman of the district, asks you for lunch to discuss the following letter he received from the Sioux Falls Jaycees.

JAYCEES Mr. Jim Frazer, Chairman
Recreation and Park District
Sioux Falls, South Dakota

Dear Mr. Frazer:

Our reason for attending this park board meeting is to defend the reputation and integrity of the Jaycees, a civic organization. In our opinion, this reputation was publicly and wrongfully damaged in an article that appeared on the front page of the *Sioux Falls Times* on February 20. We were rather shocked at some of the statements made by the park board members, in particular the statement that, "You don't need our lousy $1,000." Apparently, the Sioux Falls board is under the impression that we were grandstanding. We can assure you, gentlemen, that we had no intent to grandstand. There has not been any communication from the Sioux Fall Park Board concerning delays on improvements in Jaycee Park. We are certain that if the park board had indicated that it would be impossible to complete the requested improvements by the stipulated date of July 15, there would have been a favorable response by our general membership. There was, however, no attempt made by the park board to advise the Jaycees of the delay.

Although the Sioux Falls Park Board reported they made a concerted effort to complete the improvements by July 15, they neglected to indicate why a deadline was necessary. We feel sure that if you will review your board meeting minutes, you will note the many requests made by the Jaycees for action on Jaycee Park.

One of your board members indicated that the required improvements on Jaycee Park were virtually completed by July 15, with the finishing touches made in August. However, gentlemen, further in the article it was mentioned that playground equipment was not installed until after the deadline, due to bad weather and forced delays. The latter statement was more accurate, since on July 15 the only improvements made were the planting of some trees and bushes and the development of two circular areas, one with a large pole in it.

So let's call a spade a spade. You did not complete the installation of playground equipment by July 15 as outlined by our proposal of June 13. You did not make any attempt to communicate with the Jaycees, indicating our date of July 15 could not be met.

Last fall we spent $300 for improvements on Jaycee Park, and we had every intention of donating the balance of $1,000 to you. In our opinion, we were forced to set a deadline; it was not met, and therefore, our offer was rescinded.

Although we have not gone into lengthy detail regarding Jaycee Park, we hope you clearly understand our position and recognize our severe disappointment with the manner in which the Sioux Falls Park Board selected to answer our letter of November 7. We will be more than happy to hear any further questions the board may have at this time.

Sincerely,

Richard J. Eckert
Park Committee Chahman
1331 Cumberland Circle West
Sioux Falls, South Dakota

Problem

What is your immediate reaction? Write a reply to Richard Eckert. Can this problem be more effectively handled by staff, or should board members become involved? What is the appropriate follow-up for this situation? What should the policy be regarding acceptance of gifts in money or land by the district?

Suggested Key Words and Phrases for Internet Search

Paying for public parks

Collaboration and public partnerships

Role of nonprofit organizations for
   recreation and park activity

Public policy for parks and recreation

Public and private sector
   relationships

Case Study 99
The Lifeguards Will Strike

Situation

As city recreation director in a Florida town with a population of 30,000, you are concerned about the threatened strike by 42 lifeguards who patrol the city beach area. The lifeguard representative, Mark Simpson, has met with you a number of times during the past year and informed you of the grievances. The main issues are higher salaries for the guards and more and better equipment. You are inclined to agree and feel that their demands should be accepted. On a number of occasions you have presented their demands to the mayor, but he has been opposed because it would raise taxes and he "is simply not in favor of that."

Because the Easter vacation begins tomorrow, you anticipate a large number of students from the northern and Midwestern colleges. You know it will be almost impossible to close off the beach area. Closing the area will likely cause the students to riot. Naturally, you plead with Mark not to strike during this time; however, he indicates that you have had a year to convince the mayor that something needs to be done and no action is in sight. He tells you that either salaries are increased and new equipment is installed at the beach today or there no lifeguards on duty tomorrow. You report this to the mayor and his reaction is, "Let them strike."

Problem

What would be the first thing you would do to alleviate this situation? Would you attempt to get Mark and the mayor together to discuss the issues? Would you request "readiness" on the part of the National Guard and state police? Would you attempt to close off the beach area? Would you use volunteer lifeguards? What action might you have taken during the year to convince the mayor that the demands were legitimate? Should public employees be permitted to strike? Why? Give a complete description of how you would handle the immediate crisis.

Suggested Key Words and Phrases for Internet Search

Lifeguard laws and regulations
Lifeguards threaten to strike
Collective bargaining with lifeguards

Negotiation with lifeguards
Negotiation with employees

_____ **Case Study 100** _____
Personnel Policies at the Next Meeting

Situation

You have just accepted a position of director of recreation and parks in a city with a population of 50,000. The previous director has recently retired. Due to illness during his last 5 years in office, he was unable to make necessary changes in program, personnel, and finance. At the first meeting with the board, you are requested to review and update the existing personnel policies. Board members reported that a number of problems arose last year that could have been settled without much difficulty if the policies had been updated. One problem in particular dealt with suspension procedure; another concerning employment practices indicated that the department was violating a number of state and federal laws.

Problem

Write personnel policies that you could recommend to the board. Write policies for the following: employment practices, time and attendance, overtime, vacations, absences, absence due to armed-services obligation, special leave, jury duty, dismissal and suspension, grievances, staff training, salary policy, and retirement.

Suggested Key Words and Phrases for Internet Search

Issues and practices - Personnel policies

Personnel management - Theory and practice

Personnel policies and procedures

Personnel policies - Objectives, principles, procedures

Human relations - Personnel policy development

INDEX

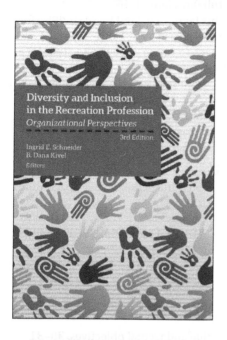
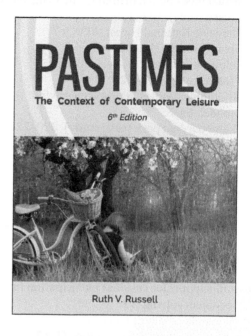
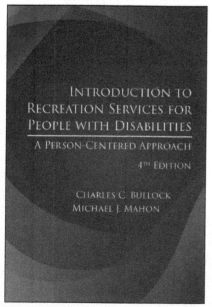